NOT ALWAYS WITH THE PACK

NOT ALWAYS
WITH THE PACK

Dennis Walters

Constable · London

First published in Great Britain 1989
by Constable and Company Limited
10 Orange Street, London WC2H 7EG
Copyright © 1989 Dennis Walters
Set in Linotron Sabon 11pt by
Rowland Phototypesetting Limited,
Bury St Edmunds, Suffolk
Printed in Great Britain by
St Edmundsbury Press Limited,
Bury St Edmunds, Suffolk

British Library CIP data
Walters, Dennis
Not always with the pack
1. Great Britain. Politics. Biographies
I. I. Title
320.'092'4

ISBN 0 09 469310 2

To Bridgett

Contents

Illustrations

The general election 1983 with Bridgett (*photographed by Wessex Newspapers*)
My five children (*photographed by Tina Walker*)

Acknowledgements

In writing this book I owe a great deal to many people. Chicchi Mattei, happily rediscovered after so many years, was exceptionally generous with her time and advice. Being able to talk to her at length brought back to me in a way nothing else could have done the events and the emotions of that period of my life in wartime Italy. This was particularly valuable where I did not have a diary to lean on. Chicchi's brother Camillo and other members of the family were very helpful and supportive.

Maria Luigia Guaita Vallecchi also kindly gave me some of her time and reminded me of several forgotten episodes. I am most grateful to her for having allowed me to use one of the stories from her book *Storia di un Anno Grande*.

Of the several people who have been good enough to discuss aspects of the book with me I would especially like to thank Lord Erroll of Hale, the Rt Hon Enoch Powell, Lord Aldington, Lord Rees-Mogg, Lord Fraser of Kilmorack, Count Giovanni Tadini and my son Nicholas.

I owe particular thanks to Ian Gilmour who, like my wife Bridgett, kindly read all the manuscript. His detailed comments and criticisms were immensely helpful and led to its considerable improvement. Characteristically he asked me to delete the passage which refers to the transformation of the *Spectator* under his editorship as being unduly flattering. I have refused to do so as it is wholly accurate.

Quintin Hailsham gave me carte blanche to do as I pleased. I hope he will not be too disappointed with the result.

But of all those who have helped me Teddy Hodgkin is in a special category. Without him the book would not have been written. From the start, he has helped me to plan it and we have discussed every stage and practically every page. His historical sense and literary skill have been invaluable to me but perhaps most of all his enormous kindness and constant encouragement throughout have been such that no words can adequately express my gratitude to him. I have taken advice from many besides those I have named but naturally the opinions expressed are mine alone.

I would also like to thank Diane Johnstone, Helen Grubb and Stephanie Jarrett for their help in typing and retyping the book, and my publisher Robin Baird-Smith for his interest and constructive encouragement.

A Personal Note

Although this is not intended to be an autobiography and certainly is not an easily recognisable one, it is inevitably autobiographical. A personal note therefore seems to be necessary.

In 1955, when I was twenty-six years old, I married Vanora McIndoe, the younger daughter of that splendid man Archie McIndoe who sadly died at the height of his powers in 1960. We had two children, Nicholas and Lorian (Lolly). Nicholas, who married Emma Blamey, fought Merthyr Tydfil for the Conservatives in the 1987 general election, thus confirming that he had inherited the political bug. Lorian seemed an unusual and attractive name at the time, but it must be said that except for the odd occasion when she was a child and I was cross with her, Lolly she has always been to me and practically everyone else. Attractive however she is.

In 1968 Vanora decided that she wanted to marry somebody else and we were soon divorced. Two years later I married Celia Kennedy, Duncan Sandys' second daughter by his marriage to Diana Churchill. Celia's sister Edwina was a great friend, but I had met Celia once only before she returned to England in 1969. Married very young she had then lived in Kenya. When I met her again, her marriage had broken up and she had come back to London with her two year old son, Justin.

We were married in May 1970 at the British Embassy in Paris where Christopher Soames was then Ambassador. The Soames family became and have remained close and dear friends of mine. Celia and I had a son Dominic, now seventeen, and I looked upon Justin as another of my children. After seven years of what seemed a happy marriage Celia unexpectedly decided in 1977 that she wanted a change, and in 1978 she left me. It was a stunning blow and the divorce that followed a year later was not an easy one. I had not wanted either divorce. To be the so-called 'innocent' party is no comfort and in English law since 1970 no help either.

At that immensely bleak moment everything changed. I met Bridgett Shearer. She was much younger than I was. I had been married twice before. I did not appear a very suitable candidate for matrimony. Be that as it may, she restored my life and we were married in January 1981. Two more children have followed, Camilla and Oliver. To be the father of five children, five and a half with Justin, ranging from thirty-one to four presents a number of problems, but it is not a situation that I would ever wish to change.

Preface

This book is intended to be less a political memoir than an attempt to describe some episodes or events which I have seen, which may interest others than myself, and which I believe to be in different ways relevant today.

The book is divided into three sections, each one very different from the other two. The first covers my time as a boy in Mussolini's Italy during the war. The second records some of my experiences as Lord Hailsham's personal assistant between 1957 and 1959 when he was Chairman of the Conservative Party, and then during 'the fight for the Tory leadership' in 1963. While going over well trodden ground my account of that strange but immensely important event which had a momentous effect on the future course of British politics does, I hope, add a few new angles and facts which have so far not appeared in print. The third part gives some account of my close involvement in the affairs of the Middle East which began in 1965, and my long battle against political Zionism. The latter started a couple of years later after the 'Six Day War' in 1967 and, like so many things in life, was unexpected and unplanned. But since then the Middle East, and in particular the Palestine problem, have dominated my political life.

So there they are, the three distinct themes – resistance to totalitarianism, Conservatism, the Middle East. I am conscious that people who are already interested in one of the three themes may expect not to be interested in the other two. But I feel strongly that there is a natural link between them; I do not just mean myself but that, in a much broader sense, they are essential parts of the political history of our country in the last forty or fifty years, and so of real concern for everyone. I hope it will not be regarded as presumptuous if I claim to have been able to make a contribution, however small, to all of them.

The title of the book is drawn, a little out of context, from a talk I had with Rab Butler at what was for me an unhappy moment many years ago. 'Whatever you do,' he told me, 'if you intend to get on in politics, never show that you have been wounded. In politics you must always keep running with the pack. The moment that you falter and they sense that you are injured, they will turn on you like wolves, biting and savaging you.'

This rather melancholy but percipient piece of wisdom has come in useful to me on one or two subsequent occasions, and I hope that I have complied with the advice in the sense that Rab intended. However, I have not wished to conform with the majority view or the conventional orthodoxy of the moment as a matter of course, and this has not helped me to maintain a good position in the pack. That I do not regret.

One other point is perhaps worth making. I grew up watching Europe doing its best to destroy itself. This seemed to me to be madness, and a madness for which Fascism and Nazism were almost entirely to blame. I find it logical that a political career which started in active anti-Fascism should have developed into a strong commitment to a Europe which will, I hope, become increasingly and in every way united. It is equally logical that I should have found myself so deeply involved in advocating the neglected rights of the Palestinians, for they too are indirect victims of Nazism and Fascism. Because of the unforgivable sins perpetrated by the Nazis on the Jews, the wholly innocent Palestinians have been expected to atone on behalf of the guilty non-Palestinians. This convenient but hypocritical rationalisation is not one which I have been willing to accept.

PART I

Introduction

MORE than forty years have gone by since the end of the war. Probably most schoolchildren know a few names of those principally involved in it – Churchill, Hitler, Stalin. From time to time political events like the trial of Klaus Barbie and the accusations levelled against Kurt Waldheim will pull back the curtains as the trial of Adolf Eichmann in 1961 did for an earlier generation. Serious television programmes may attempt to describe the horrors of the Holocaust or the drama of a place like Colditz, and television comedy can be extracted from prisoner of war camps or even from occupied France. But how many of the young in Britain know much – or indeed anything – about Mussolini? And for every dozen to whom the name of Mussolini means something I doubt if there is one who knows anything about the Italians who opposed him.

This, I think, is a great pity. 'Fascism' is a word that is bandied about very glibly and usually with little understanding of its origins and real meaning. But it was my direct personal experience of living in a country ruled by Fascism which first aroused my interest in politics. How, I asked myself, could a country get into this state? What are the alternatives? Are the citizens of any country really the sheep and cannon fodder which Mussolini and his evil disciple Hitler assumed them to be? Is parliamentary democracy the decadent and doomed system Italians were constantly being assured it was?

Anyone living in Fascist Italy had no need to be particularly alert or mature to appreciate that Fascism was not only mistaken in its theory, often ludicrous in its manifestations and cruel in its application, but also inefficient in its performance. Mussolini, increasingly isolated and impervious to criticism, was the only person permitted to make

19

decisions, and most of his decisions, in peace or war, were disastrous for Italy. Yet in spite of that he held sway for twenty years and for a time was much admired abroad.

It has to be realised that many honourable and patriotic civil servants, brought up in the tradition of Giovanni Giolitti,[1] continued to serve the Fascist regime, which they accepted as embodying the State. It had, after all, received the blessing of King Victor Emmanuel III, and after 1929 with the signing of the Lateran Treaty which recognised the integrity and independence of the Vatican State, the acceptance of the Catholic Church. They served it loyally and well. The same applied in varying degrees to the captains of industry, the diplomatic service and the armed forces. Artists like Toscanini and philosophers like Croce began by giving Fascism their support, though, quickly horrified by the way in which it was developing, these two were to become leading opponents of the regime.

Not all Italians were prepared to take the easy road of conformity. There were those who from the outset understood the real nature of Fascism, and who repudiated it. Some went into exile; others, who stayed, refused to join the Party, though this made them marked men and women for whom promotion, if they had anything to do with the government, was blocked. To survive, they needed above all courage, and if possible sufficient resources to give them independence. This meant that anti-Fascists in those early days were an élite, but a very small élite. The lead which this élite was to give later, when in 1943 virtually the whole nation turned against Fascism, was to prove invaluable.

I cannot do better than describe one such anti-Fascist family, with some of whose members, as will appear, I was to become closely associated in the wartime Resistance. The father, Ugo Mattei, had been in the Navy and in 1918 at the end of the war became manager of the telephone company serving Milan. His family were liberals (with a small 'l': the Italian Liberal Party was on the right), belonging to the tradition which in the nineteenth century had fought for the unification of Italy and the establishment of a parliamentary democracy. It fell to him to have an early introduction into the nature of Fascism.

---

[1] Prime Minister between 1906 and 1922 and responsible for giving Italy a non-regional and non-party-political civil service.

One day in 1919 Benito Mussolini, then still editing *Il Popolo d'Italia*, the newspaper he had founded in 1914, stormed into Mattei's office. He wanted, he said, several new telephones for his newspaper and he wanted them immediately. Mattei told him that he would naturally be happy to supply the telephones, but there were others already waiting and they would have to be served first. He must take his turn. Mussolini became threatening: if the telephones were not forthcoming it would be the worse for Mattei's company, and for him personally. Mattei said he was sorry to hear it, but exceptions could not be made.

Mattei suffered no terrible fate. Mussolini's threats on this occasion, like so many before and after, proved to be bluff. Others were not so fortunate. Once he was installed in power his *squadristi* (commando squads) continued to beat up and even murder their opponents, break up their meetings and administer their favourite castor-oil punishment. Terror tactics culminated in 1924 with the kidnapping and murder of Giacomo Matteotti, the leader of the Socialist opposition in Parliament. This caused such widespread shock and outrage that, had the opposition been more united and decisive, Mussolini might well have been overthrown. But he survived, and Fascism consolidated.

Mattei's was a private business, run with partners who shared his views, and they switched to do most of their work abroad and not in Italy. All the Mattei children were brought up to regard the Fascist regime with contempt, and were prepared to take risks to demonstrate their opinions. Thus in 1936, when all schools were given a day's holiday to celebrate Italy's conquest of Abyssinia, Teresa (Chicchi) Mattei, a teenage daughter, discovering that there was no legal authority for the holiday, turned up at the usual time at the Liceo Michelangelo in Florence where she was studying and demanded to be let in. She was the only one of the six hundred and fifty girls in the school to do so, and the janitor, an old member of the now illegal Socialist Party and a victim of Fascist thuggery in its early days, begged her to stay away like the others. 'If I open the school for you,' he said, 'they'll beat me up again.' 'In that case,' said Chicchi, 'they will have to beat us both up.' He reluctantly agreed to let her in, and she sat there until the school closing time at twelve-thirty, both unmolested. One out of six hundred and fifty is not very many, but the proportion of those who at that time were prepared to show active opposition to Fascism was probably a lot smaller.

Anti-Fascists like the Matteis, whose position became even more perilous once Italy had entered the war, had, when I came into contact with them, enormous admiration for Britain. They admired the fact that our country had refused to surrender when to all appearances defeat was inevitable. They admired the fact that Parliament still met and debated, that government actions could be criticised there and in the Press, that sacrifices of comfort and of life itself were volunteered and not extorted. They admired Churchill this side idolatry and took the BBC as their mentor. After all, they would say, Italy had once been a democracy and closely tied to Britain by history and affection. They were determined that this should be so again.

For me, then a boy aged fourteen or fifteen, this was a heart-warming experience. Though most of my childhood had been spent in Italy and my mother was Italian I had never thought of myself as anything but English. The sharp tension between Fascist Italy and Britain which arose as a result of the invasion of Abyssinia and sanctions in 1935–36 had inevitably increased the isolation and the Englishness of our home in North Italy. The idea that there might be any conflict of loyalties never occurred to me. I wanted us to win the war as quickly as possible, to go back to England, to get a normal education, and find some way of putting the practical lessons I was then learning to good use, which I assumed would mean if possible going into politics. Partly because of Churchill, and partly through suspicion of all 'isms' – Socialism as well as Fascism – and what seemed to me the strident teaching of class warfare on the Left, another assumption was that the party I would join would be the Conservatives, though not Conservatism of an extreme or dogmatic variety.

If those members of the anti-Fascist Resistance with whom I was in contact admired Britain, my admiration for them was at least equally great. Certainly the courage and stoicism of ordinary people, and the extraordinary heroism of many individuals, like that shown by Gianfranco Mattei, who, as will be seen, plays a leading part in my narrative, deserve wider recognition. A strong motive in writing this book has been to pay my tribute to them and to attempt to rescue them from the near-oblivion which I fear has overtaken them in this country.

There are a number of reasons why this has happened. Italy, after all, entered the war as an ally of Germany, and for three years the British and Italian Armies, Navies and Air Forces fought each other. Wavell's defeat of the Italian armies in the Western Desert in October 1940, the reconquest of Abyssinia in the spring of 1941 by a small and greatly outnumbered force of largely British and Indian troops, the humiliation of the Italian Navy at Taranto in November 1940 and Cape Matapan in March 1941, were cheering victories over an enemy it was easy to deride as lightweight compared with their grim and dedicated Nazi allies. Thanks to the posturing and bombast in Mussolini's conduct of the war there was a natural tendency to assume that all Italian combatants were tarred with the same brush. That was a grave and damaging mistake.

The truth is that, with few exceptions, the Italian people had no stomach for the fight against Britain – or against France or Greece for that matter – and that when they had changed sides they showed an entirely different spirit in the fight against the Nazis occupying their country.

Mussolini sent them into war in 1940 grotesquely unprepared. He boasted that he could put eight, or even ten, million men into the field, but there were not even uniforms for a tenth of that number. When he launched his attack on Greece at the end of October 1940 he talked of achieving victory 'in a few hours', but the troops were sent to fight a campaign in the freezing Albanian mountains with no winter clothing or equipment, and after six months had not even crossed the Greek frontier. (The Italian divisions sent later to fight in Russia were just as ill provided for.) Across the Mediterranean the Italian troops in Libya lacked the weapons, vehicles and ammunition suitable for a desert war. The soldiers on the ground had to endure the consequences of years of neglect, corruption and incompetence against a background of propaganda claims of imminent triumphs thanks to the inspired and invincible leadership of the Duce. Small wonder that there was no enthusiasm for a war which was supposed to revive the glories of the Roman Empire under a reincarnation of Julius Caesar.

I had a first-hand account of the plight of the army in Greece from a friend, David Leese, who had been born in Florence, the son of Dorothy Leese (his father was Gordon Craig) who was giving me English lessons. He had been educated at Italian schools and was an

Italian citizen, and when Italy entered the war had been duly called up. He was posted to an Alpini regiment, one of those serving in Albania, and I used to see quite a lot of him when he was home on leave. His mother was a passionate British patriot, desperately anxious about her only child, but consoled to some extent by the thought that in Greece there would be no risk of his having to fire on English soldiers.

The Alpini were crack troops and so relatively well equipped, but even so, David told me, their boots were ill-fitting, many of them not made of proper leather, and their uniforms seemed to be all either too big or too small. Ammunition was in short supply, and the whole strategy, if it could be called that, seemed to him absolutely crazy. For most of the rest of the troops conditions were much worse. They suffered terribly from the cold and there were many cases of frostbite. The Alpini had managed to mount one or two engagements against the Greek enemy, but for the rest it was simply a question of survival.

The Italian Resistance was a completely different story. The heroism shown by ordinary people everywhere, supplying the partisans, sheltering prisoners of war, performing spontaneous acts of sabotage against the occupying Germans, fully conscious that all the time their lives and those of their families were at risk, was quite remarkable.

Another explanation for the undeserved neglect of the part played in the war by the Italian Resistance is, I suppose, the fact that the Normandy landings on 6 June 1944 came just two days after the liberation of Rome, seen in a sense as the climax of the Italian campaign, and inevitably thereafter the attention of the world was focused on the battles in France and the joint assault on Germany by Allied armies from east and west. The magnificent achievements of the French, Polish, Dutch, Czech and other resistance movements co-operating with these armies captured the admiration of the public. The war in Italy, and in consequence the achievements of the Italian Resistance, were overshadowed. But it was to be another long year before the Germans were finally driven out of Italy, and before Fascism was ended. For all North Italy these were twelve months of bitter civil war in which the civilian population, as well as the by now admirably disciplined partisan units, suffered reprisals, torture and starvation, but remained steadfast.

Some excellent books, such as Eric Newby's *Love and War in the Appenines*, John Miller's *Friends and Romans*, and John Verney's

Going to the Wars, have been written by British officers who had personal experience of the devotion and resourcefulness of the Italian people. Another vivid description of what life was like in this period can be found in the late Iris Origo's *War in the Val d'Orcia*. The first part of this book should be regarded, as I have said, as my testimony to the Italian people's struggle. As will be seen, I have particular reason to be grateful to the part played by the Church in helping the opponents of Fascism. In his last years Mussolini called the Vatican his main enemy, and many priests, from the humblest to the most exalted, justified his accusation.

With the Italian Resistance

ONE day towards the end of December 1943 I was walking through the streets of Rome, then occupied by the German Army as well as policed by their Fascist allies. I carried documents which identified me as a fifteen-year-old Italian called Mario Cambi, born in Naples and resident in the town of Corigliano in Calabria. I also carried a long appreciation written by the underground Committee of National Liberation which outlined plans for an uprising by the Resistance forces in and around Rome which would paralyse German communications, to be combined with a sea and airborne landing by the Allies. This I was to translate for transmission to the Allied command in the south of Italy. If stopped by one of the numerous German or Fascist patrols I would probably have got away with my Neapolitan identity, but not with the papers for translation. A little over a year later, back in England, I was beginning, under my own name, my first term as a public schoolboy at Downside. This abrupt transition needs to be explained.

In 1908, as a very young man, my father, Douglas Walters, had gone to Italy with the task of setting up a European operation for the old-established firm of Nurdin and Peacock which, starting in the reign of George III by importing eggs from France to England, had during the nineteenth century greatly expanded the scale and nature of its work. He subsequently became its European director, and in 1924 he married Clara Pomello, the only child of Annibale Pomello, who had died a few years before.

My Italian forebears were people of rare quality and strength of character. My grandfather Annibale Pomello died, a comparatively young man, of a kidney ailment aggravated by a riding accident.

Curiously enough, my English grandfather, Walter Walters, also died as the result of a fall sustained while out hunting with the Quorn, not far from his home in Leicestershire. He died in 1890, when my father was only five years old. A passionate and financially rather extravagant love of horses, riding and racing shared by my two grandfathers had provided an initial bond between my parents.

But my grandmother, Stella, widowed at an early age, influenced me greatly, and I was devoted to her. She died in 1967 aged ninety-five. She was a woman of great strength and nobility. Profoundly religious herself she, like my mother, was immensely tolerant of other people's actions and beliefs and wholly unbigoted in her faith and convictions. I cannot recall ever hearing her utter a complaint or reproach about anything affecting her. I look upon her as being as near to my conception of a saint as I am ever likely to meet in this world.

My mother was equally resolute in her fierce loyalty to her family and friends, in her religious faith and her extraordinary unselfishness. She was an acknowledged beauty in her youth, but her apparent fragility concealed a tough physique to match her strong personality. Until a few weeks before her ninetieth birthday she remained active, vigorous and wholly lucid. In the late summer of 1987 she was struck by a serious illness which twice called for major surgery. Sadly, but inevitably, her recovery has not been complete. As a young woman she was an accomplished rock climber, and the family photograph albums abound with snapshots of her on some Alpine ridge. As children, when on holiday in the Dolomites, my brother and I used to go with her to the point of departure for the actual ascent, riding on mules provided by the guide who would accompany her on the climb. The guide's son, who was in charge of the mules, and either our nanny, Baba, or one of our English governesses, would then take us back to the resort where we were staying, Madonna di Campiglio, Cortina d'Ampezzo, or Nova Levante.

My father, who intensely disliked heights, would sensibly enough have escaped to the nearest golf course, usually in the company of Alan Napier, Consul-General in Venice and a great friend of the family, or Giovanni Cicogna, another good friend from Venice. The three of them played fairly regularly all the year round at the Alberoni, the Venice Golf Club on the Lido. My father was a determined and enterprising man of business who enjoyed his work, but remained entirely English in outlook, perhaps even to an exaggerated extent to compensate for having to live abroad and under a political regime that he found totally obnoxious. His headquarters were established at Lonigo, about twenty kilometres from Vicenza in North Italy, where my grandmother owned a fairly grand house which she handed over to her daughter and son-in-law, keeping only the top floor for herself. It was here that I was born on 28 November 1928. Most of my childhood was spent in Italy, though my brother Jack and I – he was two years older than me – used to come back every year for the three summer months to stay with a great-uncle who lived at Lyminster Court near Arundel, and with the Peacocks near Itchenor, also in Sussex.[1] A marvellous Italian nanny was followed by a succession of English governesses, so that I grew up bilingual.

I suppose my first moment of political awareness came in the autumn of 1935, when the League of Nations imposed economic sanctions on Italy in consequence of Mussolini's invasion of Abyssinia. As Britain, and in particular Anthony Eden, then Minister for League of Nations Affairs in the Baldwin government, had taken a lead over sanctions, the British became extremely unpopular in Fascist Italy. The walls of our house were regularly daubed with offensive slogans and sometimes loutish village teenagers threw stones at my brother and myself as we bicycled round Lonigo. We and the house were the only British presence in the area, and perhaps inevitably as a result an irresistible target.

Both my parents had great scorn for the Fascist regime, and young though I was it never appeared to me anything other than contemptible. There was, for example, the 'sabato Fascista', the Fascist Saturday, when week after week everyone, unless they were very brave or very foolish and had not joined the party, had to put on a black shirt and take part in marches or physical jerks, all of which made the fat 'gerarchi', the party bosses, look highly ridiculous. Another example of what struck me as the utter absurdity of Fascism was when the order came from on high that people were no longer to address each other in the usual way with the formal 'lei' or the informal 'tu', but had instead to use the collective 'voi' which was practically never heard except in parts of the south. But the decree was

---

[1] Jack Peacock was the managing director, later chairman, of Nurdin and Peacock. He and his wife Phyllis were great friends of my parents.

adamant: '*Il lei è abolito; usate il voi.*' (The '*lei*' is abolished: use the '*voi*'.) It was as if a British government was to forbid the use of 'you' and insist on 'thou'. Yet wherever you went, in government offices or banks or public places, you were confronted with a printed notice ordering you to use '*voi*'. I felt this to be such nonsense that I continued to address everyone with '*lei*'.

The outbreak of war on 3 September 1939 found us on our annual visit to England, but we returned to Italy in December. Back in Lonigo my father consulted the embassy in Rome and others whose opinions he respected, and they all expressed the reassuring but, as it turned out, disastrously misleading opinion that Italy was unlikely to become involved. In May 1940, with the German breakthrough in France, the situation abruptly worsened. Alan Napier advised us to move to Florence because he understood there might be a train from there to repatriate British civilians, but owing to the swift German advance through France and Belgium the train never materialised. So it was near Florence, staying with friends in a villa at Poggio Imperiale, that, on 10 June, we heard of Mussolini's declaration of war on Britain and France. Most of the British in Florence were immediately rounded up and put in prison. We were lucky enough to escape, because we were not registered in Florence and by the time the authorities, having drawn blank in Lonigo, discovered where we were, internment had been substituted for imprisonment.

After some delay, during which we were allowed to stay in Florence under police surveillance, we were interned in the small village of Antella, about 15 kilometers from Florence, and it was there that we were to spend the next three years. This was a typical Italian village of about five hundred inhabitants, houses and shops set round the square with a rather charming church. There was a tram which ran from Antella to Florence, and to begin with I was allowed to go to a private school there, the Domenge Rossi, but after a while this privilege was withdrawn. Jack and I were also given lessons by an English lady called Dorothy Leese, the mother of David, who had been the *Times* correspondent in Florence, and a Mme Garzes taught us French. A retired and rather distinguished Marlborough master, Arthur Brownjohn, whose son, General Nevil Brownjohn, subsequently became Vice-Chief of the Imperial General Staff, was interned in a not too distant village and on occasion provided a sophisticated gloss to my lessons. I kept up my Italian studies with a local teacher. As a result, with the exception of mathematics and science and albeit in very bizarre circumstances, I probably enjoyed as good an academic training as the one my contemporaries were receiving back in England.

It was sometimes possible for children to be repatriated. Both my brother and I were keen to get back to England, and when the first opportunity arose it was decided, after some debate, that my brother should go and that I should stay. He was nearly sixteen, and should the war go on for a few more years he would become of military age, in which case the conditions of his internment would be made much more severe. I don't think my mother could have borne to let us both go. It cannot have been easy for my brother to leave us all, but he showed great fortitude and good humour throughout, and in 1942 he departed on a special train for repatriating internees bound for Lisbon.

My parents were not allowed to move outside the limits of the *comune*, and my father had to report to the *carabinieri* headquarters a mile away once a week. Also, about every ten days, the *maresciallo* of the *carabinieri* would come to the house we were in to check that we were all still there. For my father these were three years of almost intolerable frustration and boredom, compounded by a feeling of guilt at not having taken his family back to England while that was still possible, and at being unable to do anything for the war effort.

We had little money apart from a subsistence allowance paid through the protecting power, Switzerland. The food was bad, and although my grandmother was able to help us financially from time to time we were relatively poor, and being enemy aliens had little access to the black market. The only thing that kept my father sane was listening to the radio. All we were officially allowed was a low-powered wireless set, capable of receiving only Italian stations, but we managed to secure a stronger set on which we could receive the BBC. This became quite an obsession with my father; five or more times a day doors and windows would be tightly closed for the illicit and attentive ritual.

In one thing we were lucky. The house on the top floor of which we were lodged belonged to a family called Alemani, and it gradually became apparent that they were staunchly anti-Fascist. The father, Gigi Alemani, had, through his wife who came from Ivrea near Turin, got a job with the big Turin-based firm of Olivetti, and was now in charge of their Florence factory and office. Because of poor eyesight he was exempt from military service. He was one of the brave few who had refused to join the Fascist party, and after a few months he and his wife, Paola, would regularly come up and join us in listening to Italian broadcasts from the BBC. Apart from the radio and reading, our only other diversions were some kitchen bridge and poker, of which my father was particularly fond.

One episode stands out clearly in my memory. It must have been some time in November or December 1942 that our family solicitor from Lonigo, Avvicato Ferraretto, a firmly anti-Fascist, was given permission to visit us to get my mother's signature on some legal document. It was a visit that gave enormous pleasure to both sides, and he was able to stay the night. Gigi and Paola Alemani were invited to join us for supper, and Gigi Alemani and Ferraretto seemed to strike up an immediate rapport. There was an animated discussion about the course of the war, how long it would last, and about the chances of overthrowing the Fascist regime.

I could see that Gigi was trying to discover how far Ferraretto was prepared to become involved in active anti-Fascist work. Ferraretto said he was prepared, and so Gigi went downstairs and came back with a lot of papers. Having sworn us all to the utmost secrecy – not that there was any real need for that – he revealed that these were copies of the clandestine newspaper *Italia Libera* and pamphlets put out by the underground political group Giustizia e Libertà. Many of these were handed over to Ferraretto, who was asked to distribute them in likely places, such as the universities in Padua, Vicenza and Verona. Gigi explained that though his organisation, now part of the Partito d'Azione, was strong in places like Milan and Turin, it lacked contacts in Veneto. This was where Ferraretto could help. I remember the delight Ferraretto expressed at the prospect of at last being able to do something positive, whatever the dangers. For me, this was the first time that I had actually seen any of these clandestine publications, though I had quite often heard their names, and I found it a thrilling experience.

So life dragged on until the summer of 1943. On 7 May Tunis fell to the Allies and North Africa was cleared of Axis troops. On 10 July British and American troops landed in Sicily, and thirty-eight days later the whole of the island was in Allied hands. While that battle was going on there came, on 25 July, the wonderful news of the meeting of the Fascist Grand Council at which Mussolini had been deposed and arrested. A new government was formed under Marshal Badoglio, and though ostensibly it was committed to continuing the war by the side of the Germans it was generally – and correctly – assumed that negotiations would begin with the Allies to take Italy out of the war.

In the circumstances, the decision taken at that time by the Allied command to subject a number of Italian cities, which because of the prevailing confusion and uncertainty were almost wholly unprotected and defenceless, to a series of ferocious and indiscriminate air attacks is not only impossible to justify but even to begin to understand. In retrospect these attacks and their timing can only be explained by a mixture of callous stupidity and inexplicable incomprehension of the situation.

On the night of Friday, 13 August 1943, for instance, a merciless air bombardment was launched on Milan which killed over a thousand civilians and razed some five thousand houses to the ground. Quite apart from the senseless killing and destruction, such attacks only made the task of the Badoglio government, which was seeking to negotiate with the Allies without at the same time provoking an immediate German attack, infinitely harder. Equally, they added to the many difficulties of the embryonic anti-Fascist resistance movement, which was beginning to gather its forces for the coming battle with the Germans.

The armistice came on 8 September, but this great event was tragically mishandled. Although I think the real culprits were the King and Badoglio, who immediately removed themselves from Rome to Bari, now Allied headquarters, leaving the Italian armed forces with no clear instructions as to what they should do, a good deal of blame must also attach to the Allied negotiators who, mesmerised by the now officially adopted slogan of unconditional surrender (though Churchill had wanted it applied to Germany only, not to Italy), never really trusted the Italians and so failed to co-ordinate any military strategy with them. The consequence of this bungling was that the whole of Italy was not to be freed for another two years, instead of the two months which at first people were assuring each other was the probable timetable.

But to begin with all seemed to be going well. After 25 July anti-Fascists came more and more into the open. Fascist mayors and other senior officials were being replaced, not by anti-Fascists but by rather faceless bureaucrats, who were at least a great improvement on their predecessors. I began going into Florence increasingly often, and soon came into contact with a group of anti-Fascists introduced by Gigi Alemani, who had already been active underground, printing leaflets attacking the Fascist regime. These came out under the banner 'Giustizia e Libertà', and were distributed in the universities, among army formations, and so on.

After the fall of Mussolini the group in Florence increased the scope of its activities and the nature of its appeal. Its leaflets, run off with the co-operation of some of the jobbing printers in Florence, were now directed principally at the Badoglio government, exhorting it to negotiate quickly with the Allies and to prepare for action against the Germans. They also demanded the right to free assembly and to form trade unions, as well as freedom for the Press. Leading anti-Fascists should be acknowledged and given positions of authority. They were also trying to get in touch with the Italian High Command in the Florence area, but this was made more difficult because the only orders that had been received by the area commander, General Armellini, were to continue to collaborate with the Germans.

One of the leaders of this group was a Professor Raffaello Ramat, who was to play a prominent part in the later Resistance, and it was joined by our host in Antella, Gigi Alemani, but the two whom I got to know best were a remarkable brother and sister, Gianfranco and Teresa (Chicchi) Mattei. Gianfranco was then aged twenty-six, a brilliant chemist who had just been made a Professor at Milan University. Chicchi was four years younger, and there were five other brothers and sisters. As I mentioned earlier, their parents had brought up the children to hate Fascism. The nucleus to which these people belonged was affiliated to the Partito d'Azione, the Action Party, one of the many political groupings which carried on a precarious existence in the underground opposition.

Its precursor, Giustizia e Libertà, was founded in the early 1930s by opponents of Fascism including the famous Rosselli brothers who were later murdered. It called itself 'Liberal-Socialist' – a contradiction in terms if both words are properly interpreted. But if the party's political philosophy was a bit confused, this enabled it to draw on a wide membership of the left and right, united in their single-minded determination to work for the overthrow of Fascism. Gianfranco and Chicchi became Communists but continued to work as part of the group. After the liberation of Italy the party's *raison d'être* was gone, and it quickly faded away, but while the war continued the Partito d'Azione and the Communists were probably the best organised and most active of the Resistance parties.[1]

I helped this Florence group in every way I could. I monitored BBC broadcasts, made out and translated summaries of them, gave these to Gigi Alemani to type, and then brought the finished version into Florence, travelling almost every day by tram or bicycle. I also helped in distributing leaflets and in checking on German troop movements, for after the fall of Mussolini many new German divisions had been switched to reinforce the Italian front. To begin with all this activity was pretty Heath Robinsonish, but we learned by experience and the later Resistance became extremely professional. I knew that my parents were worried about my activities, though after leaving Antella, partly for reasons of security and partly because of space problems, we were living in different houses, so they were not aware of all that was going on.

During these heady August days we all assumed that the armistice would come soon, and that though the Germans might cause serious trouble in the north, most of Italy, including Rome and Florence, would be quickly liberated. Our group was busily making preparations for the arrival of the Allied armies, and as translator and interpreter there was obviously a role for me to play.

We were, of course, absurdly optimistic, but when on 8 September 1943 Badoglio announced that an armistice had been signed our optimism seemed justified. I kept a diary during this time, often little more than scrappy notes, but after the liberation of Rome in June 1944 I transcribed them into notebooks, a number of which have survived. I quote from this at times rather juvenile production with some embarrassment, but it does give better than anything I could write now an idea of the atmosphere of those days. The first entry is for 8 September:

8.15 p.m. Badoglio's broadcast. The Armistice. Good God, it is all over. Relief, joy, just wild reaction. It's over at last. Soon everything will be all right. British troops will march into Florence, a few weeks of utter bliss, and then England! Three years of longing and hoping. England! It's a dream, but it's

[1] For a closer examination of the part played in Italian politics by the Partito d'Azione see Appendix A.

coming true. Wild cycle ride to Florence. Mad scenes in the streets. It's all over. Spent the night at the Giachettis'. [Signora Giachetti was English, and her two daughters, Robin and Pauline, belonged to the Ramat-Mattei group.]

A few more days pass. Why aren't we landing? The few German troops which seem to be around are worried. We are told that they are very scared at the possibility of being cut off. More and more rumours. Facts also, unfortunately. German troops start marching through. Fascists appear again in the streets. Everything is utterly confused. German troops. British and American PoWs. Italian Army troops. Some Fascists.

All appear to be thronging in and around Florence. News bad. We have landed at Salerno. Why? God, why? We have been flung back on the beaches. The 8th Army is apparently rushing to the rescue, but Florence is a long way off. What a blunder. If we had landed at Livorno at once, possibly the whole of Italy would have been taken over quite easily. The Italian Army would have rallied. As it is, it seems to be crumbling fast.

What to do about Italian soldiers and escaped Allied prisoners of war was one of our greatest problems. Badoglio's armistice broadcast had ended with the words: 'The Italian armed forces will therefore cease all acts of hostility against the Anglo-American forces wherever they may be met. They will, however, oppose attacks from any other quarter.' The German command called on all Italian units to hand over their arms, and some complied, but most simply disintegrated, the men trying to make their way home, or forming partisan units in the mountains, or taking refuge in the big cities. The gates of the prisoner of war camps had been opened, and though some of the inmates had been rounded up by the Germans and deported, more were wandering through the countryside, hoping to make their way to the Allied armies in the south.

On 12 September in a daring rescue operation a Storch aircraft with Hitler's personal pilot, Colonel Otto Skorzeny, landed near the ski-lodge on the Gran Sasso mountain 100 kilometres north-east of Rome, where Mussolini was being held prisoner, and carried him off. After spending some days with Hitler at his headquarters on the Russian front Mussolini returned to Italy at the end of September and set up the so-called Republic of Salò (a small town on Lake Garda). This was supported by the most dedicated and ruthless Fascists and tyrannised north Italy until the end of the war.

35

I am staying with the Giachettis. Two American prisoners hiding in their house, one from Arkansas, who finds it very amusing that I call it AR-KAN-SASS. Meeting with the Matteis, Ramat, Gigi Alemani and friends of the Giachettis to discuss possible action. The Resistance is beginning to take shape. Following day another meeting when the Partito d'Azione leaders were present: Ragghianti, Ramat, Gigi Alemani, Enzo Enriques. I was asked to provide photographs for false identity cards. A splendid, very attractive young woman, Maria Guaita, who seems to be in charge of providing false documents, deals with this. Gianfranco and Chicchi Mattei I met the day after, with Ugo Mattei and Raffaello Ramat. Further meeting at the Giachettis. Incidentally, a couple of days before, fighting had broken out in Florence between the remnants of the Italian garrison and the Germans, but it doesn't last long. At this meeting a nice-looking chap speaks to me, but his name is not given. He says: 'The Germans have now taken over completely. Most of the escaped British PoWs round Florence have got away. The British are temporarily blocked but are bound to advance soon. Meanwhile, first task: collect arms where possible off Italian soldiers who are fleeing and gather them in certain fixed places. Two, collect civilian clothes and distribute them to escaping Allied prisoners of war. Also maps and medicines.'

Our group prepared a standard kit for distribution among the escaping prisoners of war. If possible it contained a map, but failing that – and maps were hard to come by – information about the latest position of the British and American forces and the most promising route by which they might be reached, giving distances and noting the areas where the Germans were concentrated, and so to be avoided. The kit also contained some food and basic medicines as well as a few useful Italian phrases.

I speak to him after the meeting and when I tell him about my English connections he asks me to speak to F., who is organising part of the PoW relief and aid campaign. Rush off to Bianchis [friends of my parents]. Daddy is now hiding there. It really is a shame that he should go through this sort of thing.

F. [Marchese Piero Fossi] a nice fellow, rather distinguished-looking, quiet, efficient, perfectly calm under pressure. Conference in flat where I had spent the night. Three men and three girls, Franca, Orsola,[1] Tina. They are perfectly cool and matter-of-fact.

We discuss buying medical equipment from the chemist by the Ponte de

[1] Orsola De Cristofaro Biasutti. She was later arrested, but escaped and resumed her underground activities in Florence.

la Carraia, getting hold of two motor-cars and a van, and then, having got through the cordon, driving beyond the Certosa [about 15 km from Florence], where apparently there is a large group of prisoners stranded. Some of the people hiding apparently were not well. I am feeling fairly cool. I must at all costs stick it. F. gives us maps and of course I have the identity cards.

I now had three forged cards, two identifying me as Mario Cambi, one a railway pass and the other an identity card. The third, which purported to have been issued by the Ministry of Agriculture, named me as Giorgio Aldo. Its purpose was to facilitate entry to farms where escaped PoWs might be hiding. I had chosen Cambi as my principal alias because at that time I was staying with an old lady called Bianca Violani Cambi who lived in the Piazza Viesseux. The railway pass had been provided for me by a member of the Resistance working in the Florence office of Thomas Cook, called Signor Tabacco; the others by Maria Guaita.[1] My birthplace was given as Naples and my residence as in Calabria because they were in that part of Italy now under Allied occupation, so that the Fascist authorities would have had no means of checking the accuracy of these statements.

Franca, a pretty girl of about 20, calmly remarks that the German soldiers would appear to be stopping people on the outskirts and searching them. Those found with arms or equipment which cannot be explained are in serious trouble. It would be better, she says, that two people be appointed for each job. F. agrees that it was a good idea! Nasty sinking feeling in the pit of my stomach as I walked out. Very conscious of the maps.

My job was relatively easy – just buy a great number of medical supplies and wait for the car to appear. Franca was getting it. I had been given plenty of money by B. but I think the chemist was rather surprised at the order which I gave! A little Fiat drives up with Franca at the wheel. I shove the parcel of medicines in the back, sit next to her and we were off. A German staff car roared by. I looked at myself in the mirror. I looked all right, but a sinking feeling in the tummy, difficult to describe. I smiled at Franca as she crashed gears. A feeling of superiority came over me. Women can't drive, just can't. I kept repeating that to myself. Funny how little details seem to stick out.

We are at the roadblock. A German soldier signals us to stop. I think I am

---

[1] After the war she described her life with the Resistance in a remarkable book. See Appendix B.

feeling relatively cool again, and after a cursory glance at the papers he waves us on. Arrive beyond Certosa. Some Americans who seem to make no sense. Thank God I could explain the situation to an intelligent South African. He tells me that the position is very sticky. Three of their chaps terribly ill. I told him that they just must give themselves up. They couldn't remain there any longer. It was too risky. We had been directed to their hiding-place by people on the road at the village before Certosa. Gave him the medicines and a map and explained the layout of the country. As decided at the meeting, I suggested two courses of action – a) join with the Italian soldiers flocking to the mountains, and eventually become partisans; b) make an immediate break for the south; to remain stationary was mad. He agreed and said they would discuss it and come to a decision at once. We shook hands. What a life, what hell. Such splendid fellows too. So many families waiting for them far away. Fourteen – God, I feel about 40. Return uneventful. Further conference. We have been lucky, and plan the next move. I ask B. to find out about my position. The fact that we have got away from Antella must have been observed and they may well be on the look-out. He has a friend at the police station and is going to make necessary enquiries. Am going to stay with Countess Fabricotti whose house is near the English cemetery. Mummy is OK with Daddy at the moment at the Bianchis. I wonder whether I am doing the right thing. Yes – feel it is my duty, speaking Italian like a native and being English. Also I feel that I seem to be able to keep relatively cool.

Countess Fabricotti's house in turmoil. Several people hiding there including her brother, a smart, typical cavalry officer. Robin Giachetti drops in to see me. Another splendid, marvellous girl. She is doing absolute wonders. Charming and intelligent. We have a long talk. There is another job to carry out, but Franca is not available.

Night rather bloody. I am sleeping on the floor and don't like it at all. The following morning, contact the British nuns.[1] They are wonderful old girls. Mother Superior is already organising clothes supply for prisoners of war, also medicines, and has ransacked the convent school for maps. She is also prepared to take wounded prisoners into the convent, she tells me.

Together with L., one of F.'s men,[2] cycle out loaded with maps, also food and medicines for the Ugolino [where the golf course was, about 16 kilometres from Florence] where another group of stranded prisoners of war

---

[1] Two institutions in Florence, a hospital run by the Blue Sisters and the fashionable girls' school, Santa Reparata (where Robin Giachetti among others had been educated), included among their staff a small number of English and Irish nuns, whose work had not been interfered with.

[2] No longer identifiable.

is situated. We have rather a narrow shave when we are stopped for documents and they don't seem to like L.'s. I feel sheer physical fear for the first time, a horrid feeling, and when we get away a cold sweat is pouring down my back. L. is worse and seems to be panicking, so I give him a lecture, which amuses me. We get to the PoWs, New Zealanders, and fine fellows. A repeat of yesterday's performance. The officer in charge says he would feel guilty to leave the men and make a break for the south. I point out the alternative, give him maps and explain the situation. Such a nice fellow. He asks me about myself and tells me that what I am doing is suicidal. With a touch of bravado I tell him that that is my business, but actually I am very touched by the way he shakes my hand.

Conference at F.'s Position getting worse. The Italian soldiers who have taken to the mountains with fighting intentions have lost most of their officers and are apparently returning in vast numbers to their homes, and many are being rounded up on the way by the Germans. Also, supposedly, most of the British officers have made a break for the south. Tommies are terribly lost. Poor chaps, it is quite understandable, not speaking the language and not knowing where the hell they are. We tune in to the BBC. News bloody. The intervention of the Navy and the arrival of the Eighth Army has prevented us being pushed back into the sea, but we are blocked at Salerno. God, why land at Salerno? I remember thinking I will have it out with our fellows if ever I see them again. Two more fellows and a girl apparently caught and shot. There are so many rumours, one does not know which to believe. F. absolutely cool but obviously worried. We have a talk on the side. Apparently he fears we are being tracked down. Notices appear on all the walls, signed by the military commander, 'Any Italian harbouring escaped PoWs or internees will be shot at sight and house burnt down. An award of 10,000 lire.' Talk with him and also Chicchi Mattei, and we agree this will make things tricky. So, when I return to Countess Fabricotti's house I have a guilty feeling, and can't help thinking that it is my duty to clear out as soon as possible.

Supplies to PoWs near Ugolino again. Rather tragic scene, all Tommies again very lost, and very difficult to explain the situation to them. It would be splendid if one could remain with them. One fellow entreats me to stay and show them the way south. I feel horrid, but explain the impossibility of this. Point everything out clearly, and leave. I suppose they will all be caught soon. Still, if they follow my instructions and scatter at once, some at least may get over to our lines, but hell, they are a long way off. We are utterly bogged down south of Cassino. God alone knows when we are going to move. Go and see Daddy – he is worried and irritable. I don't blame him. Just as well he thinks I am hiding and doing nothing.

Back to F.'s, and further conference. Certainly an effective organisation is getting under way. The Communists and Partito d'Azione men seem the most efficient. I talk quite a lot at the meeting and they don't seem to mind. A man rushes in and gives us bad news. Part of a group has been captured and he fears that the house where we are may be the next. We decide to scatter, but not all in a bunch, and so we go down one by one. The strain of having to wait is awful, but at last it is my turn, down those stairs. It couldn't have taken me half a minute, but seemed an hour. Every detail as clear as daylight. I was thinking what I would say if I was caught at the bottom of the stairs. Very little to say, with two false documents in my pocket. I was determined not to speak. Remember thinking that I must remain calm. I was at the front door and then turned quickly to the right and walked away. I hadn't gone very far when I heard the shrieking of brakes, but I daren't look round and so I don't know whether it was the police or just an ordinary car. I continued walking in a haze and then up to Bianchis' to Daddy. He was worried and felt he couldn't remain there any longer. Mummy had now joined him. The servants must be getting suspicious, and what the Bianchis were risking weighed on him. We had a long talk and decided that if the British didn't land within the next day or two, he should make a bolt for the south with Mummy, and I could follow a few days later. She could easily get into a convent in Rome, with all the contacts she had. It was the 5th of October. I looked at myself in the mirror and was shocked to see how haggard I seemed. Well, they had been three eventful weeks.

Later, meet F., who had also got away. He has bad news for us personally. His friend at the police has reported that the Fascists are aware that Dad and I are hiding in Florence and that I have been active in the Underground. Bolsi, of the Italian Questura, tried to put them off our track, saying that Pop had gone north where he had friends, and that I was only a child, but that won't last long, I fear. Am feeling shaken and take further addresses from Chicchi Mattei and others, of people in Rome so that we could go there, when we reach Rome, in an emergency. It is obvious that I must follow Daddy and Mummy in a matter of days.

Rush off to R., who is directing the Underground printing press. Give him all the latest information and collect some money. It is getting late and curfew will be very soon, so I leave for Countess Fabricotti's. She opens the door, as pale as death. The police had called, less than an hour ago, at the flat where her brother was in hiding, and although they missed him, she expects they could come round to her house at any time. They may be watching the house still, she tells me. I am quite aware of that, so collect a mac and decide to leave a few odd things there. Curfew any moment now, so I must rush. I shake her hand – she really has been splendid and I feel very moved. She embraces me, muttering 'Così giovane, così giovane, (so young, so young)' and I am off.

There is not a moment to lose and I can't go very far. Turn down a side street. Not a very nice quarter of Florence. See a notice, 'Pensione Albergo'. I enter rapidly. Just at that moment the hour strikes. Not much time had been left. I instantly realise that this is a very low kind of place, more a sort of brothel. The receptionist girl seems to leer at me, but eventually provides me with a room. I hadn't had any sleep the night before and am feeling ghastly. The hall seemed to be moving round in circles, round and round. When I go upstairs, on the landing, some rather disreputable people emerge from a door. I remember fumbling with a key and finally opening, closing and locking the door. It was a filthy-looking room, and I just threw myself down, dressed, on the bed, wondering whether my behaviour might have excited the receptionist's suspicion. I remember thinking 'I may have been stupid' but at that a feeling of exhaustion came over me and I went to sleep.

Woke up with a stifled panicky feeling – the feeling of being hunted, which I will never entirely forget – or will I? Brush my hair and go downstairs. The place doesn't look quite so bad by daylight. New girl at the door. I pay for my room and hand her the key. It is about 7.30 a.m. on the 6th October – Jack's birthday. The hunted feeling gets worse and I feel I am being followed. Must pull myself together, the next few days are very important and I must have my wits about me. I feel very worried about Daddy – he looks so obviously English and his accent could easily betray him. Have arranged to meet Orsola in a small café. She turns up with false documents, one for Mummy and one for Daddy. She had already given me mine some days before. Am not so worried about Mummy – she can do the talking for him. Whatever happens, she will be utterly cool and resourceful. They are now both staying at Bianchis'. I give them the false documents and it is agreed that with the help of Bianchis and the Manentis,[1] they would decide to try to get through to Rome tomorrow morning. Mummy managed to contact Maglia Dainotto, an old friend and a very distant relative, and she could stay there with Daddy for a few days. I said that I would follow as soon as possible but I was determined to continue with the translations and other things that I was involved with at that moment.

I say goodbye to them and feel very broken-hearted as I am terribly worried about Daddy. It is so much worse worrying about other people, and he is not cut out for this sort of life.

[1] Mario Manenti was an architect and sculptor who, among other things, had built the 'Italian village' (studios) at the end of the Fulham Road. His wife Bushka belonged to an Anglo-Jewish family. Their villa was on the Erta Canina in Florence. They gave help to the Resistance, were both sculptors and both charming.

The end of internment had, of course, come as an enormous relief to my father. Soon after the armistice the local policeman had come up and congratulated him: 'Now we are at peace.' He was at last able to go to Florence for the first time in three years and he proposed to stay there until, in a few weeks' time, as he and so many others confidently expected, the Allied armies marched in. Disillusion was swift. It was the Germans who marched in and took over. Because of his English appearance and accent it would have been dangerous for him to go about in the city, and dangerous too for his hosts to go on concealing him.

So the decision to move to Rome was taken. In the train my mother would do all the talking. If I travelled separately there would be less risk of our all being caught.

My father had become a Catholic when he married my mother, more, I suspect, to please her and her family than from any deep conviction. In fact I think he remained at heart an agnostic until the last years of his life (he died in 1964) when religion did become important for him. A priest in Florence had arranged through a sort of Vatican underground that if my parents succeeded in getting to Rome my mother was to be housed in the Vatican-protected Villa Lante convent. Later, as will be seen, it was possible to make a similar arrangement for my father.

Further meetings with F. and the Matteis. He gives me names of the relevant people I should contact when I get to Rome, but most of all Gianfranco, whom I had met at some of the early meetings and who was now already in Rome. The first base would be at the Calvinos',[1] at an address which I was given. The time has now come for me to go to Rome too. I am staying the night with Signora Cambi in Piazza Viesseux. A splendid old lady of 70, who is also coming to Rome with me tomorrow and I have spent several nights there since the crisis started. I am passing as her nephew, and one of my false documents gives me her surname. Gianfranco will issue me with some others when I get through to Rome – if I do. Am feeling tired – the strain is beginning to tell. The last four weeks have been hell, in the real sense of the word. Mrs C. is a brilliant woman, and a Professor of Literature, is quite cool and calm, but then she is 70! We discuss literature – Shakespeare, Dante and Macchiavelli.

[1] Friends of the Matteis. It was in their house that I first met Giorgio Amendola and was given by him an expertly forged identity card.

We agree that the chances of getting through are better than even, but not much more than that. The main hope being that the railways are in utter turmoil, packed with refugees and constantly being bombed by our fellows. At 4 a.m. the curfew is lifted and we leave her house. Am carrying a light kitbag and mac. No taxis or buses, and we walk through the darkened streets. The first light is just appearing on the horizon. Now that the waiting is over I am feeling cool again, but I keep on thinking of Daddy. I assume that they have arrived safely. I had caught a glimpse of him just before he left. He had dressed himself as I had told him to, in badly fitting cheap Italian clothes and a ridiculous grey hat. He didn't look too strikingly English. I remember thinking that Uncle Norman [of Lyminster Court, a rather correct stock-broker] would have had a fit if he had seen him.

I am packed in the corridor like a sardine. An old peasant, stinking of garlic, on my right, and rather an attractive girl on my left. Am pretty constantly looking to the left! We pass through bombed and smoking villages. The roads are packed with German military convoys rushing south. They travel before daylight will break, as they get rather a pasting in the daytime from the RAF and from the Americans. Find myself thinking of the past weeks in Florence and of all the splendid people I have been working with, and whether I shall ever see them again. I don't even know most of their names. We pass a German convoy which had been quite literally blasted by an attack. Half-mangled corpses are still scattered all over the road. I am surprised how little emotion I feel. After all, they are human beings too! Still, this sort of life is not the right kind to make one sentimental. The thought of all those wretched Italians in Tuscany and the stories I have heard already about what was happening to people harbouring prisoners of war makes me feel that the more Germans that are killed, the better.

The train jogs on. At Arezzo German guards get on to the train and I feel my heart beginning to beat faster, and that dry feeling in the palate. They are slowly approaching along the corridor, inspecting documents. It is very difficult to express my feeling to anybody who hasn't been through it. I was wondering whether the same had happened to Daddy and whether he had got through. '*Ne pas se pencher au dehors*' keeps on dancing before my eyes. The train halts and then suddenly there is a frightful shout or scream from a carriage further down the train, and from the window we can see a man being pushed off the train by the German guards. It is pretty bloody and the girl next to me has gone white as a sheet. The old peasant next to me keeps repeating '*brutti vigliacchi, brutti vigliacchi*' (horrid cowards) under her breath. Suddenly there is a thud, and another, and yet another, and we can hear aeroplanes above. One flies over fairly low, and I feel a knot in my throat and want to cheer. Funny wanting to cheer someone who's probably going to kill you within half a minute. Then the Germans jump off the train and we lurch forward. The train is off, and for the first time since we started, moving fast. The sound of bombs pursues us into the distance.

The journey goes on and on, but finally at 6.45 in the evening, after 13 hours' travelling without a bite of food, we draw into Rome. Get out of the train with Mrs Cambi, who had been sitting on a box very patiently at the end of the carriage, and never seemed to move. We walk rapidly down the platform. At the barrier there is an Italian policeman who gives a cursory look at my identity card, and hers, and nods. As I walk out of the barrier, my heart gives a great leap. For a second I feel almost light-headed and want to shout with joy.

It was a beautiful evening, warm and summery, Rome looking lovely. The driver of our carrozza is talkative, and with a few questions I get him to tell me what is going on. Apparently the Florence 'reign of terror' has not started at all here, and as yet, as the British are expected to arrive within days, people's spirits are high. At that moment we stop at some traffic lights and I see posted on the wall one of the notices about harbouring escaped prisoners and internees as well as escaped Italian soldiers and officers, and I think of Maglia [Dainotto, close friend of the family] where I am now heading. A German staff car draws up next to the carrozza and I look down on the faces of the four arrogant bullies sitting in it. These two things have been sufficient to quell any temporary enthusiasm and the hunted feeling comes over once more.

Arrival at Maglia's. Daddy and Mummy already there for five or six days. No emotional scenes but immense relief. Not much time to lose, curfew at 8.30 p.m. and we obviously can't all remain there. Mrs Cambi leaves for a friend's house. Daddy and Mummy will continue to stay at Maglia's for the moment. I will be staying at Mario Mossolin's, a distant cousin of Mummy's. Maglia's daughter, a pretty girl of 20, accompanies me. Very cool, and I should think very resourceful in an emergency. Am getting to admire more and more these Italian girls. They seem to rise to the occasion.

Mario's flat in Via Siacci just off Villa Borghese. Family consists of Mario and wife, and two daughters, one about 12 and the other 21 and very attractive. She is terribly worried because her fiancé was in a garrison to the north and she has heard nothing from him since the Armistice. Rather untruthfully I assure her that most of the Florence garrisons and those around there have got away and that he is probably hiding in the country. Long conversation with Mario, a wealthy, very successful lawyer, intelligent and charming. He obviously is not in touch with the Resistance, but gets a lot of useful information. Listen to the BBC – we are bogged down south of

Cassino.[1] Very worrying, and the thought of the thousands of PoWs stranded in Tuscany distresses me. They will be forced to give themselves up in large numbers and will all be rounded up if we don't hurry. Poor chaps, they were so game and full of spirit.

First good night's sleep for weeks, also a hot bath. One learns to appreciate small comforts. In the morning, go to Calvinos'. Address had been given to me in Florence by B. and the Matteis. There I meet some of the leading men of the underground and others whom I knew. Ugo Mattei, who had already gone to Rome some days before; Giorgio Amendola and Sanguinetti of the Communists; Bassani of the Socialists. Chicchi Mattei was also there. She had been, I am told, one of the couriers between the Milan CLN [Comitato di Liberazione Nazionale] and the Rome CLN. She is certainly a pretty girl with attractive spaniel eyes. Meet again Gianfranco, Chicchi's brother. It is strange that such an important instant liking should have sprung up between us. After all, he is eleven years my senior and the most brilliant scientist that Milan University had produced for many years – and I know nothing at all about science. Not that that really matters a bit.

We had a long talk. He had just arrived from Milan a few days before, and his job is now to organise the Rome Resistance Movement. We compare notes about Milan and Florence, and he insists on treating me as an equal though I point out that I was merely a very insignificant cog, as indeed I am. He says, 'I have heard one or two things about what you have been doing in Florence, and I am very impressed.' Amendola is a very imposing fellow and a striking figure of a man. He is the son of the famous Giovanni Amendola [a leading Liberal anti-Fascist deputy, beaten to death by a Fascist mob in July 1925] and has only recently arrived in Rome, and now that Togliatti, the leading Communist, is in the south, he is in charge. I am very impressed by him. He dominated the meeting and when I contradicted him regarding something he had said about the Tuscan situation, he took it very well indeed. I take my hat off to him for that. Sanguinetti is obviously very clever and very able. He is a multi-millionaire and is helping to finance the Rome Resistance Movement. Ugo Mattei, whom I got to know in Florence, is a fine, very direct person, an ex-naval captain with a splendid record of anti-Fascism and a charming smile. Bassani able, but I should say more of a talker than a man of action. Gallia of the Republicans I should say clever, brave and highly resourceful. Sandullo a talkative, pleasant Sicilian.

[1] Following the Salerno landings on 9 September, the Allies had advanced to the main German defences, the so-called 'Gustav Line', which ran along the Garigliano River on the west coast, up to Cassino, across some of the highest parts of the southern Apennines, and then along the Sangro River to the Adriatic.

Gianfranco and I go out to lunch. He is really without nerves. We enter a restaurant and in spite of the fact that there are several German officers he appears completely relaxed.

See Daddy in the afternoon. Mummy has already got into a convent, the Villa Lante on the other side of the river. She has been having trouble with her legs and can hardly walk. Daddy and I discuss plans. He is of the opinion that Rome will be freed very soon and that attempting to cross the lines now would be asking for trouble. We decide to stay put for a few days and look for a safe hiding-place, the Vatican perhaps, or an extra-territorial monastery. Take Daddy to meet Bassani. Gianfranco also there. They suggest contacting Monsignor O'Flaherty, who apparently has been doing splendid work for escaped prisoners of war. I go and see O'Flaherty, with an introduction from Bassani. He is pleasant, but not particularly helpful. It is not his fault. He is a marked man, I am told, and I am also told that he is hiding three British generals including, I believe, the famous O'Connor, who had escaped at some stage from Vincigliata.[1]

Monsignor Hugh O'Flaherty, an Irishman long resident in Rome and an official of the Vatican's Holy Office, a man of infinite courage and resource, was largely responsible for a clandestine organisation which arranged for hundreds of escaping prisoners of war, who had made their way to the city or its environs, to be hidden, fed, financed, encouraged, and generally looked after. (See *The Rome Escape Line* by Sam Derry. Harrap, 1960.)

Monsignor O'Flaherty sent a message to me on one occasion, asking me to come and see him in his office at the Collegio dei Tedeschi, which had become the nerve centre of his PoW organisation. He wanted to discuss some translations I had been doing which concerned the escape routes. After the liberation of Rome I was able to see him several times and to thank him for his help.

Am getting worried about Daddy again. Maglia is marvellous but we know the risk she is running and it isn't fair to her. Furthermore there is a shit of a porter, and apparently he might blab. It's all right for me, language OK and I

---

[1] The castle of Vincigliata near Florence was the place of detention for high-ranking Allied officers captured in the Western Desert, including General O'Connor, who escaped, and General Carton de Wiart, who was sent with an emissary of the Badoglio government to Lisbon in August 1943 to help over negotiations for an armistice.

can stay with the Resistance crowd. I just can't expect poor old Pop to act like a film gangster. He is looking older and not too well.

Another day passes and I am beginning to feel desperate. Gianfranco and people have their hands full as it is and I can't ask them to search for safe hideouts. Enter into a church and pray. This is the sort of time when God and religion really mean something and I find it a comfort to believe. I must stop this philosophic nonsense or these notes will never end. Go and see Mummy at the convent. I know just how she must be feeling, but she is simply terrific. How I admire her. Am getting more and more worried about Daddy. This is absolute hell.

Spend the afternoon with Gianfranco and translate a very important document into English, apparently absolutely top secret. I should think Kesselring [Marshal Albert Kesselring, appointed German Commander-in-Chief in Italy in November 1941] would give a lot for it, and that pleases me intensely. A man is going to cross the lines with it tonight. Busy as he is, Gianfranco has had time to enquire about hideouts, but it is so difficult. Every religious institution seems to be packed with people hiding. Gianfranco is so charmingly boyish that I can hardly believe he is the same man that has tricked the German police in the north and is doing some extraordinary work at the moment in Rome. According to Sandullo, he was conducting some wonderful scientific research and also will certainly be a leading figure when the Liberation takes place.

There has been another raid on the ghetto, and as Gianfranco and I walked past a side street, we could still hear the sound of wailing children, and also we saw German troops pushing people like cattle into trucks and beating people on the back. One man, who was next to me and Gianfranco, took a step forward, and I think he was going to go berserk. We seized him by the arm and hurried away to a small café. The man was muttering incoherently. We ordered three stiff brandies, and Gianfranco and I looked at each other. He was quite calm and cool, but there must have been absolute horror stamped on my face, for he stretched out his hand and patted me on the back, and his words stand out as clear as daylight: 'Don't worry, they shall pay. Don't forget, either, for that would be stupid. (*Non aver paura; pagheranno. Ma non dimenticare perché quello sarebbe stupido.*)' The other man had now calmed down, and as pale as death was drinking brandy. I followed Gianfranco out blindly into the street, too shaken to say anything.

As his alliance with Hitler (the 'Rome/Berlin Axis') became more firmly based Mussolini was increasingly anxious to demonstrate his solidarity, and this included adopting some of the Nazi racial policies. Although by 1937 Jews were already being discriminated against over employment, the promulgation in July 1938 of his 'Charter of Race', which decreed that Jews as well as Ethiopians and Arabs belonged to an inferior race, came as a shock to many Italians who had no hostility towards the small but old-established Jewish community. When I came to know some of them I felt the greatest sympathy and admiration for them, so many being strongly anti-Fascist and active in the Resistance.

When the Nazis took control after the Badoglio armistice the plight of the Jews greatly worsened. I put together some scattered notes from my diary:

On September 27 the Germans raided the home of Ugo Foà, head of the Jewish community, and took him to Gestapo headquarters. He was told that the community had 24 hours in which to raise fifty kilos of gold, to be handed over to the Germans. If they failed to produce this, five hundred Jews would be deported to a concentration camp in Poland immediately, and others would follow. Thirty kilos were collected by the evening and Foà pleaded for an extension of the time limit. This was granted until noon the following day. In fact the twenty missing kilos were provided by an anonymous donor, generally believed to have been the Pope. Two days later the Germans entered the synagogue and seized lists of names of members of the community. They were systematically rounded up in a brutal manner and deported to camps in Germany and Poland.

October 16. Persecution of the Jews has apparently started today. It is said that Senise [former head of the intelligence services, but a civilised and humane man] refused to hand over lists of the names and addresses of Roman Jews to the Germans. He is said to have been arrested and deported to the north. Without these lists the Germans have to rely on informers. They raid houses where Jews are thought to be living, compel the porters to say how many Jews there are in the building, force open the doors of the apartments, hustle and kick the unfortunate people into closed lorries, and take them off to an 'unknown destination' – i.e. concentration camps in Germany. People here who on the whole liked and got on well with the Jews are shocked, and terrified that more widespread persecution will follow.

October 24. Many Jews have managed to escape. The Pope has given instructions that they should be welcomed in Vatican protected institutions and religious institutions. There are several hiding in Collegio San Giuseppe, the Villa Lante, San Paolo, and countless other monasteries and convents. But the night raid on the ghetto has accounted for very many being deported to Germany.

Back to my main diary.

Daddy has had a narrow shave with the curfew. Very worrying. It is 15th October. Our lads still blocked south of Cassino. The 'reign of terror' starting up in Rome. Rome absolutely packed with people hiding: escaped PoWs, Italian Army officers, Italians who came out against the Fascists in the brief Badoglio spell, Jews, etc. Fascist blackshirts consisting of the worst type of scoundrel led by two sadists, Bardi and Pollastrini, have formed two Italian SS brigades, very dangerous for us. On the 16th, through Mummy's convent, I meet Brother Robert Pace, a splendid fellow who is doing some wonderful work for PoWs. He suggests contacting the Collegio San Giuseppe, which enjoys a certain amount of Vatican protection and which belongs to the same order as his, the Brothers of the Christian Schools. He takes me along to meet the Superior, Brother Sigismondo, a tall, fine figure of a man. He will take us. Relief beyond words.

The Collegio San Giuseppe Istituto di Merode belonged to the Order of Christian Brothers (Fratelli delle Scuole Christiane) founded by St Jean-Baptiste de la Salle, the seventeenth-century educational pioneer and patron saint of schoolteachers, a French teaching order which was particularly strong in Ireland and had some houses in England. The Brothers, who included some very distinguished men, wore clerical dress – that is to say, a black soutane with white tabs at the throat. They were not full priests, but had taken vows of chastity and obedience. There were about twenty Brothers in the Collegio, all Italians, and an equal number of lay teachers who used to come in daily. As there were only about two hundred boys in the Collegio – admittedly fewer than usual owing to the war – this was a remarkably good teacher/pupil ratio and helps to explain why the Collegio had as high a reputation as any educational institution in Rome.

San Giuseppe was divided into two parts – the Collegio which comprised the five Ginnasio grades for boys between the ages of eleven and fifteen, and at the back of the building was the Istituto with the three Liceo (sixth-form) grades. The Rector, Brother Sigismondo, was in overall charge, with one deputy, Brother Ugo, who headed the Collegio, and another, Brother Mario, who headed the Istituto. I was placed on arrival in the top grade of the Ginnasio and then promoted to the Istituto.

About forty refugees had been given asylum in San Giuseppe,

49

including Italian officers who had not been able to get out to join the partisans, also some belonging to Colonel Montezemolo's monarchist underground, quite a few of them old boys of the Collegio. There were in addition a number of Jews and several Yugoslavs. Only the Rector and a handful of the more senior Brothers knew the identity of those in hiding. The rest certainly knew that something very odd was going on, and may have been unhappy about it, but those of us engaged in Resistance activities had no impediments placed in our way. Realising that if we were caught, and it was established where we were living, the Germans would have been provided with an excuse for a raid and all the refugees might have been picked up, we took every possible precaution.

Obviously the porters at the gate of the Collegio knew of our comings and goings, and one of them, a typically loquacious Roman with bulging eyes, called Vincenzo, seemed particularly on the spot. Equally, the servants could see much of what was going on, but Brother Mario Grottanelli told me that at least two of them were soldiers on the run, and any Italians of military age had the strongest possible interest in keeping quiet, since once outside the gates of the Collegio they would have been conscripted back into the Army or sent to forced labour in Germany. All the same, it is remarkable that there was never any leak or treachery. Besides, in those unreal days, when there was no such thing as 'normal life' and everyone lived in a sort of nightmare, probably three-quarters of the boys had relations, or knew of people, who were on the run somewhere, or belonged to families which were opposed to the regime, so a natural discretion prevailed. As for me, there was no reason why any of the boys should have questioned the reason they had been given for my appearing among them, and none of them ever asked me about my supposed Neapolitan and Calabrian backgrounds. Boarders worked and slept in the Istituto, and as their number was considerably reduced the extra space was made available to those in hiding.

We boys had communal meals, such as they were, but the food was appalling – not quite concentration camp level, but not far off. It largely consisted of ersatz black bread, extremely indigestible, and gave me a bad attack of colitis which made me quite seriously ill for a couple of weeks in March. The Brothers kindly arranged for a second bed to be put in my father's room.

The men in hiding had their meals in a sort of refectory, and except for those of them engaged in Resistance work there was little to do to pass the time except read, write and listen to the radio. Brother Mario had quite a strong set, and we used to gather in his room to listen to the BBC. The winter of 1943–44 was one of the coldest in Italy for many years, and there was little heating in the Collegio. Cold, hungry and fearful men do not have the appetite for the sort of recreational activities generated in many prisoner of war camps.

Brother Robert Pace was Maltese and belonged to the Order of Christian Brothers, but to another of their houses. He was a most impressive man, speaking perfect English and very good Italian with a slight English accent. He was running a network for escaped PoWs similar to Monsignor O'Flaherty's and no less effective. It was thanks to his intervention with the Rector that my father and I were given sanctuary in the Collegio. There was, perhaps, no great difficulty in the Collegio's accepting me, who could pass anywhere as an Italian schoolboy, but taking in my father simply added one more to its already overwhelming problems.

Brother Robert came to see us in San Giuseppe when we were established there to ask if there was anything more he could do to help us and to see if there was any way in which I could assist him in his work. I was able to do some translation for him and to act as messenger between him and some of the religious institutions which were co-operating with him. After the war he came to see me in Cambridge and I have always regretted having then lost touch with him.

What a marvellous bunch of chaps these monks are. There are about forty people hiding in the college, all without ration cards, and Rome rations absurdly small, so the brothers halve their rations and it is just enough to keep alive. Rush along and collect Daddy and we enter the precincts of the Collegio San Giuseppe. It is 18th October. Daddy is given a small room at the back of the college. I am to pass as one of the boys just arrived from another of their colleges, and so that to start with I needn't talk too much with the others I am told that I have a senior position with the boys and also that my health is not good and therefore I have to receive special medical attention. My name, Mario Cambi of Naples. Daddy, Aldo Danieli of Corigliano Calabre. He is my uncle. So on the night of the 18th find myself walking up and down a badly lit dormitory, strictly blackout, telling some of the boys to get into bed. It is a remarkable experience, but am getting used to remarkable experiences. The memories of the past five weeks whirl around in my brain, enough to last me a lifetime. If only our chaps could get through, but we have messed things up so badly and more and more German troops are pouring south. I think of Florence. There is a sudden sound of shooting and I remember that Gianfranco had told me that there might be some firing tonight. I am meeting him tomorrow and I know he will be amused to hear my story about the dormitory.

A new page of the diary covered less amusing events.

At 10 p.m. all the people hiding gather in a big room and are addressed by Frère Sigismondo. It is a strange scene – the rather large bare monastic room filled with people, of all types and ages, dimly lit, and at the end of the room, clad in his long black robe, stands Frère Sigismondo. It all stands out extremely vividly. Daddy is next to me. He looks haggard and unshaven. Poor old Pop. That stifling panicky feeling, the acute hunted version, comes on and is most unpleasant. Frère Sigismondo speaks quietly and pleasantly: 'The Germans must know that people are hiding here. The boys, the servants – it is impossible to keep things entirely secret. Some of the people hiding may even have spoken carelessly.' A little shiver seems to run through the gathering. You can't even trust the man next to you – nasty feeling. 'A raid must therefore be accepted as a possibility or even a likelihood. The Vatican protection certainly helps but I do not believe there is any absolute guarantee of immunity. Should the Germans come, as soon as they enter an alarm bell will ring,' and he demonstrates. A bell starts ringing. 'That means they are at the door, and I think I can give a minimum of five minutes in which to scatter and hide. No traces must be left in the rooms. Everybody must make his own arrangements and, as you know, there are arrangements here for hiding, and some may perhaps try and get out.' I am thinking of what this entails – a gruesome game of hide-and-seek in the long dark corridors of the College, and the stake one's life, and the dreadful tortures of the SS. A shiver goes straight through me and I gasp for breath. I keep repeating, 'Pull yourself together.'

Frère Sigismondo says, 'Meeting finished, but will the people who arrived today please stay on.' About a dozen of us remain. He then comes up and tells us, in a gentle conversational way, that he will show us the secret hiding-place under the cellars. It is like a nightmare. We follow him along the dark passages and down the stairs into the cellar. At the end of the cellar there is a special contrivance and part of the wall seems to swing in, and behind it there is another room, damp, cold, dark and musty. The wall is then replaced in position and nobody can tell the difference. I remark to Daddy that I didn't think it would be a good place to go. It would be like rats in a trap. Daddy, who suffers from claustrophobia, agrees with me. I can picture the scene of thirty or forty people tumbling to get in and the SS after them. Most unpleasant. We walk up again and scatter. I go back to the dormitory. A nice evening, end of a perfect day!

Night all right. I could sleep well, but as soon as I woke up the hunted feeling would come again. Meet Gianfranco for lunch at the Re degli Amici, a little restaurant on Borgo della Croce. He was amused by my tale of the first evening in the College, but realised it was no picnic. He is working on a scientific experiment, a sort of powder which is spread on the road and will make the tyres of cars either burst or flatten. As soon as he has perfected this, he is going to get things properly organised and get lots of our men to become improvised road sweeps. Then, when a German convoy goes through, the road will be spread with the stuff and the convoy paralysed and so become easy meat for the R.A.F. which is strafing the roads. It sounds great fun! We agree to meet in four days' time at Milo's house for a conference which he tells me is going to be quite important, in order to raise funds. Back to the San Giuseppe. Food really awful. I discover again what it means to be hungry. Weather getting colder and our lads solidly blocked at Cassino. We hope they are going to land soon. Hope, always hope. In the evening we gather in the room of a young officer, Santarelli, who, after having fought against the Germans at Siena, had been captured and then escaped from a train by jumping out of the window when the train was on a bridge over a river. We listen to the BBC on his little wireless. Cassino, Cassino, Cassino, Volturno.[1] Blast these names!

Meeting at Milo's house quite fascinating. Milo, Sanguinetti's brother-in-law, and also a multi-millionaire. Three big film magnates, Gallone, Tamburella and another. They had been associated with the Fascist regime and are now anxious to rehabilitate themselves by assisting the underground Resistance movement with finance. As Gianfranco remarked to me, the money is vital. What is going to happen to them later on a matter of supreme indifference. I entirely agree. Gallone was there with his mistress, a very beautiful woman about 35, had been a Hungarian actress. On the whole an unsavoury atmosphere. I remarked to Gianfranco that I wouldn't trust any of them further than I could kick them. He agreed but said it didn't matter, all that mattered was to get their money. Negotiations were getting sticky. Pretty late, we decided to meet in a few days' time.

[1] The Allied advance had been for a time held up by German defensive positions behind the Volturno River, 30 kilometres north of Naples and south of Cassino.

One evening in late November I had a long talk with Frère Sigismondo, a very interesting man and most attractive. He had travelled widely and had none of that pettiness of outlook which spoils so many Italian priests. He told me that his name was already on the German blacklist but he wasn't worried at all. He was only frightened for us. He was terribly nice to me. I think he may have found it strange to see an apparently nice lad turning into a man by hard experience, and I remember his words: 'Mario –' (they all called me Mario and I would hardly have turned round at my real name) '– this will finish some day and then you will have all your life ahead of you and it will have been an exceptional experience for you.' I smiled at him, a knot in my throat. And then, suddenly, the alarm bell began to ring. I can never forget that sound, never. He stood up. 'You'd better go off and help your father, and also warn people. As I explained to them all, I will keep them at bay as long as possible, and also bluff as long as possible.'

I rushed out of his room and down the corridor, every sense perfectly alert, and really quite cool. Tore through the passages, the bell still clanging hard, towards Daddy's room. Met people hustling down the stairs towards the cellar. Santarelli stopped and asked me, 'Aren't you coming? Not much time, you know.' I nodded and told him that in any event I probably wouldn't be hiding with them, and rushed on. On the stairs collided with one of the fellows. He was a strange little man, I think a Yugoslav. He was in a blind panic, and a terrible sight, as pale as death and jabbering. I got hold of him by the collar – he was a smallish fellow – and shook him like a rat. He then began to whimper. Two chaps rushed out, and I handed him over to them and continued to Daddy's room. Dear old Dad, quite calm. I pointed out that perhaps we should get moving. He put his arm through mine and we walked out and I rushed him towards the nuns' quarters. They used to cook and do all the laundry for the boys. An old nun took Daddy and said, 'Yes, of course. Come right in, and I will find a place to hide you.' I left him, tore back to his room, cleared everything and took the incriminating papers to the room of Frère Mario Grottanelli. It was too late to hide and in any event I was supposed to be one of the boys, so I walked back towards the centre of the College. In the main passage I met Frère Sigismondo and Frère Ugo with three German officers. I smiled politely and passed on, to wait for an hour, an hour of agony. If they caught one, we were all going to be caught. Daddy with the nuns possibly, hopefully all right. Inaction, hell. Then the All Clear bell started to ring. I got up, feeling like a wet rag and went straight to Sigismondo's room. He said the bluff had worked – he had kept them talking while Frère Ugo telephoned the Vatican. Cardinal Maglione's secretary had then rung back and had insisted on speaking to the officer in charge. They said they were looking for a German officer who had deserted. They insisted on going through the College, but had done so in a fairly cursory way. They had found nothing. The rooms, he said, had all been cleared admirably. Tore down to Daddy, looking a bit shaken, but quite calm. He told me that he had been put in the boiler. That was not exactly good for his claustrophobia, but he said that he now had a great admiration for nuns and would never make a nasty remark about them again. End of another perfect day!

Within a few days I meet Gianfranco at the Re degli Amici again. Another meeting to be arranged with Tamburella, again to raise money. Apparently he has a number of pretty actresses on tap which is very useful, for they get information off German officers. Time goes slowly on. Getting late. Cold and damp. Food — well, one can't call it food — and am hungry and thirsty. November slowly drawing to a close. Getting colder and rains a lot. Hope of an Allied landing is slowly fading and with it hope of ever getting out of this alive quickly. Had a long talk with Santarelli, an extremely charming fellow and a sentimentalist.

Have some very important documents to translate for Gianfranco which had reached him from Allied HQ, so important that I go and collect them in the Via Giulia, his secret hiding-place which he does not want anybody to know about. They give me a splendid opportunity of getting an insight into the Allied headquarters mentality. The one thing they seem to lack is imagination. I meet Montezemolo,[1] now called Prof. Cataratto. Splendid chap. They are on his track and he has had some terribly close shaves. He is a handsome and dashing officer and even in his civilian clothes has class. When he shakes hands to say goodbye I feel myself tingling all over. Hero-worship, I suppose. Also met Piero Dodi who is working very closely with Montezemolo.

Gianfranco and I see each other regularly and I continue doing work for him, particularly translations. One evening we have a long talk. I treasure these moments of intimacy. Nothing is more revealing than a man-to-man talk. I ask him if he is really a Communist, and his reply is revealing. 'I am profoundly anti-Fascist, and passionately believe in overthrowing tyranny in Italy. The Communists are the best organised Resistance movement, and they have been fighting Fascism for a long time. They started before anyone else,

---

[1] Colonel Giuseppe di Montezemolo was a monarchist and representative of the Badoglio government in the Rome underground. But though the CLN was opposed to the King and Badoglio they had a great respect for Montezemolo and worked closely with him. He was a very courageous and active leader until he was caught on 25 January 1944. He was taken to Gestapo headquarters in Via Tasso, tortured, and later murdered at the Ardeatine Caves. After the liberation of Rome General Alexander, Allied Commander-in-Chief in Italy, wrote to his widow: 'No man could have done more, or given more, to his country's and the Allied cause than he did.'

and I believe they want to make life better for everyone. So – I am a Communist.' We discuss Via Tasso and the tortures of the Gestapo head-quarters, just as if it wasn't at the back of my mind subconsciously most of the time. To be put against a wall and shot, I can understand. You could shout out 'Viva Italia' or 'God Save the King', but to be slowly and horribly tortured in the white-panelled hospital-looking rooms of Via Tasso – I still sweat at the thought. Those tortures – my age, I believe, would be terribly against me. Apparently the best age is when you get older. Still, I could in my imagination stick some of them but it was always the monstrous attack on one's genital organs, one of the last to come, apparently, which I could not conceive being able to resist. There was something particularly bestial about it, the agony too frightful to imagine, and also something else psychological and horrid. They have thought of most things, these sadistic criminal swine.

Gianfranco told me that most of the torturers were sadists and some homosexualists. Little mercy to be expected. 'I doubt if I could stand it,' I said. 'I would kill myself,' he answered. There was a girl of the Resistance who had become a prostitute so as to get into one of the torture places which was used by the Milizia Repubblichina. Her descriptions, according to a friend, are just too incredible. In one room there was a torture chamber and communicating an officer's study and then a big room where drunken orgies would take place. Some of the officers would leave the room, proceed to the torture chamber and then return smiling to continue their fucking and drinking, and when the doors were opened, the agonised screams of the wretched people could be heard. What bloody sadistic bastards.

Time goes on. Food bad. Haven't seen Mummy for weeks. Occasionally she makes a rushed visit to the College and leaves food parcels. I only discovered later that she used to get them from Trastevere black market. A very wonderful performance, a very wonderful woman. We start toying again with the idea of crossing the lines but winter is on and in the Apennines it must be almost impossible to go through. Santarelli is very keen on the idea but I don't think Daddy could survive it at the moment. He is looking pale and worn out, and I am not exactly at the top of my form. December is slowly dragging on.

Gianfranco tells me that he has to go to Milan for a brief visit to collect some important material. Before leaving he gives me a pistol with six bullets to be used in a desperate emergency.

A few days later I get an urgent message from him. We are to meet a British agent outside the Café Greco for a very important meeting. We are to carry copies of the Osservatore Romano. This is rather exciting. It is the first and only time that I feel any of the so-called thrills which are so often described in fiction. Tall man with glasses, about 30 to 40, with a scholarly air, approaches. He looks at us and then throws away his cigarette, as pre-arranged, which appeared to have been just lighted. We go into the café and pass through into the second room. Gianfranco most eloquently puts forward our position and then says that he will give him the document. The necessity of capturing Rome soon, before the full force of winter sets in. Points out the psychological necessity of this – how if Rome does not fall, the German and Fascist puppets in the north will gain strength increasingly and hunt down the thousands of remaining prisoners of war who are free, and the Italian troops who are at the moment hiding. The partisan morale would also be vitally reinforced, and in any event he doesn't think they are receiving enough help from the Allies.

He then pointed out the possibilities which were in the plan, of landing north of Rome with an airborne force, and put forward the plan which has been drawn up by the CLN, most of which I had translated. All this time the man was watching Gianfranco and never opened his mouth. Finally, when he did, in perfect Italian, he was very evasive. I broke in and pointed out that he would have to rely on partisan information. It was reliable. They had proved it, time after time. And finally, looking straight at him, said in English, 'God, if ever people deserved to be trusted, they're these Resistance men here.' A slight sign of interest came into his eyes. He hadn't realised I was not Italian. He said that he would like to speak to me alone after the meeting. Gianfranco proceeded with his elaboration and then handed the papers over. He then said to me, 'You must convince him that they can rely on us and that our information is correct. We wouldn't betray them.' As if I didn't know it, and I felt humiliated that he had to apologise, but I could also see the other side of the argument which perhaps Gianfranco could not. HQ would coldly and dispassionately examine the information and then probably decide, 'Too uncertain – too much depends on the actions of the Resistance and on the information of the Resistance. It may be correct, but we can't take the risk. The consequences of failure would be too disastrous.' And of course they were right in their own way, just as Gianfranco and the Resistance men were absolutely right in theirs.

X. – and I call him X. for I never knew his name – came back to the Collegio San Giuseppe. I asked Frère Sigismondo whether we could use his sitting-room and he said we could. I briefly told him my story and I caught another momentary flicker of interest before that impenetrable look came back again. He repeated exactly the same argument that I had thought he would, but he said that he personally would trust Gianfranco and his crowd entirely. He asked me about them and I let him have it straight from the shoulder: they were marvellous, absolutely completely reliable, and 1) we had been bloody blind fools not to trust them before; 2) we were not helping them enough; and

3) would be bloody blind fools if we didn't trust them again now, and follow their plans. He asked me to write a short note covering Gianfranco's report, and said that he would pass again in a fortnight, as he was now leaving for the north. He spoke in a quiet pleasant cultured English voice and Italian with a Roman accent. When he was going, I repeated urgently, desperately, 'You must convince our people to trust the Resistance. You must, you must.' He looked at me rather coldly. 'I do. They won't, I don't think.' 'No,' I replied bitterly, 'they won't.'

I was left feeling embittered and frustrated, and yet he was right all the time, I suppose. Emotionalism did not come into this sort of thing. It was a mathematical analysis, and yet how impossible it would be not to feel as the people around me felt. After all, we were living this together, going through it together.

Christmas. What a bloody depressing day. Far worse than any other, because Christmas tends to bring recollections of happy days, crackers and champagne, the only time when I used to be allowed to drink as a child. We spent most of the day listening to the BBC in Santarelli's room. Christmas carols and all that bunk. We tried to be cheerful, drink some very good wine somebody had brought into the College.

A week later, a surprise visit from X. He had just come from across the lines. He tells me that the Resistance plan was considered too ambitious and risky. I had been expecting this, so it left me only slightly disappointed. Gianfranco had of course already been informed, he told me, as had the CLN previously. I remarked that I wasn't going to stick this much longer and would try and cross the lines soon. He then replied, 'No, don't do that yet. You are doing good work here, and I can assure you something will happen soon.'

Unfortunately the rest of my diaries, covering the period from January to June 1944, have been lost. The last page of all the diary that survives ends it on a lighter note:

It seems I'm not the only one taking risks. Daddy appeared this evening looking remarkably spruce, and the explanation is an episode which might have gone badly wrong – and nearly did! He has more than once told me that on his occasional sorties from the Collegio he has gazed longingly at the barber's shop in the Via Condotti, a very elegant establishment he used to frequent when he was in Rome before the war. He has always enjoyed his visits to the barber in London or Vicenza or wherever he is, getting the full treatment of friction, massage etc. But since 1940 he has had to put up with a monthly visit to the shop in Antella kept by the man we know as 'the butcher' because of the way he chops our hair. But it never occurred to me that he would risk a visit to the Via Condotti where he might easily be recognised.

But that is precisely what he has done – and what has happened. While he was being ministered to, another client came in and took a nearby seat. When Daddy eventually looked round, he recognised the aristocratic features of an old friend from Vicenza, Giuseppe Roj, who was having his short black beard neatly trimmed. [Marchese Giuseppe Roj and his brother Antonio and his wife were old friends of my parents, but needless to say they had not seen each other since 1940.] At that precise moment Giuseppe Roj also turned round, and their eyes met. Giuseppe's face lit up with pleasure. He called out, '*Carissimo!*' Daddy immediately barked back, '*Aldo Danieli! Aldo Danieli!*' With considerable aplomb and without batting an eyelid Giuseppe continued, '*Carissimo Aldo, come mai avrei potuto dimenticare il tuo nome! Che piacere rivederti!*' [My dear Aldo, how could I have possibly forgotten your name! What a pleasure to see you!]

When Daddy was about to leave Roj shook him warmly by the hand without saying a word, but handed him a visiting card. On it was written the address of his apartment in Rome and a short note: '*Non penso di vederti per un po', ma appena arriverà quel bel giorno fatti subito vivo e vieni a pranzo da me.*' [I don't expect to see you for a while, but as soon as that happy day comes, get in touch immediately and come to lunch.] Daddy is very aware that a much less welcome person might have taken the nearby seat, so I didn't rub it in.

My father did not visit the Via Condotti barber again until after the Liberation. He did, however, telephone Giuseppe Roj soon after 4 June, and when Roj heard that my mother and I were in Rome too he insisted that we should all three lunch with him. It was a most enjoyable and festive occasion, at which Elena Molon, another old friend from the Veneto, and one of the Valmaranas, a well-known Vicenza family, were also present. We drank champagne, with a special toast to the barber in the Via Condotti, whose name was Giovanni.

When 'X' had said to me, 'Something will happen soon' he must have known about the Anglo-American landing at Anzio, 50 kilometres south of Rome, which took place on 22 January. The intention was to force a German withdrawal behind Rome, but though the landing took the Germans by surprise they were able to mount counter-attacks which at one moment threatened to drive the Allies back into the sea.

News of the landing caused a fresh wave of optimism in Rome. We had hoped it would be linked with an airborne landing, and I was engaged in the preparation of many documents listing possible sites for landings and drops, which bridges should be held and which blown, where partisans would operate, where the Germans were concentrating, and so on. But sadly there was no breakout from the Anzio beach-head and no landing from the air. A good deal of evidence has since come to light to show that if the Allies had pressed ahead after their initial success the Germans were in fact preparing to abandon Rome.

The Allied armies further south were being held up by strong German positions on Monte Cassino, topped by the historic monastery, founded in 529 by St Benedict, 'the father of monasticism', and where the saint himself is buried. The decision was taken, though reluctantly, that the monastery would have to be destroyed from the air, and on 15 February 450 tons of bombs reduced it to rubble. A great deal of play was made by the Germans about the supposedly wanton destruction of this national treasure, but the Italians' hatred for the Germans was so intense that I cannot recall even a ripple of protest among laymen or clergy. The abbot of Monte Cassino monastery came to Rome and to the Collegio after the bombing, where I met him and was struck by his complete lack of bitterness.

One serious consequence of the Anzio landing was that people in the Resistance tended to become rather careless about security, and several of them were picked up. But it was probably an act of betrayal that was responsible for the severest blow that our group had to suffer and which deprived me of a man whose character and example had been my inspiration for the past six months, and whose memory I would treasure for the rest of my life.

On the evening of 1 February a detachment of German SS broke into the house in the Via Giulia where they found Gianfranco Mattei, Giorgio Labò and others. There they discovered a large quantity of arms and ammunition as well as explosives which had been prepared under Gianfranco's direction. All were arrested, savagely beaten up, and carted off to Gestapo headquarters in Via Tasso, from which none of them was to emerge alive. Gianfranco was tortured continually for three days but gave away nothing, though he knew the names and hiding-places of all the leaders of the Resistance in Rome. On the third day an Italian officer who had been arrested in mistake for someone else was put in the same cell as Gianfranco. This officer had a cheque-book and a pencil in his pocket, and on the back of a cheque Gianfranco wrote a brief farewell message to his parents: 'My dearest parents – Owing to very unfortunate circumstances for which one can only blame fate I fear that these will be my last words. You know what ties of enormous affection have linked me to you and to my brothers and sisters and to everybody. Be strong, knowing that I have been able to be strong. I embrace you – Gianfranco.' The officer was wearing a belt, which he gave to Gianfranco who, fearing that he might not be able to stand up to further torture and hoping that the others would be able to claim that he alone knew the secrets, hanged himself.

Unlike some of the Gestapo's other victims, Gianfranco's body was not handed over to his family. But after the liberation of Rome the following bare notification was found in the records of the city morgue: 'Unknown, apparent age 32, from Via Tasso. Body received 4 February 1944, delivered for burial at Prima Porta cemetery 17 February 1944. Cause of death, asphyxiation by hanging.' There, at the extreme end of the paupers' burial plot, two friends found the resting place of Gianfranco Mattei. His body was subsequently re-buried in the part of the Verano Cemetery in Rome reserved for the Partisan dead.

After the liberation of Rome Gianfranco's mother Clara, a woman of exceptional intelligence, warmth and goodness, gave me a photo-copy of Gianfranco's last message and a photograph of him inscribed with the words from St John's Gospel: '*Nessuno ha un amore più grande di colui che da la vita per i suoi amici*' (Greater love hath no man than this, that a man lay down his life for his friends) – '*Al caro Dennis con molto affetto, la mamma di Gianfranco.*'

As his mother was later to write on what would have been her son's fortieth birthday, it was only his 'burning desire for justice and strict awareness of his responsibilities which cut him off from his family and his studies to which he was devoted.' The Italian Resistance produced no more heroic figure than Gianfranco Mattei.

Some weeks after Gianfranco's murder a group of five Communist partisans in Florence planned and carried out the assassination of Giovanni Gentile. Gentile was a distinguished philosopher – not to be ranked with Croce, but still with an international reputation. He had always supported Fascism, had been Mussolini's Minister of Education and was even prepared – why, it is impossible to guess – to go along with the appalling Republic of Salò. He was shot as his car drove into the gates of his house in Florence. It may be that this group felt treason in an intellectual was worse than in, say, a policeman; and certainly Gianfranco's relatives and friends could have felt no mercy towards his killers and their associates. At the time the Partito d'Azione in Florence issued a communiqué saying that this was not a proper way to fight Fascism. Bearing in mind the climate filled with hatred and violence of those days, this was a civilised and magnanimous gesture.

Some time after the execution of Gentile a group to which Chicchi Mattei belonged was involved in another case of summary justice. The Fascist chief in Florence was a leading collaborator with the Germans, ruthless, greatly hated and greatly feared, called Colonel Ingramo. His headquarters were in a hotel near the Ponte Vecchio, and he always moved between there and his heavily guarded villa outside the city at high speed in an armoured car with a massive armed escort. There seemed to be only one chance of getting at him. Sometimes as the Colonel was about to leave the hotel people were allowed to approach the armoured car and present petitions. The window of the car would be lowered and the envelope containing the petition handed in. It was the Colonel's boast that such petitions always received proper attention.

So it was arranged that someone should approach the car with what purported to be a petition, and that at the moment when the window was lowered another member of the group, Paolo Martini, should shoot the Colonel. All went according to plan. The envelope was presented, the window was lowered, and the shot fired. All, including Chicchi, escaped on bicycles. But soon it was learned that, though severely wounded, Ingeramo was not dead, and Martini feared that he might have been recognised. So Chicchi was sent to the hospital to make enquiries. She spoke to a nun, who asked her if she was a friend of the family. No, said Chicchi, just interested. 'Well,' said the nun, 'the Colonel is certainly critically injured and is certain to die, but it is possible that before he dies he will be able to speak. Come back tomorrow.' This Chicchi did. It may be that somehow Chicchi had betrayed the true nature of her interest, because at this second meeting the nun told her: 'My family are poor peasants from Calabria, and I am on your side.' She again asked Chicchi to come back the next day. At this third meeting the nun told Chicchi: 'The Colonel died during the night. I had to give him laudanum to relieve his pain, and I fear I gave him too much. So he died peacefully. But I made certain that before he died he received the Last Sacrament. And I feel that what I did will be of advantage to him on the Day of Judgement, because if he had recovered and given away the names of your friends this would have meant that he committed yet another crime which he would have had to answer for.'

Shortly afterwards Chicchi was arrested on a train between Florence and Rome. She was very badly beaten up and put into a makeshift prison on one of the roads leading out of Rome. There one of the Fascist collaborators, shocked at seeing this young girl covered in blood, told her that he would look the other way for five minutes, so that she could run across the courtyard and climb over a wall. 'But if you make any noise I shall have to shoot you,' he added. She escaped.

News of the arrest of the Matteis naturally made all those who knew and had worked with them more cautious than ever, and tighten up security which had grown slack as a result of the euphoria after the Anzio landings. I continued to carry out such tasks as seemed to be essential for those members of the underground with whom I was still in touch. One among several contacts I made at the time was Franco Malfatti, a leading operational member of the Resistance, who was linked to the CLN through Amendola, though this was something I was not aware of until after Rome had been liberated. As in all clandestine operations, the fewer names of people and places that are known the smaller the likelihood of discovery, and I was well enough trained not to ask questions.

I knew of the existence of the CLN but not the names of any of its members. It had been set up in Rome at the beginning of September 1943 under the chairmanship of Ivanoe Bonomi, later to be Prime Minister of the first coalition government, and contained leaders of the six principal parties in the underground opposition, including many names of men who were to dominate the political scene in post-war Italy – men like Alcide De Gasperi of the Christian Democrats, Ugo La Malfa of the Action Party, Mauro Scoccimarro and Giorgio Amendola of the Communists, Meuccio Ruini of the Labour

Democrats, Alessandro Casati of the Liberals, Pietro Nenni and Giuseppe Romita of the Socialists. Remarkably these men were able to meet fairly regularly in occupied Rome without being discovered, though Bruno Buozzi, one of the leaders of the Socialist Party, was caught and shot just outside Rome. The politicians were not directly involved in the operational side of the Resistance, which was delegated to a separate executive committee. Their main concern was to prepare the political structure of Italy after liberation.

Two other incidents at about the same time as Gianfranco's arrest emphasised the need for the utmost discretion. At the beginning of January the Germans raided a convent of the Franciscan Friars where they captured General Caracciolo. A few weeks later German troops and Fascist militia raided the Benedictine monastery of San Paolo where they pulled in General Monti and several other senior officers as well as a number of Jews. The Fascist Press made a lot of propaganda out of this, printing numerous photographs of Italian generals dressed as monks, jeering at them as cowards who had abandoned their troops and hidden in disguise. No mention was made of the fact that San Paolo, like San Giuseppe, had extra-territorial Vatican protection. Their discovery caused the Vatican some embarrassment, and inevitably we in San Giuseppe feared that the Germans and their Fascist collaborators, having shown no scruples about raiding San Paolo, would turn their attention once again to San Giuseppe.

Those of us who went out lived in particular fear of what was called 'rastrellamenti'. This was the name given to the sweeps mounted by the German Army against the partisans in the mountains, sometimes at division strength, but it was also applied to the random searches carried out by German troops and Fascist militia in Rome and other occupied towns and villages. Suddenly a certain area of the city would be sealed off by army trucks and police cars, and anyone moving in that area would be arrested and taken off for questioning. They would not necessarily be tortured, and if they were shown to be in the clear they might be released – though not invariably; sometimes, however innocent, they might be held as hostages.

It was impossible to predict when or where a rastrellamento was going to take place. I once narrowly escaped being caught up in one. I had been to see my mother in the Villa Lante convent (I only risked visiting her twice in all these eight months) and was walking back through the Via Condotti which leads into the Corso when I heard someone shouting *'Rastrellamento!'* Two cars belonging to the Fascist Police which operated under German control (the Carabinieri almost to a man having refused to co-operate) appeared at the end of the street together with some German troops. I turned round, and began walking in the direction I had come from. After about 50 yards I broke into a run and made a wide detour by the Piazza del Popolo to the Piazza di Spagna and the Collegio. By the time I reached the Via Babuino people were beginning to move freely again, so I realised that the *rastrellamento* was probably over. I gathered from what I heard that the Via Condotti and all the nearby streets leading to the Corso had been sealed off and quite a lot of people taken away.

What would have happened if I had been a little further on my way back, and so among those rounded up, it is impossible to say. I carried two identity cards in the name of Mario Cambi – the excellent forgery given me by Amendola and a genuine card from the Istituto stating that I was a pupil there. So if the inspection had been fairly cursory I should have got away. On the other hand, I also had some papers taken from my mother which had been given to her by a former English nun called Dorothy Dobson, who was also hiding in the Villa Lante convent. These came to her from another refugee in the convent, the wife of a senior Italian officer, and contained information about German troop movements which she wanted me to translate and pass on to our circle for transmission to the Allies. These would, of course, have been highly incriminating for me and the Collegio if discovered, and I remember debating in my mind, without much success, how you destroy papers inconspicuously while walking along a street.

The longest document I had to deal with was handed to me in the middle of January, just before the Anzio landings and the arrest of Gianfranco, and amounted to an almost passionate plea to the Allies to get moving. Drawn up by a committee of the CLN of which Gianfranco was a member, it was a follow-up to the document we had handed to the British agent in December and reinforced the same sort of arguments with more detailed and up-to-date information. As usual, I translated this document in my father's room, writing it up in a school notebook, which I then handed to one of the army officers in hiding, a former journalist who had a typewriter and who typed out the English version. This I took back to Gianfranco, it being safer for me to move around than it was for him (there was no school uniform, so my appearance was that of any Italian boy of my age), though he changed his lodging frequently. He made arrangements for a courier to take it south. I kept a copy of this, but some time later, when there was an alarm about an expected German raid on the Collegio, I destroyed it. It would be very interesting to know whether my translation ever reached Allied headquarters, as the earlier documents clearly had, and, if it did, what they made of it.

As the Allied armies seemed to be still bogged down in their advance, some sections in the Resistance, particularly the Communists, impatiently demanded a more militant policy against the Germans and their Fascist partners. It was a Communist bomb hidden in a rubbish cart which exploded with terrific force at two o'clock in the afternoon of 23 March as a column of German troops belonging to the Bözen Regiment, which formed part of the guard on Gestapo headquarters, was marching, as it always did at that hour, down Via Rasella to the bath house. Thirty-two soldiers were killed outright or died shortly after. We in the Collegio heard the explosion, which rattled our windows, and when we learned what had happened our first feeling was one of admiration for the success of so dramatic a coup. However, this was quickly followed by fears about the inevitable German reaction.

None of us, I think, could have foreseen the gruesome form which this was to take. The following day the SS rounded up three hundred and thirty-five men and women held in their Via Tasso headquarters and in the Italian-administered Regina Coeli prison, including a few ordinary criminals as well as political opponents of the regime and members of the underground. These were marched through the streets with their arms tied behind their backs to the Ardeatine caves at Domitilla outside Rome where they were all machine-gunned, the slaughter going on through several hours of the night. The mouths of the caves were then blown up with mines and blocked, so that any who had survived were finished off by asphyxiation. The list of the dead included diplomats and professors, clerks, peasants, students, bankers, shop assistants, prostitutes, painters, lawyers, engineers – no section of Rome's population was spared in the German tenfold revenge. While the horror caused by news of the massacre did not stiffen the resolve of the Resistance – there was no need of that – it did, I think, convince the priests and nuns and all those who had been sheltering potential victims of the Nazi butchers of the enormous value of the work they were doing.

General Alexander's spring offensive, Operation Diadem, opened on 11 May. By 18 May Cassino had fallen to General Anders' Polish corps, and on 23 May the Allies broke out of the Anzio beach-head to link up with the advancing armies. At long last we realised that the liberation of Rome was imminent.

Advance units of the American 88 Division entered Rome on the evening of 4 June, and I went to meet them, though in fact the soldiers to whom I identified myself turned out to be Canadians. I found an officer and persuaded him to detail some of his men to come with me to Via Tasso, so that we could see whether any of the Gestapo's victims were still there. German snipers were still active, but we got into the building and checked through all the cells, finding nobody. The Gestapo had cleared out the day before, taking most of the incriminating evidence of their tortures with them. Nor, though we had long known that Gianfranco was dead, did we then discover how he died; that came out later.

These were for all of us wonderful and exciting days. After three years of internment and nine months in hiding, during which I had had to shoulder more responsibilities than usually fall to someone of my age, it was an enormous relief to be able to move about without fear and under my own name, to be able to read newspapers expressing every variety of opinion (except support for Fascism), to meet and celebrate with some of the friends I had made in the Collegio. There was one in particular I saw a good deal of, Franco Bruno, whose father, an admiral and one of the ADCs of the Prince of Piedmont, had also been hidden in the Collegio. With him I attended all the major political rallies which were addressed by the newly emerged party leaders, Togliatti, Nenni, Parri, Cianca, De Gasperi, Saragat, also Sforza and Don Sturzo, now returned from exile.

My father had come out of the Collegio on 5 June, and reported to the first headquarters he could find. He was immediately recruited into the civil administration of occupied territories (AMGOT) and given quite a senior position. This was a great consolation to him, as he could now at last feel that he was doing something in the war for his country. It also meant that he had access to Army rations, so that we could eat proper food again – by no means the least blessing of liberation.

During the time that I spent in Rome after the Liberation and before returning to England I often called at the Collegio San Giuseppe to visit those Brothers I had become most attached to, in particular Brothers Mario, Stefano and Sigismondo, although the latter was heavily engaged in a major reorganisation of the College. One note I made at that time survives – I think it must date from early July.

I called to see Frère Mario, and stopped to chat with the loquacious Vincenzo. As we spoke my attention was momentarily caught by two individuals who didn't look Italian and who scurried past rather furtively. I asked Vincenzo who they were. He looked at me mischievously and said: 'I don't know, but I suspect they may be two English officers hiding from the Americans.' (There had been some reports in the newspapers about bad feeling between British and American officers in Rome.) Then he roared with laughter at what he considered his funny joke.

Vincenzo had been most amused at discovering that I was English. He admitted that, though he had always suspected that there was something fishy about my father, I had fooled him completely.

I repeated my question to Frère Mario a few minutes later, who replied rather guardedly: '*Mio caro Mario, come tu sai molto bene, ci sono tante cose che i miei occhi non vedono.*' [My dear Mario, as you very well know, there are many things that my eyes do not see.] At that moment I realised in a flash and with something of a shock that the College was now providing asylum to 'the other side'. I felt certain that they would be far fewer in number, but equally certain that some people were hiding there once again. I decided that I would not pursue the matter any further. In spite of my detestation of the Germans and the Fascists I could not possibly have acted as informer against my protectors and saviours of yesterday.

As I was subsequently able to establish, they were not many and there were certainly no war criminals among them. It also has to be recognised that the first trials to be held after the Liberation, both of the Repubblichini (Fascists who supported the Salò Republic) and of Fascists of the pre-1943 vintage, resulted in some very rough and ready justice. The harmless ex-Governor of the Bank of Italy (Azzolini) for example was sentenced to thirty years' imprisonment, although in a retrial not long afterwards the sentence was quashed and he was acquitted.

I continued to be called upon from time to time to act as interpreter, and one episode in particular comes to mind. Marshal Badoglio had owned an apartment in Rome, which had been confiscated by the Fascists, and he wanted it back. For some reason this involved AMGOT as well as the Italian authorities, and as my father was not available I was brought in to interpret. Badoglio asked me what I had been doing, and when I told him he seemed quite impressed and presented me with a large signed photograph, which now hangs on the wall outside my study.

My father had immediately put in an application for us to return to England, but this proved not to be possible until December, when we got passages in the troopship *Scythia* which sailed from Naples. Meanwhile we had the use of a flat belonging to friends of my mother's who had gone to stay with relations in Naples. My father was very insistent that I should at last get a proper and formal education, and as I was keen to go to university I entirely agreed with him. 'You don't want to be a fish out of water for the rest of your life,' he said.

By now Jack had finished at Stowe, where he had been sent because our great-uncle was a friend of the first headmaster, J. F. Roxburgh, the educational pioneer, and was doing a short course at Cambridge before going into the RAF. It had originally been planned that we should both go to Downside, and when Cardinal Griffin, the Archbishop of Westminster, came to Rome in the summer of 1944 I met him with my parents. On his return he got in touch with that wonderful man Christopher (later Bishop) Butler, who was then headmaster of Downside, and who kindly agreed to make a place for me as soon as I got back, only stipulating that he should meet me before he finally confirmed the place. We met, and I was accepted. So that was the end of Mario Cambi.

Appendix A: The Partito d'Azione

THE Partito d'Azione, which was formally established in 1942, had its origins in earlier anti-Fascist movements, the main ones being Giustizia e Libertà and the Movimento di Rinnovamento Politico e Sociale Italiano. Giustizia e Libertà was formed in the twenties by Carlo Rosselli and others including his brother Nello, Alberto Tarchiani, Emilio Lussu, Ernesto Rossi, Riccardo Bauer, Ferruccio Parri, Aldo Garosci and Carlo Ragghianti. After repeated acts of resistance Carlo Rosselli and several more of the organisation's leadership were arrested by the Fascists and interned on the barren island of Lipari, but regained their freedom in a daring escape masterminded by Alberto Tarchiani in 1929. Carlo Rosselli continued the struggle against Fascism with renewed vigour, both in Italy and later during the civil war in Spain where he formed and commanded the Rosselli Brigade.

In 1937 Carlo and Nello Rosselli were assassinated by Fascist agents at Bagnoles de l'Orne in France. The Central Committee of Giustizia e Libertà issued a statement at the time accusing Mussolini of having ordered Carlo Rosselli's assassination and of having been personally involved in organising it. Certainly Carlo Rosselli, because of his outstanding qualities of intellect and leadership and his great physical and moral courage, had become one of the enemies Mussolini most feared and hated.

One of the more spectacular acts carried out by Giustizia e Libertà, and one which caused a sensation at the time, was when in 1930 an unarmed biplane piloted by Giovanni Bassanesi flew over the centre of Milan in broad daylight scattering some of its leaflets. Pursued by three Italian Air Force fighters with orders to shoot it down, the plane just managed to cross the Swiss frontier and land safely on the same air strip from which it had earlier set off. Fate was not wholly kind however and, sadly, Bassanesi crashed and was killed later the same day when attempting to fly the biplane back to Geneva. A similar mission was carried out not long after over Rome by Lauro De Bosis.

It would be a waste of time to try to analyse the complicated intellectual, philosophical and political processes which eventually resulted in the formation of the Partito d'Azione in 1942. But what should be remembered is that its founders, including those from Giustizia e Libertà, together with some from other political groups like Ugo La Malfa, Randolfo Pacciardi, Oronzo Reale and Alberto Cianca, provided the focal point of opposition to Fascism right from the start. They were the élite which contributed that essential element of continuity which then expanded dramatically after 1942, particularly in the Resistance and the War of Liberation between September 1943 and April 1945, when the Partito d'Azione was preeminent.

After the Liberation and return of democracy to Italy the Partito d'Azione continued to flourish for a very brief period, and one of the first post-war coalition governments was headed by Ferruccio Parri, a founding member of the party and a great Resistance leader. But it quickly fragmented, its leadership being absorbed by other parties or disappearing from active politics. Some, like La Malfa and Reale, joined the Republican Party; others like Lussu joined the Socialists, others still the Social Democrat and Liberal Parties. By 1949 the Partito d'Azione was no more. Its life had been short but magnificent; its contribution to the fight against Fascism without equal.

The Liberal-Socialist concept which governed its political thinking was almost certainly an irreconcilable contradiction in terms – a contradiction which could be concealed or put on one side while the intellectual and political battle against Fascism was being fought, and during the period of armed resistance, but which could not long survive the return to open politics and the demands of a democratic electoral process.

However, it may be worth examining briefly some of the ideas put forward by Riccardo Bauer, one of the party's leading theorists. In his writings, Bauer refers to the dualism which plagued the party from the start – that is, between the democratic wing to which he, La Malfa, and several others belonged, and which wanted to deal with social problems free from the 'rigid abstract Marxist concept of class warfare', and the wing headed by Emilio Lussu which wanted the party to declare itself as being 'explicitly socialist' in all the traditional meaning of that term.

Bauer considered the concept of the class struggle outmoded, aiming to replace it by 'that spiritual process of freedom which determines economic facts and is not determined by them.' He maintained that 'abolishing the class structure and social classes is not important; what matters is preventing their fossilisation and resisting the tendency for classes to become rigid and so oppressive.' Bauer thought the Partito d'Azione neither could nor should define itself as a 'class party' but should present itself as 'a progressive and reforming force, a democratic and interclass force of the left comprising white and blue collar workers, farmers and intellectuals, all brought together by a common awareness of the urgent need to achieve social justice.' Optimistically – and as was to be revealed before long, mistakenly – he wrote at the time of the party's inception that 'our socialism coincides with our liberalism. They are two aspects of a similar ideal which converge to form a common political attitude and goal.' It might be argued that two of Bauer's friends, Gobetti and Rosselli, who had headed earlier different anti-Fascist movements, 'Liberal Revolution' and 'Liberal Socialism', might have used the same language and even made some compromise between the two work. But once the hard left of the party had become dogmatically socialist and fundamentalist, no compromise was possible.

And so the Partito d'Azione came to its swift demise. Its life had passed with the speed of a meteor but the influence it exercised for a brief but immensely important period of Italian history was much more significant and lasting than that of any mere shooting star.

War has often been the forcing-house for new political groupings. Thus the Civil War produced the Levellers and the Diggers and many other political-religious movements, but these almost all died a natural death with the return of more normal conditions. To come to more recent times, a comparison might be made – though circumstances were so different – between the Partito d'Azione and that short-lived political child of the war in Britain, the Common Wealth Party. This was launched in 1943 by a Liberal MP, Sir Richard Acland, and was supported by an Independent MP, Vernon Bartlett, as well as by left-leaning members of the public including J. B. Priestley and Tom Wintringham who, like Carlo Rosselli, had fought with the International Brigade in Spain. The aims of the party were said to be 'greater equality of work, sacrifice and opportunity between soldiers and civilians, men and women, employers and workmen', the elimination of managerial inefficiency and civil service red tape, and preparation for post-war emphasis on better education, full employment, and 'civilised standards of living'. Later the party became more explicitly socialist than liberal, advocating the nationalisation of land, building societies and insurance companies.

The party had considerable successes in wartime by-elections, largely because the National (predominantly Conservative) Government had been in power for so long and public opinion, as the 1945 election was to show, was eager for a change. But though the Common Wealth Party fought that election with high hopes it returned only one member, and soon, like the Partito d'Azione, disappeared altogether.

In France too the war spawned new parties, such as the United Resistance Movements (MURF) and the Christian Democrat MRP which, together with the Communists, dominated the first post-war Assembly. But in France, of course, the person of de Gaulle, whether in office or retirement, commanded the political scene in a way that was not paralleled by any single figure in the Italian Resistance.

Appendix B: A walk with the Germans

I AM very grateful to Maria Luigia Guaita Vallecchi for allowing me to use one of the stories from her book, *Storia di Un Anno Grande*.

As my diary records, I met Maria Luigia Guaita on two occasions only, and then very fleetingly, in Florence in September 1943. Those encounters however made a lasting impression on me, partly no doubt because she was an extremely attractive young woman, but much more so because she seemed to typify the outlook and style of so many people, the women in particular, whom I met within and around the Italian Resistance between September 1943 and June 1944. Their professional competence was matched by an enthusiastic and even lighthearted amateurism. Although their dedication to the struggle was absolute, they were never either dour or oppressively serious. The combination that emerged I found enormously attractive.

I think the short story, '*In viaggio con I Tedeschi*', portrays this atmosphere and attitude remarkably well and vividly. The whole ethos of that period in German-occupied Italy springs to life in a way which is to me both funny and moving.

As the fifteen-year-old daughter of the house described it, that little bit of Tuscany which lies between Bagni di Lucca in the south and the Radici Pass in the north, and between Fiumalbo in the west and Abetone in the east, was becoming as vast as Arizona. She chattered on enthusiastically about her brother-in-law, the partisan leader, commander of the First Rosselli Brigade – perhaps she was even a bit in love with him, and why not? Her sister had insisted on riding out to join him in the hills round Abetone. There was certainly plenty to be enthusiastic about.

But I was only half listening to what she was saying. It was June 1944. We had received a message that the Allies wanted to know the strength of the partisan groups controlled by the Tuscan Comitato di Liberazione Nationale, what arms they possessed, and so on. Our headquarters had immediately despatched couriers to obtain this information, my assignment being precisely with the First Rosselli Brigade.

I had arrived in Pescia at sunset and gone to the house of the man we knew as Pippo. He was not there, but his father-in-law, who was a butcher, went down to the cellar and brought up a steak of a size which we in Florence could only dream about. It was while his wife prepared the evening meal that his younger daughter had joined me at the window where I was looking down at the main square of Pescia, in which the swallows were swooping and twittering.

I could see a group of German soldiers sitting at a table in one of the cafés, moodily drinking beer, while at another table some Fascist (Repubblichini) soldiers were putting on a great show of cheerfulness. Apart from these there were few men about in the square, and even fewer women. Soon it would be quite dark, and all artificial lights would have to be extinguished. I was torn between wanting to keep the window open and the need to observe the blackout. My nerves were on edge. Over and over again I mentally listed all the things that had to be done, and matched them with the handful of people we had available to do them. In those days there was never any time to relax or sort out one's thoughts.

Only the day before a careless word had almost betrayed me. I was in Florence and on my way home, carrying a bag which contained a dozen of the little yellow bombs which we called *scacciacani* (dog-scarers) because they were really of not much practical use. Three Fascist soldiers had stopped me and asked what was in my bag. It had been a hard day; I was very tired and felt almost feverish. 'Bombs!' I told them, and then suddenly realising what I had said gave them a feeble smile. They grinned back at me, and then burst out laughing. '*Ciao, bellona,*' said the boldest of them, giving me a friendly smack on the bottom.

Thinking about it afterwards I tried to analyse why I had given such an extraordinary answer. I came to the conclusion that I had simply been incredibly lucky. My youth and a smile had fooled them. But now, as I watched the shadows lengthen in the square, I felt I could not always expect my luck to hold.

The next morning I got a lift on the crossbar of his bicycle from one of our group who took me to the crossroads where I was to board the bus for Abetone. There were four German soldiers on the bus, an officer and three other ranks. Automatically I went and sat as far away from them as I could, and put the bag containing the clandestine papers I was to deliver under my seat. Then I spent my time looking out of the window, trying to identify the place where I was supposed to get off.

But when we came to it, to my dismay the Germans got off too, and I could now see that they were carrying red and white striped poles and that there were maps sticking out of their leather haversacks. I started out along the track that led to the village, and the Germans followed me, walking slowly and talking in loud voices. Obviously they were heading for the same village, and that, as I well knew, was where Pippo and probably most of his men were to be found.

I lengthened my stride and as soon as I could turned off along a path which I hoped would prove to be a short cut. The path climbed steeply, and after a few minutes I could no longer hear the Germans' voices. But I had somehow to increase the distance between us. I was haunted by thoughts of what had happened to Mommio, a small village not far away in the Apuane hills which had recently been burned and then razed to the ground by the Germans.

I had a vivid picture in my mind of arriving at Mommio, which was then the capital of a small partisan republic. The partisan commander, known as the Black Devil, was a splendidly courageous fellow and not in the least devilish. His second-in-command was his brother-in-law, Domenico, an expert radio-telegraphist who had served in the Merchant Navy, as large and hairy as an ape but as gentle as a lamb. Domenico had managed to cross the lines after the armistice on 8 September, bringing with him one of the radio sets provided by the Allies, and had then organised the partisans in the mountains near his village, and had arranged for the first Allied parachute drop of arms in the Florence *provincia*. I had had to go to Mommio to ask Domenico to make some changes in a message he was to send for us, and as I approached the village a strange figure jumped out from behind a bush and asked me for the password. He was dressed like a cowboy, festooned with guns, with a big red handkerchief round his neck and with tasselled boots that would have been the envy of any small boy. The whole village had a holiday atmosphere, the children all wearing red handkerchiefs and playing at being partisans and Fascists, though it was proving difficult to find anyone prepared to be the *repubblichini*. Some days later had come the terrible retribution.

Fearing a similar fate for the village I was heading for, I tried desperately to think what I could do in the brief interval that would elapse between my arrival and that of the Germans. Though the incline grew steeper, I broke into a run. I was dazed by the heat and the noise of the cicadas; my temples were throbbing, my heart was in my mouth, and my eyes felt ready to pop out of my head at any moment. Why hadn't I been spotted by one of their lookouts? What did the idiots think they were doing?

I left the path and ran through the bushes towards the first house in the village which I could now just see. Its garden had a hedge round it, but one last leap and I was over. Charging through the door into the dark interior I found myself gripped tight by someone. It was Pippo. Gasping for air, speech was almost impossible, but I managed to stammer out, 'The Germans! the Germans!' pointing frantically in the direction I had come from. 'Let them come,' said Pippo. 'But what about you?' I asked. 'What about the partisans?' 'They won't come to this house,' he said, 'and there are no partisans in the village.' He grinned, made me sit down and have a drink. A little girl came in, took off my shoes and helped me to put my feet in a basin of warm water. My legs were covered in scratches and my heart was still thumping. 'But why wasn't there a lookout?' I insisted. 'I didn't see anybody.'

'You weren't supposed to,' said Pippo. 'We saw the Germans as soon as they got off the bus. Anyway, this lot are harmless. They'll just take a lot of useless measurements and go away again. They won't concern themselves with anything else. But I couldn't think who the mad woman careering up the hill could be. It wasn't until you leapt over the hedge that I recognised you. What a stylish entry!'

'I suppose I must have looked ridiculous,' I said, rather crossly. 'Yes, you were quite funny,' said Pippo, turning to a tall blond young man, probably one of his lieutenants, who was also laughing.

Pippo – his real name was Manrico Ducceschi – was one of the most influential and respected partisan leaders in the whole of Tuscany, and the only one whose men were subsequently to be kept fully equipped by the Allies so that they could fight side by side with them. Already in June 1944 he had over a thousand men under his command, and they represented the strongest formation in the Pistoia area.

I recalled Pippo as I had first known him, ten months ago. He was then a serious and rather shy undergraduate, reading classics, the youngest of my brother's friends. He had come to see me, and told me that he was going to the mountains with three others. 'Lulli isn't coming,' he said, 'because he thinks there will be more to do in the city. Well, we'll see.' (Lulli was the leader of the small anti-Fascist cell that had arisen in Pistoia.) 'You can bet he won't do anything. But I shall need lots of things – shoes, clothes, money.'

I had given him my own and my brother's mountaineering boots and a revolver that an officer had asked me to look after. My mother had insisted on giving this delicate-looking boy two thick sweaters, though the weather was still quite warm. Since then I had not seen him, though I had often had news of him and of the daring operations he had successfully master-minded. I tried to recognise the former student in the present guerrilla leader. He was even thinner now than he had been, perhaps a little balder, but bronzed and with an unmistakable air of self-confidence. Watching him while he spoke to his men I could see that they trusted and admired him.

I told Pippo the things that headquarters wanted to know. He gave some rapid and precise orders to the blond lieutenant, who turned on his heel and went out. We were left alone in the large, cool, dark kitchen, and he asked about all of us – how we were and what we were doing. He seemed rather disappointed by my account, but perhaps I hadn't explained properly. Then he asked me about the poets De Robertis, Montale and Saba. I told him I had found a safe house for Saba to hide in. He was a great poet and a noble old man, but nervous and with an extremely irritating wife. Pippo quoted from a poem in which he had compared her to a chicken. From Saba he passed on to Montale, almost all of whose works he seemed to know by heart, reciting them more to himself than to me. He sat on the step of the hearth while I sat on the bench, thoughtfully stroking the scratches on my legs.

The blond lieutenant came back with a thin strip of paper on which he had written the information headquarters were asking for. He asked me where I was going to hide it, and I told him I would put it in one of my shoes. 'Good,' he said.

I turned to Pippo. 'Can I leave you these leaflets?' I asked. 'Will you promise to hand them out and explain them?' I showed him the different leaflets I had brought, some containing the political programmes of the Partito d'Azione and some with various propaganda messages. From the point of view of the politicians it was just as important that the partisans should develop their political thinking along the right lines as that they should fight. But it was difficult to convince the partisan leaders of this. Even the more mature among them, like Pippo, were totally taken up with much more urgent and dramatic matters.

I saw that both Pippo and the blond lieutenant were smiling. 'You won't throw them away, will you?' I begged. 'I'd rather take them back with me than let that happen. They cost us a lot, both in worry and money.'

'And goodness knows how much in talk!' said Pippo, laughing. But I sensed that at heart he was sad and disillusioned. So I broke out into a description of our work in Florence, of our hopes and fears. I told him of our wish to work as closely with them as possible, even if we were often not much good at meeting all their needs. I told him we were so worried about the dangers they had to face that we almost forgot our own. If this was not the longest speech I had ever made it was certainly the most eloquent.

'My dear Maria Luigia,' said Pippo, 'you are a very splendid girl.' And he shook his head sadly.

(Translated from *Storia di Un Anno Grande, Settembre 1943–Agosto 1944* by Maria Luigia Guaita. La Nuova Italia, Florence, 1975.)

PART II

With the Chairman

M

Y return to England was a great joy – the fulfilment of a four-year-old dream. London was the first stop, where a few weeks at a crammer's brought me up to the required standard in mathematics, and a doodle-bug, falling near Marble Arch where I should have been at the time, nearly undid my successful avoidance of the Nazi war machine in Florence and Rome. Then Downside, a dramatic change from the Collegio, but one made easier for me by the fact that the headmaster, Christopher Butler, seemed to take a special interest in this unusual new boy, and by my own determination to do well enough academically to get into Cambridge, something on which I had set my heart.

In this I was successful. School Certificate came almost immediately, then Higher Certificate in which I did well enough to get what was then called a 'state scholarship'. Most places in Oxford and Cambridge at that time were reserved for men coming out of the forces, and most school leavers had to go on to do their two years' national service, but I was fortunate in getting a formal chit from the Foreign Office and Ministry of Labour which stated that in view of my Italian experiences I was exempt. I took an exam for entry into a group of four Cambridge colleges, and at the age of seventeen won a languages exhibition to St Catharine's.

Politics was now my main interest. At Downside I had been active in the school debating society and in a sixth-form club which was devoted to politics. As soon as I came up to Cambridge I joined the University Conservative Association and was repeatedly elected to the Committee of the Union, being twice narrowly defeated for the secretaryship, which would have almost automatically led on to the presidency. I was involved in the Federation of University Conservatives, in those days a much more responsible body than it seems to be today, and became its chairman. This meant, among other things, that for a year I was an ex-officio member of the National Executive of the party, and as its youngest member found myself sitting next to Churchill when he gave the Executive lunch at the Savoy. That was something which, when interned in Italy or in hiding, I would have seen as a summit of my ambition but impossible of achievement. He was charming. We talked about Italy, where he had just been on a painting holiday, he drank a good deal of brandy and told me it was a great mistake to think that brandy was not an excellent lunch-time tipple, and presented me with a cigar which I kept reverently for many years. But when I ventured to try it the cigar had become unsmokable.

There is one event that took place while I was at university which I should mention here, because, although peripheral at the time, it had some relevance to my later interest in the problems of the Middle East.

My period at Cambridge overlapped with the establishment of the State of Israel and all the troubles that accompanied it. To begin with I had few views and no knowledge about Palestine. What views I did have were instinctively sympathetic to the Jews. My experience in Italy had seen to that, and moreover I had many Jewish friends who understandably enough supported the Zionist cause. But a chance encounter with two Arabs changed my thinking.

One was Musa Alami, a Cambridge-educated member of one of the most influential Palestinian families. He had held a senior post in the mandatory government but resigned in protest against its policy on immigration. Later he was to devote his energies and fortune to the creation of a magnificent project in the Jordan Valley for the rehabilitation and training of orphan boys from the refugee camps, but at that time he was engaged in setting up offices in London, Paris and Washington which aimed at trying to ensure that the case for the Arabs in general and the Palestinian Arabs in particular did not go completely by default. The other was Edward Atiyah, a Lebanese Christian, long a teacher in the Sudan but now a leading member of Musa's London Arab Office and the author of a fascinating autobiography, *An Arab Tells His Story*. From them I discovered what Arthur Balfour had failed to realise – that in Palestine, where he blithely recommended the setting up of a 'national home' for the Jews, there were

Palestinians, that the Palestinian Arabs were the overwhelming majority there, and that they did not wish to lose their country to alien settlers largely financed and encouraged by the United States. Colin Ross-Munro, now a distinguished Silk, then reading history at King's and a great friend, still vividly recalls the sharp impact this discovery made on me at the time.

Musa Alami and Edward Atiyah were in no way hostile to the Jews; in fact, they and their forefathers had lived happily side by side with the Jewish communities in Palestine and Lebanon for hundreds of years. They were certainly not anti-Semitic; how could they be, since they were Semites themselves and proud of the fact. Anti-Semitism was to them an alien doctrine, rampant in Europe (where its most horrific manifestation had been the recent holocaust perpetrated by Nazi Germany), America and other parts of the world. But they were Arab patriots, who wanted to see Palestine, in common with every other part of the Arab world, emerge from foreign tutelage into an independent state, which should reflect the views and aspirations of the overwhelming majority of its population.

They presented me with facts, not with emotional arguments, and the facts were irrefutable. As a result, during that time when the fate of Palestine became a subject for debate and discussion in Cambridge as well as in Parliament and the Press and at the United Nations, I aligned myself with the Palestinian Arabs and against the Zionists. That issue was soon pushed into the background by more urgent aspects of the Cold War, and my involvement in it ended. Little did I then realise in what an unexpected and overwhelming way it was going to be revived for me in 1967.

After Cambridge I became one of the founding members of the Bow Group, often and with some reason regarded as a sort of Tory equivalent of the Fabian Society, others being Edward Boyle, who had been President of the Oxford Union in 1948, and Geoffrey Howe, slightly older than me but coming up to Cambridge two years later owing to national service. We were to enter the House of Commons together in 1964. Another opportunity for meetings and discussions with like-minded young Conservatives was the Coningsby Club, which I joined, as did others such as William Rees-Mogg, Peter Goldman, David Windlesham, David Howell and Peter Tapsell, who were to become enduring friends. Nigel Lawson, though somewhat later, was also Chairman of the Coningsby, and I saw a great deal of him and his wife Vanessa.

In 1952 I was chosen to attend the Harvard International Seminar, presided over by an unknown academic called Henry Kissinger. He struck me as a rather Germanic professional type, living in pleasantly bourgeois surroundings in a small house outside Cambridge with his pretty, demure Austrian wife. There I was occasionally invited to dinner, but neither I nor anyone else could have foreseen that he was going to become in twenty years one of the most powerful men in the world. When I met him again, first in 1966 when, now a Member of Parliament, I was a member of the UK delegation to the United Nations, and again when our paths crossed over the Middle East, the friendly dialogue continued.

I had read languages in Part 1 of the Cambridge Tripos, and then switched to law for Part 2, it being my intention to read for the Bar. At a society dinner in Cambridge when the guest speaker was Brendan Bracken it fell to me to propose a vote of thanks. He asked me what I planned to do when I went down, and when I said politics and the Bar he commended my choice and told me that I should aim at getting into the best chambers, which meant Walter Monckton's, and that he would do something about it. I assumed that this was the sort of promise easily made during a good dinner and just as easily forgotten after it, so was astonished when a few weeks later I got an invitation to lunch with Bracken, where he told me that I was to go immediately to see Monckton. I did, and was duly offered a place in his chambers.

This would have been a splendid start, but not one of which I was to avail myself. I soon realised that I was already engaged in too many political activities which I could not have kept up in the probably briefless, and so incomeless years at the Bar. After Harvard had come a study group at the Council of Europe in Strasbourg and other political concerns, all interesting but none bringing any financial rewards. So, with some regret, for I think I would have enjoyed the Bar, I decided not to waste any time on working for my Bar finals and instead to get a job which would provide an adequate income and which would not be too demanding of my time and energies. I was taken on as a junior executive in Pritchard, Wood and Partners, which at the time was one of the leading British advertising agencies, and it was while I was still there that Lord Hailsham, then Chairman of the Conservative Party, asked me to be his personal assistant.

He had become Chairman in September 1957 at a moment when, as he was later to admit, 'every rational analysis of the situation led me to suppose that the effect on my fortunes would be to make my name for ever associated with ignominious failure.' When accepting the post he had made it a condition that he would have to be provided with the services of a personal assistant 'of the highest character and ability', and he consulted Oliver Poole, Michael Fraser (now Lord Fraser of Kilmorack), Joint Director of the Conservative Research Department, and Peter Goldman, by now Director of the Conservative Political Centre, about names. Mine was one of those they put forward for this improbable paragon, and fortunately the one Hailsham chose. Needless to say, when the offer was made to me I jumped at it. Although the financial reward would be small I could not have hoped for a more fascinating position at the very centre of politics at a crucial time for the future of the government and the Conservative Party.

Meanwhile I continued to pay fairly frequent visits to Italy. My father had at first struggled gamely to get his business back on its feet, but it never recovered from having been sequestrated by the Fascists and then pillaged by the Germans. No realistic compensation was ever made for his losses, nor for those suffered by my mother. Not surprisingly my father felt bitterly about all this and eventually, as his health was deteriorating, he decided to sell out, though only for a fraction of the company's pre-war value. (He had had a fifty per cent share in it, as well as being a director of the parent company in England.) He and my mother had paid severely both personally and financially for Mussolini's adventurism but, as my mother frequently remarked, we had all come out of it alive, which was more than could be said for so many others. We should consider ourselves very fortunate, she would add, and no doubt she was right.

When Hailsham took over the chairmanship at the end of 1957 morale in the Conservative Party was lower than at any time in this century, not excepting the aftermath of the Labour landslide of 1945. Suez had been a disaster both for the country and for the government which, through a series of miscalculations and deceits, had led the nation into a humiliating defeat. Anthony Eden had stepped down and left the country with his reputation in tatters; and this was the man who had for years been, second only to Churchill, the brightest star in the party's firmament. The new Prime Minister, Harold Macmillan, was relatively unknown in the country – certainly less well known than his number two, Rab Butler who, as a very successful Chancellor of the Exchequer in Churchill's 1951 government, had done away with wartime controls, and who, in the opinion of many, deserved the post that had gone to his rival. Meanwhile, the opposition Labour Party could claim that their stand over Suez had been justified by events, and in their leader, Hugh Gaitskell, they had a man who had not only established ascendancy in his own party, but who was widely respected in the essential middle ground of politics where elections are lost and won.

'During the summer of 1957,' Macmillan wrote in his memoirs, 'the state of the Party and the current of public opinion were still moving against us.' He felt he had almost consolidated his government's position in Parliament, 'but in the country we were still weak and divided. It seemed to me that the best chance lay in a change in the chairmanship which would be sufficiently dramatic to create something of the improvement effected by Lord Woolton after our electoral disaster of 1945. Hailsham appeared to have all the qualities required.'

Quintin Hailsham was very different from Lord Woolton in every way except in dedication to the task set him. Woolton had become a politician only by chance, brought in by Churchill to apply his managerial skills to the problem of feeding a nation at war. As Minister of Food he had become 'the popular "Uncle Fred" who gave people, especially housewives, the impression of personal concern for them – taking them into his confidence, warning them in advance of shortages, admitting and correcting occasional errors of judgement. Many a child who was wayward with his food was threatened with the displeasure of Lord Woolton.'[1] Later, his appearances at party conferences were to produce the same glow of confidence and affection in his audience.

Hailsham on the other hand had politics in his blood and bones. Academically brilliant, steeped in the history and literature of his own

[1] Entry in the *Dictionary of National Biography* by Lord Redcliffe-Maud.

country as well as that of Greece and Rome, he had an intellect of great depth and immense agility. Whereas Woolton was said to have 'taken the party machinery to bits and rebuilt it from top to bottom' Hailsham was not primarily concerned with party organisation or with the day-to-day running of Central Office. This was left to Oliver Poole, his predecessor as Chairman and now Deputy Chairman, a very skilful businessman and politician, who understood exactly how the party machine functioned and what was needed to maintain and improve its efficiency. Hailsham's role was rather that of a prophet, reaching out directly to the people, and he at once set about planning his campaign with the thoroughness and resource of a staff officer preparing for a battle or a barrister mastering a complicated brief.

At my first meeting with Hailsham he had outlined the difficulties that lay ahead. The party's confidence in itself, and the electorate's confidence in the party, had to be revived. There would have to be a close examination of the state of the party up and down the country. And above all there was a practical goal to be aimed at, one which most people then assumed to be unattainable – to win a third election in a row, something which must come before the end of 1959 and might come earlier. Dramatic methods would have to be employed if the imagination of the party was to be captured and this goal achieved.

Hailsham's first chance to show what he could do came at that year's party conference in Brighton. I was there, although my appointment as his personal assistant had not been officially announced, so that Central Office could have time to notify anyone who might be affected by it. Naturally, I was present to hear him speak at what was then, and perhaps remains, the most important of the conference fringe meetings, that arranged by the Conservative Political Centre. It was a superb speech, both in its content and delivery, and was received with enormous enthusiasm. The final passage in his peroration is worth giving, not just as an example of his highly effective oratorical style, but as a reflection of his personal beliefs which, because they were so strongly held, found a ready response in many who heard him expound them.

If we in the Conservative Party are to fulfil our mission we must appeal to deeper instincts in the national conscience. For we are concerned fundamentally with the defence of spiritual values when they are in danger of being overwhelmed by the powers of darkness. In an age of infidelity, Conservatism is concerned with faith. In an age of dissolving allegiances, it upholds loyalties. In a fog of material considerations, it points to integrity. In an atmosphere of self-seeking, it preaches self-sacrifice. Its demands are greater than its rewards. It stands for honour and dignity in public life, for decency and purity in private relations, for the family, for patriotism, for religion. Of course, we claim no monopoly of these great words. But, whether rightly or wrongly, we are Conservative because we seek to conserve the values they express.

A party which sets itself such ultimate standards is better equipped to change with the times and to meet the challenges and opportunities of a new age than one which is tied to ephemeral slogans and shibboleths. That is why the Conservative Party alone of British parties has survived and surmounted adversity from generation to generation. That is why I can say to you who serve it today: this is my message to Conservatism. This is my message to Britain. Lift up your hearts, together we have great work to do. Be as eagerly confident of the future as you are justly proud of the past.

I recall one MP at the end of the meeting – and this was of course long before any 'leadership issue' had arisen – saying, 'Well, if the PM ever goes, *there* must be the alternative leader – if only we can get him out of the Lords.'

The imagination of the public was captured in a simpler but no less dramatic fashion; pictures of the party Chairman in a bathing costume entering the water on Brighton beach appeared in all the papers. And then there was the business of the bell. The normal ritual at the end of the party conference is that the Chairman of the conference hands over to the Chairman of the party the bell which he had used during the week to keep order over debates. The Chairman of the party gracefully accepts, and that is that. But not this time. Gripping the bell and swinging it vigorously to and fro Hailsham roused his audience to a frenzy of enthusiasm.

The enthusiasm on the floor was not entirely shared by the Prime Minister who had, following custom, absented himself from the conference hall during the week, to appear godlike on the platform on the final Saturday afternoon. This tradition was ended by Edward Heath and has not been revived, although the leader's speech remains the *pièce de résistance* of the conference. That was always intended to be the climax of the proceedings, but on this occasion the climax had come in the morning. Macmillan was still in his first year as party leader, and this should have been his big opportunity to impress himself on the faithful, but now he found himself upstaged, and there can be little doubt that he resented it. He wrote in his memoirs: 'Indeed, so successful was Hailsham's conduct of the Conference and so eloquent his final speech that some of the Press and other commentators felt that the new Chairman had put the Prime Minister somewhat in the shade. I had, of course, no feelings of reproach.' It is possible to suspect that the forgiving spirit of the memoir writer does not reflect the true feelings of the politician at the time. Some weeks later I had to attend a meeting at Number Ten in which Macmillan and one or two other Ministers were present. Hailsham was late, and I was shown in alone. 'Ah, the bell-boy,' said Macmillan, and there was not a great deal of cordiality in his voice.

Brighton was the beginning of the campaign, and during the next two years Hailsham was to set himself a gruelling programme. He was determined to visit every one of the fifteen areas into which, for the purposes of Central Office and the National Union (the organisation of voluntary works), the country is divided. Each area had a full-time agent appointed by Central Office and held an annual or biannual meeting of party workers and supporters. Hailsham attended these meetings, or, if none was due to come up, called for a special one.

His speech at these meetings would usually fall into four parts. He would start by looking at the special problems of the area, and this would be followed by a good knockabout turn attacking the opposition, which always went down very well. Then there would be a passage about the policies of the government and the philosophy of Conservatism. He would expand the thesis that only the Conservatives were capable of making private enterprise and public planning work together, thus avoiding the rigidity of socialism, which saw nationalisation as the cure-all, and the ineffectiveness of welfare in the United States which widened the gap between rich and poor. As he summed it up in one typical speech:

To reconcile the communal loyalties and obligations which men and women owe to society with their claims for personal freedom is the eternal problem of democracy. To achieve this balance has throughout history been a formidable task, and we are rightly proud of the example and inspiration which our own practice of democracy has given to many other lands. But freedom is not a gift of the gods. It must continually be sustained and defended. And in our own present age of scientific and technical revolution the conquests of Man over his physical and material environment carry with them new threats to freedom potentially more dangerous than any in the past. The fact is that we are seeking to produce in Britain a balanced society. It is precisely because it is balance we seek in our political policy that we have so many enemies among the cranks and extremists. The necessity for the modern state to play a much larger part is generally admitted. But it is the extent and method of state intervention which creates the deepest division between Conservative principles and those of their opponents.

He tried to ensure that this part of the speech was linked to his next speaking occasion, so that a coherent pattern of argument would emerge. Finally, there would be an emotive peroration, which almost always brought his audience to its feet – no mean achievement in the days before television had debased the standing ovation to the point where pretty well every platform speaker at the party conference, however inept, is accorded one.

About ninety per cent of Hailsham's speeches would be written out in full in advance. Moreover, of that ninety per cent, by far the greater part was entirely and laboriously written out by him in his beautiful italic script and then typed, corrected meticulously by him and re-typed. From time to time I would contribute to the balance of ten per cent, as would Peter Goldman, Michael Fraser and Ronald Sims, head of publicity at Conservative Central Office, depending on the occasion. But he was so practised an orator that he always appeared to be speaking extempore – and indeed was quite capable of doing so for as long as necessary when the occasion arose. One advantage of this advance preparation was that the Press could be given a much more extensive handout than usual. He also made a point of speaking at least once at every by-election, of which there were no fewer than twenty-four, or an average of one a month, between his becoming Chairman and the general election of October 1959. Another self-imposed duty was to visit any area where a particular local problem had become acute. Unemployment in Scotland was one such; the textile industry, then under dire threat owing to cheap imports from the Commonwealth another, and Cyril Lord, the colourful textile magnate, was waging an energetic and skilful campaign calling for government action to protect Lancashire. The numerous journeys Hailsham made to Manchester, Bolton, Oldham, Rochdale and other centres did a lot towards keeping the North-West steady – though the Rochdale election of February 1958 was one of only two Tory losses to Labour.

I went everywhere with Hailsham, gaining in two years a more thorough knowledge of the country than could have been acquired by any other means. It was an exacting programme for both of us, but Hailsham was always an amusing and intellectually stimulating companion, if on rare occasions capable of displaying the temperament of the artist which is one facet of his many-sided character. As he wrote in a letter to me after my association with him had ended: 'I am afraid that at the best of times I am not an easy man to work for; but you were not working for me at the best of times. You were working for me at a time when I was desperately worried, much criticised, and therefore probably much more difficult.'

Take, for example, an incident on the eve of the party conference of 1958. This was held in Blackpool, and we were joined in our reserved compartment on the journey up by Peter Goldman, not only a close friend of mine but on form one of the most amusing people I have ever known. We naturally discussed the coming conference and current political issues, and Hailsham went through his boxes with his usual despatch, but when that was done he found time to turn the conversation to his favourite topics – history and religion – teasing me about the Catholic Church (to which he was in fact most sympathetic from his deeply held Anglican point of view).

Arrived at the Imperial Hotel, Hailsham said that the least he could do to reward the two of us for the work we had been putting in was to entertain us to a really good dinner, something one restaurant in the hotel was then capable of providing, having not only a good kitchen but an excellent wine-list. We ate well and drank quite a lot of claret, attaining a state of benevolent relaxation. Hailsham noticed that a nearby table was occupied by Gerald O'Brien, Deputy Director of Information at Central Office, two journalists, and a young girl who worked in Central Office, Susan Chataway, sister of Christopher Chataway, another friend of mine and then a star television commentator.

In December of the previous year Miss Chataway had become

involved in something that was hailed as high political drama but which turned out a very damp squib – the so-called Bank Rate Tribunal. On 19 September 1957 the Bank of England raised Bank Rate by two points from five to seven per cent. Almost immediately some Labour MPs, led by Harold Wilson, claimed that there were 'clear indications of a leak', that people in the City had known this was going to be done and had taken advantage of their knowledge. An enquiry by the Lord Chancellor came to the conclusion that nothing improper had occurred, but that did not satisfy Labour, and on 12 November a left-wing MP, Sir Leslie Plummer, asked in the Commons 'whether or not prior information of his [the Chancellor of the Exchequer, Peter Thorneycroft] intentions had been given to Mr Poole.' Oliver Poole was Deputy Chairman of the Conservative Party, and Harold Wilson spoke menacingly of his 'vast City interests'. Here, it seemed, was a wonderful opportunity to discredit the Tory Party and one of its leading members.

Behind these allegations was a chapter of comedy, almost of farce. On 25 September Miss Chataway had met a cousin of hers, John Pumphrey, then head of the Establishment and Organisation Department in the Foreign Office, on Woking station platform and travelled up to London with him. She told him she was now working in Conservative Central Office, at which he said, 'What fun! Do you get a lot of advance information?' She jokingly agreed that she did, and according to Mr Pumphrey (though Miss Chataway told the tribunal she could not remember this) went on to say that she wouldn't be surprised if they didn't have the police in the office in a day or two 'about this Bank Rate business'. 'Good God,' said Mr Pumphrey, 'you didn't get that in advance, did you?' 'Oh yes, we knew.'

Miss Chataway, a lively and charming nineteen-year-old, had started work as a trainee in the Press Department of Central Office only a few days before the rise in Bank Rate, and worked in a room with five others. Not only could she by no conceivable chance have known anything about a Bank Rate rise even if anyone else in the office did – and they didn't – but obviously she treated the conversation as a bit of light banter between friends. Not so the serious Mr Pumphrey, who decided that he would have to see that a report of the conversation was communicated to Hugh Gaitskell, Leader of the Opposition – but without telling his cousin what he was doing. And so on to the setting up of a tribunal of enquiry under Lord Justice Parker and the waste of a lot of people's time and a lot of public money.[1]

Hailsham now began ribbing O'Brien about some Press story, and then declared, in what purported to be a Lancashire accent, 'Real thing I want to do is go on Racer,' meaning the Big Dipper in Blackpool Fun Fair. Then he turned to Miss Chataway. 'You're a girl of spirit, aren't you? Will you come on Racer with me?' She said she would love to. 'Right,' said Hailsham. 'As soon as we've finished dinner we'll go on Racer.'

It seemed to me that this could have most unfortunate consequences. We had always, and perfectly truly, been at pains to point out that Miss Chataway was among the most junior of all employees in Central Office, with no access to any senior officials there. If the Press was able to publish pictures of her and the party chairman together on Racer (exchanged hats? arms round waists?) they would have a field day. So I told Hailsham I didn't think it was a very good idea: 'I don't think you should do it.' This sent Hailsham into one of his occasional rages. 'I'm going to go,' he said. 'You're my personal assistant, not my nanny.' And he went across to Miss Chataway (fortunately the two journalists had left by now): 'We'll go as soon as we've finished dinner.' I repeated that I thought it not a good idea. 'I don't care whether you think it's a good idea or not,' he said, and got up to go to his room, calling out to Miss Chataway as he left to be sure to meet him in the lobby when he came down: 'We'll go on Racer.'

I was determined that Hailsham should not go on Racer but was not clear how best to stop him. I spoke to O'Brien. 'He's not to go,' I said. 'It's up to you to deal with her; I'll deal with him.' 'But what am I supposed to do?' he asked. 'Do whatever you like,' I said. 'Why not take her to play ping-pong?' (There was a sign showing the way to a table-tennis room in the basement.) So when Hailsham came down he looked around and found no Miss Chataway. 'Where's she gone?' he asked. I said I didn't know. 'What d'you mean, you don't know?' 'I mean I don't know. I'm not in charge of Miss Chataway. She's just not around.'

[1] From the Report of the Tribunal of Enquiry: 'We are quite clear that this claim to prior knowledge was made by Miss Chataway in jest, as part of a conversation begun by Mr Pumphrey in jest. How he came to take her remarks seriously is difficult to understand.'

Hailsham instantly realised what had happened. He got into a most tremendous temper. 'Right,' he said. 'As you won't let me go on Racer what we'll do is walk up and down the promenade.' It was pouring with rain. He had the small plastic mac he always carried and a cap; I had neither coat nor hat. We walked up and down in pouring rain and almost total silence for forty minutes and I came back soaked to the skin. Back in my room, I wrung out my suit like a sponge. It was absolutely ruined, but I had won my battle.

A little while later, back in the lobby, a lot of journalists came up to me. Somebody must have overheard the exchange in the restaurant, because they wanted to know if it was true that the Chairman was going on the Big Dipper with Susan Chataway. I said, 'No, of course not. You can't seriously suppose the Chairman of the party would go on the Big Dipper with a junior secretary on the eve of the conference.' Being a very generous person, the next morning Hailsham made a handsome apology.

Among other things the journalists wanted to ask me was whether the Chairman was going to ring the bell again at the close of the conference, and this was a question I could not answer. A few days earlier I had had a talk with John Wyndham,[1] Macmillan's Political Private Secretary and a most likeable ally and friend. Liaison between him and Oliver Poole at Central Office, as well as with me, had always been excellent, as had been my link with Tony Barber,[2] Macmillan's Parliamentary Private Secretary. John Wyndham told me in the gentlest way that he thought it would not be received with great joy if once again the Prime Minister's final speech was pre-empted by the Chairman. There had in fact been a number of occasions in the past twelve months when the Chairman had appeared to be getting more limelight than the Prime Minister, and that must have caused natural resentment. There may also have been a genuine lack of sympathy on Macmillan's part for the Hailsham style. Macmillan was no doubt an actor, but a deliberately underplaying actor; Hailsham was an over-

[1] John Wyndham, with Harold Macmillan when Minister Resident in North Africa, 1942–45. Private Secretary 1957–63. Sixth Baron Leconfield and first Lord Egremont 1963.
[2] Anthony Barber (Lord Barber, Life Peer, 1975). PPS to Prime Minister 1958–59. Minister of Health 1963–64. Chancellor of the Exchequer 1970–74. Chairman of Conservative Party 1967–70.

My mother's family house at Lonigo which was sold in 1969

My mother with my daughter Camilla in 1982, a few months after she
was born

Cognome	Cambi
Nome	Mario
Padre	fu Pietro
Madre	fu Daniele Anna
nato il	18 ottobre 1929
a	Napoli
Stato civile	celibe
Nazionalità	italiana
Professione	studente
Residenza	Corigliano
Via	dei Cinquecento 29

CONNOTATI E CONTRASSEGNI SALIENTI

Altezza	m. 1.55
Corporatura	snella
Capelli	biondi
Occhi	grigi
Naso	reg.
Segni part.	

FIRMA DEL TITOLARE

Mario Cambi

, li

Impronta del dito
indice sinistro

IL PODESTÀ

False identity card 1943 as Mario Cambi

MINISTERO DELL'AGRICOLTURA E DELLE FORESTE

TESSERA DI RICONOSCIMENTO

rilasciata al Sig. Dr. Giorgio Aldo

Via Firenze 48 - Napoli -

Delegato speciale per le malattie delle piante.

Roma, li 27 Ott. Anno XXI.

FIRMA DEL TITOLARE

Giorgio Aldo

IL MINISTRO

False identity paper 1943 as Giorgio Aldo

My father as a Brother of the Order of
Christian Brothers. In fact he did not use
this disguise

SACRA CONGREGATIO
DE SEMINARIIS ET STUDIORUM UNIVERSITATIBUS

Si attesta che il Signor Prof. DANIELI ALDO, fu Giuseppe e fu Berti Maria, nato a Napoli il giorno 8 Novembre 1880, domiciliato in Roma, Via San Sebastienello 3, è addetto, in qualità di Supplente di lingue straniere al Pontificio Istituto De Merode, in Roma, (Via San Sebastianello), dipendente dalla Santa Sede.

Roma, 28 Dicembre 1943   IL SEGRETARIO

U E B E R S E T Z U N G

Es wird hiermit bescheinigt dass H. Prof. ALDO DANIELI Sohn des gestorb. Giuseppe und Gestorb. Maria Berti, geb. z. Neapel am 8/XI/1880, wohnhaft Rom, Via San Sebastianello 3, der Päpstlichen vom Heiligen Stuhl abhängingen, Anstalt "De Merode" (Rom, San Sebastianello Strass, 16) angehört, als Hilfslehrer der fremden Sprachen.

Rom, den 28 Dez. 1943   DER SEKRETÄR

My father's false identity paper as Professor Aldo Danieli

RESISTANCE

Left: Gianfranco Mattei. *Right:* His last message (see p. 61), smuggled out of the Gestapo headquarters in the Via Tasso, Rome

APPEASEMENT

The Prime Minister and Foreign Minister of Great Britain, Neville Chamberlain and Lord Halifax, visit Mussolini and his son-in-law, the Foreign Minister Count Ciano, Rome, January 1939

Representing the Cambridge University Conservative Association at an Oxford dinner in 1948. In the foreground the author and Doric Bossom from Cambridge and Margaret Roberts (Thatcher), Oxford

With Quintin Hailsham and his favourite bull in 1958 at Carter's Corner, his house in Sussex

Quintin Hailsham rings the bell at the 1958 Conservative Party Conference at Blackpool

Quintin Hailsham and R.A. Butler during the Blackpool 'Fight for the Tory Leadership' Conference, October 1963

Personal Assistant to Quintin Hailsham at the Conservative Conference, Blackpool 1958

With Alec Home and the ex-Japanese Prime Minister, Mr Kaze, and Mrs Kaze
when Secretary of the Conservative Foreign Affairs Committee, 1967

Left: A characteristic greeting from Musa Alami at his Jericho farm. *Right:* Edward Atiyah

Palestinian children in a refugee camp in Jordan in 1967. In the background left to right: Derek Cooper, the late Colin Jackson MP, the
author, Robert Maclennan MP, Ian Gilmour MP

American-Jewish tourists watching from the blown-up Allenby Bridge
Palestinian refugees crossing the River Jordan in July 1967. The same
four MPs in foreground

Another refugee fleeing across the Jordan taking with him what he can
carry

With Ian Gilmour at Chairman Arafat's Tunis residence in 1985

Visiting President Sadat with Ian Gilmour in 1976

١٩٧٧/٥/١٥

Damascus 1978 with President Asad

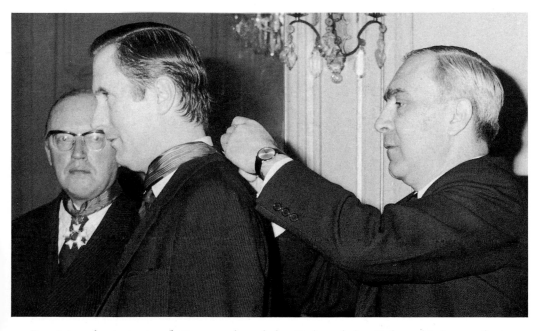

Receiving the insignia of Commander of the Order of the Cedar of Lebanon from
Ambassador Nadim Dimishkie in 1969 on behalf of the President

With Bridgett after the declaration of the poll in the 1983 general election

My five children shaped as a train. A birthday gift from them in 1988.
Left to right: Oliver, Camilla, Dominic, Lolly, Nicholas

player by nature as well as by conviction that this was the way to drive the message home.

So when that same evening Hailsham and I discussed the speech he was to make the next morning I urged him not to ring the bell. I said I did not think this was necessary, though of course it would be expected of him by the party rank and file and would certainly go down very well. But on this occasion, I said, he should pay attention to his own interests. I did not think bell-ringing would make any difference to the success of his speech but it might make a considerable difference to his relations with the Prime Minister, and I told him it had been pointed out to me that it was hoped by the Prime Minister's friends that on this occasion the Chairman would content himself with a splendid speech rather than a challenging one.

We discussed the speech for at least an hour and a half, at the end of which I was left with the clear impression that he agreed with my view and with the advice of others and would not ring the bell. However, when the moment came at the end of what was certainly a splendid speech he was carried away – I think genuinely – by the emotion of the moment. Grasping the bell firmly he declared: 'This year I am going to ring the bell in thankfulness because I was not confounded, and because the small smooth stones of David are still powerful enough to confound and fell Goliath.' The delegates' applause continued for several minutes and once again the bell rang out. This provoked roars of applause and a standing ovation, which undoubtedly showed how immensely popular he was in the party.

My feeling is that Macmillan was intensely annoyed, and, though much later he obviously must have forgiven, it took him a long time to forget. After the 1959 election the chairmanship was passed with unnecessary haste into other hands, those of Rab Butler, Hailsham being demoted from Lord President of the Council to Lord Privy Seal and handed the new and relatively minor Cabinet post of Minister of Science. This was very shabby treatment.

The 1959 election produced the third victory in a row for the Conservative Party, which earlier had seemed impossible; indeed, not only were the Conservatives returned again, but with an overall majority increased from sixty to a hundred. The main credit for this achievement must of course go to the Prime Minister who had done so much to repair the damage done by Suez – cordial relations with the

United States restored, new respect in Europe, the process begun of orderly withdrawal from empire in Africa. But the part played in victory by the Chairman of the party has tended to be overlooked. October 1959 was not a one-man victory, but the victory of a tandem. When it was all over Hailsham wrote to me: 'Ours has been an endeavour to achieve the seemingly impossible. It may be that I am wrong in telling you quite frankly that I believe it is we (by which I mean Poole and you and I) who have done just that. By that I do not mean in the least to belittle the decisive role of the Prime Minister or the Cabinet colleagues. Nevertheless, I still think, quite emphatically, that without us it would never have happened. It has never happened before, even under the most propitious circumstances, and we together made it happen in circumstances which were the reverse of propitious. I believe that this victory is one of the decisive events of our time. I have striven for it, fought for it, prayed for it. As you know, I am, perhaps, a little too prone to recognise the finger of God in human events. But I think the opposite fault from which everyone else seems to suffer is even worse. So may I say quite simply that I sincerely believe that in the past two years both of us, you and I, have been permitted through no personal virtue to co-operate in fulfilling one of the purposes of the divine will.' To write in this way about my association with his triumph was typical of his generosity.

I have cited the Racer-Chataway incident as an example of Hailsham's temperament. This should be balanced by an example of his concern for justice and the infinite pains he was prepared to take to secure it.

Nigel Nicolson had been one of the handful of Conservative MPs who opposed the Suez adventure, and this brought him into head-on collision with his constituency association, that of Bournemouth East, predictably composed of hard-liners who had been longing to see Nasser not just toppled but smashed. Being unable to get rid of Nicolson immediately they had taken the unusual step of selecting another candidate, Major Friend, in his place to fight the next election. Hailsham was shocked that this had been done without giving Nicolson a proper chance to defend himself. He had several meetings, in London and Bournemouth, with the Chairman of the association, a Major Grant, and at last won an important concession: Nicolson was to be allowed to address a special meeting of the Executive.

Should Nicolson fail to persuade the Executive, then Hailsham would launch the novel idea of holding a ballot of all the members of the Bournemouth East Conservative Association. On 14 January 1959 Major Friend, no doubt in response to the pressure being exercised by the Chairman, resigned as candidate.

Hailsham's embattled support for Nicolson was more admirable since on at least two major issues their views were in sharp disagreement. Hailsham had been First Lord of the Admiralty at the time of Suez, and though not in Eden's inner counsels, and so unaware of all the skulduggery going on, he had been in favour of quick and effective action to teach Nasser a lesson. He also disagreed with Nicolson on the question of capital punishment. Nicolson was an abolitionist (this had, not surprisingly, brought on an earlier clash with his constituency association), whereas Hailsham supported capital punishment as the ultimate deterrent. But he recognised Nicolson's qualities as a man and a member, and sympathised with him as a civilised and literate person.

Hailsham had won a further point, that he would also have the right to speak. He hoped, no doubt, that his oratory and the fact of the Chairman of the party being present would swing the day in Nicolson's favour. So we travelled down to Bournemouth for the specially convened meeting of the Executive, which was held on 24 January 1959 at 2.30 in the Bournemouth East constituency headquarters. I shall always remember the unhappy look on Nicolson's face as he greeted us.

The plan was that Hailsham should address the meeting first, without Nicolson's being present, and that he should speak afterwards. Hailsham made an excellent speech, in which he conceded to this rather unprepossessing collection of Conservative activists their absolute right to choose their own candidate and not be dictated to by the party Chairman, but he reminded them of several examples of MPs who had been supported by their constituency associations in spite of differences on policy. He reminded them also that a Conservative MP, unlike so many Labour members, was a representative not a delegate, and that this was something which presupposes the member's right to formulate his own judgement, even if many others think it a wrong judgement. He tried to strike every chord. He gave warning of the capital their political enemies would make if Nicolson was rejected; how they would be represented as tyrannical. At the end of the speech, when I looked at the faces in the hall, I thought it possible that he might just have made it.

Then Nicolson came in and spoke. This was a most depressing experience, because from the outset it was perfectly clear that there was no sympathy at all for him in the hall. He made a good speech, but the questions put to him were without exception aggressive, couched in a way which made it plain that not only were his views anathema but there was strong personal animosity against him. When it came to a vote he was overwhelmingly defeated. On the question of the ballot, however, Hailsham was successful, and it was agreed that a poll of all members of the association would be held as soon as it could be arranged.

Going back in the train Hailsham was depressed. We were joined by the very likeable and entertaining political correspondent of the *Evening Standard*, George Hutchinson, a good friend of mine and wise ally of the Conservative Party, later head of publicity at Central Office, biographer of Macmillan (*The Last Edwardian*) and Heath, and a columnist on *The Times*, who tried, not too successfully, to cheer him up. But Hailsham went on about what a sad day it had been for Nicolson, and about what he feared was a rather nasty side of Conservatism that he had seen that evening, and which he had always been loath to recognise. As he spent a great deal of time travelling round the country extolling the historic virtues of the Conservative Party, he must for a day or two at least have found it difficult to write one of his lyrical pieces about a party which included a bunch of such unattractive and bigoted people.

The ballot of members of the association was held on 25 February 1959, when Nigel Nicolson was defeated by 3762 votes to 3671, a majority of ninety-one and a much closer result than the one at the Executive meeting. There was extensive Press publicity at the time, and speculation that other constituencies might follow the Bournemouth example and adopt American-style primaries for the selection of candidates.

Meanwhile Randolph Churchill had publicly offered himself as compromise candidate and privately had lobbied hard to bring this about. Hailsham, who was fond of Randolph but like others found him hard to handle, had more than once been rung up by Randolph late at night and had told him that in future, if he had anything urgent to communicate, he should ring me – advice of which Randolph took full advantage, his telephone calls at all hours of the day and night becoming a feature of my life. However, it was not to be. The compromise candidate eventually chosen by the Bournemouth Conservatives was John Cordle, who remained their member till 1974.

Hailsham was prepared to take a lot of trouble over Nigel Nicolson because he thought he was an asset to the party and in the House of Commons. But his instinctive and practical humanity embraced, as I discovered, all sorts and conditions of men. Here is one example.

At four o'clock in the morning of 20 November 1958 my bedside telephone rang. I assumed it must be Randolph Churchill on the other end of the line, but on this occasion the caller turned out to be a reporter on the *Star*, the now defunct Liberal London evening newspaper. He asked if anyone had been in touch with the Chairman. I said at that time of the morning I was hardly in a position to know. He then told me that Ian Harvey had been arrested by the police for an indecent offence with a guardsman in St James's Park and was now in custody in Rochester Row police station.

Ian Harvey was MP for Harrow East and Under-Secretary for Foreign Affairs, an intelligent and eloquent member, High Tory and High Anglican, married with two daughters, known and well liked by many politicians, including Hailsham and myself. But as there was obviously nothing that could be done at that time in the morning I waited for a couple of hours before telephoning to Hailsham and telling him what had happened. On that morning, as on many others, the official car (the driver ominously named Hazard but in fact expert and safe and for many years afterwards Jim Callaghan's driver) was to pick me up at my house in Chelsea and drive me down to Hailsham's house in Putney. By then Hailsham had spoken to the Foreign Secretary, Selwyn Lloyd, who had already heard the news, and his first call was at the Foreign Office so that the two of them could have half an hour's discussion of the political implications of the affair.

After that meeting was over Hailsham came out to the car and said to me: 'I think what I really ought to do now is to go and visit poor Ian.' (He had been released on bail and allowed to go home.) 'He must be feeling terrible. This is the end of his career. What a disaster! I think perhaps I might be able to do some good.' So I was asked to cancel his next appointments and we drove down to Richmond, where the

Harveys lived, and I waited in the car while Hailsham went inside. He stayed for nearly an hour. When Hailsham came out he said he had perhaps been able to give a bit of comfort to Ian and to his wife, who was understandably in a state of considerable shock. He had also given some legal advice and recommended a lawyer. Hailsham told me Harvey's face was badly bruised because when arrested he had tried to run away but had been caught and there had been a violent struggle. 'I can quite understand,' said Hailsham. 'He must have fought like a tiger. He was fighting for his life – not just for his political life but for his wife and children.' And as Hailsham spoke the tears were streaming down his face.

By-elections, as I have said, took up a great deal of Hailsham's time and attention, and though Central Office could not impose a candidate on a constituency it naturally took considerable interest in their selection. When it came to choosing a candidate for a seat to be fought at the general election, although Central Office participated in the selection process it was highly unusual for the Chairman to become involved. There was nobody Hailsham was keener to see elected to Parliament than Peter Goldman, for whom he had the highest regard, greatly admiring his intellect and liking him as a person. He rightly thought he would be a great asset to the Conservatives in the House, a view shared by many including Rab, whose considered verdict was that Peter's loss to the party, when he gave up the Political Centre and politics in general, 'was as important as the resignation of any Cabinet Minister'.[1]

Hailsham suspected that some Conservative selection committees had allowed a measure of disagreeable but unspoken anti-Semitic prejudice to influence them in blocking Peter's progress to Parliament. As Peter was one of my closest friends I warmly agreed with Hailsham's views, and on at least two occasions there seemed to be something that he might be able to do about it, though on both occasions he, as well as Peter, was to be disappointed.

The first opportunity was provided by Finchley, and here the ultimate decision was destined to have far-reaching consequences not just for Finchley but also for the country. On 10 March 1958 Sir John Crowder, MP for Finchley, announced that he would not be standing

---

[1] *The Art of the Possible*, R. A. Butler. Hamish Hamilton, 1971, p. 140.

for re-election. He had the reputation of being a crusty reactionary who took little part in debates, so here was a chance to replace him with someone from a rather different mould, and as Finchley had a large proportion of Jewish voters Hailsham thought it would be very suitable for Peter Goldman. Peter Horton, the Conservative Central Office Area Agent, was asked to ensure that Peter's name at least got on to the short-list of candidates, and in due course he came to see Hailsham to report on how things were going in Finchley and some other constituencies. Horton said that he hoped Peter would be short-listed but could not be certain of that, and even less certain that he would be chosen. Also in the running was a Major Ian Fraser, a local councillor, and a very bright woman called Margaret Thatcher who had fought Dartford at the last election. 'Well, it will obviously be a good thing if Peter Goldman gets it,' said Hailsham, and left it at that.

Shortly afterwards a telephone call came through from Sir John Crowder, and as Hailsham was out of the office I took it. He said he wanted to see the Chairman immediately. He wanted to protest to him about the 'disgraceful list' that had been drawn up for his successor. He said that Central Office had blundered badly and 'everyone I know in Finchley' (how many?) was extremely annoyed. I told Sir John that of course the Chairman would see him, and when Hailsham came back he asked me to look up Margaret Thatcher's curriculum vitae. This seemed very promising. She had obviously fought a good election at Dartford, and had the advantage, in Central Office eyes, of being a woman – then, as now, really good women candidates willing to embark on a parliamentary career being hard to find.

When Crowder arrived I put the particulars of Margaret Thatcher and the local man on Hailsham's desk. Sir John took the offensive. He said the situation was absolutely intolerable. None of them was fit to be on a short-list at all; quite disgraceful. Here was a safe Conservative seat, and it ought to be an opportunity to get the right sort of people into Parliament, but this was no way to set about it.

Hailsham managed to remain courteous. 'Well, John,' he said, 'I don't really know what you are complaining about. I understand there is a local man, as there almost always is on a short-list, and though I don't know him I'm told that his is a perfectly reasonable name to put forward. Then there is Peter Goldman, who is Director of the

Conservative Political Centre and generally regarded as one of the cleverest young men in the party, a first-class intellect and a brilliant speaker, who has been doing splendid work in the Political Centre and for whom I have the highest personal regard. And then,' here he looked down and consulted his brief, having forgotten the name, 'you have this very clever woman, Margaret Thatcher, who did exceptionally well at Dartford. She's young, a barrister, and a woman. I should have thought you had a pretty good selection to choose from.' 'That's precisely what I'm complaining about,' shouted Crowder. 'In fact what you're offering us is this: we've got to choose between a bloody Jew and a bloody woman!'

Then came Southend West. This was a safe Conservative seat and had become something of a Guinness fief, having been held by Rupert Guinness (later Lord Iveagh) from 1918 to 1927, then by Lady Iveagh, and after her by their son-in-law 'Chips' Channon[1] who had represented the constituency since 1935. It was now vacant following his death on 7 October 1958. Hailsham thought Southend West would do nicely for Peter Goldman because it too had an unusually high percentage of Jewish voters.

However, it soon became apparent that a strong contender for the seat was 'Chips''s son Paul, intelligent and personable, but only twenty-three years old. Central Office took the view that Paul's selection, whatever his merits, would do the image of the party no good, a view which was conveyed to the Chairman, together with some adverse comment which had already appeared in the Press.

Hailsham didn't feel that there was much he could do about it at that stage, but told me to go and speak to Oliver Poole and find out what he thought. Oliver Poole suggested that Hailsham should see Alan Lennox-Boyd, then Colonial Secretary and Paul Channon's uncle by marriage, 'who might', he thought, 'be able to influence young Paul, though personally I doubt whether he would try to do so,' he added.

In due course Lennox-Boyd came round to see Hailsham. I had met him on a number of occasions and liked him enormously. Highly intelligent and immensely charming, he had beautiful manners and

---

[1] A glittering pre-war and early post-war social figure. His remarkable diaries, skilfully edited by Robert Rhodes James, caused something of a sensation when published in 1967.

was invariably friendly and courteous to underlings like myself. On this occasion not only did he not appear to resent my presence (it was unusual for me to be present when Hailsham had private meetings with Cabinet colleagues though on this occasion he asked me to stay on so that I could report on Central Office opinion) but greeted me in the friendliest manner.

Hailsham started by saying he hoped Lennox-Boyd would not object to his raising a rather delicate personal matter. He then explained the situation, emphasising that nothing he said in any way reflected on Paul as a person, and I reported on Central Office opinion. Hailsham said he hoped that Paul would get into the House of Commons soon, but that it would be in the best interests of the party if it was not at this particular by-election in an election year. Could Lennox-Boyd do anything about it?

'My dear Quintin,' said Lennox-Boyd, 'how very awkward for both of us. You have set out the position most fairly and you were quite right to speak to me about it. In your place I would have done exactly the same. But I must be equally frank and tell you that I am not in your place and that I do not intend to do anything about it.' He said he thought that if Paul was selected, and got in, the whole affair would be forgotten by the time of the general election. 'Southend is an excellent seat and excellent seats are not easy to come by, for, as we both know, luck plays such a part in selection. I'm very fond of Paul,' he said, 'and I don't want to try to influence him against what may be his best interests.' Paul Channon was duly selected and then elected at the by-election that followed in January 1959. It turned out that Lennox-Boyd was wholly correct in his analysis of the situation. By October 1959 few remembered anything about the previous selection process, and even fewer cared one way or another. Paul Channon has since had a distinguished career in Parliament and in government.

'Bless him!' said Hailsham when Lennox-Boyd had left. 'I would have done exactly the same.' 'Yes,' I said, 'but it's sad about Peter. We really must do something about him soon.'

Most unfortunately for all concerned this aim was never achieved. No winnable seat coming up, Peter fought the hopeless West Ham South at the general election. Then at last his luck seemed to have changed. He was chosen to fight a by-election at Orpington in March 1962, generally considered a very safe Tory seat, with a majority at the general election of nearly 15,000. But by one of those freak mid-term reversals this was converted into a Liberal majority of 7,000, and that sadly and cruelly marked the end of Peter Goldman's hopes of getting into Parliament.

After Hailsham had been replaced as Chairman in November 1959, and our association thus brought to an end, I returned to Pritchard, Wood and Partners. I remained there for about two years, and then joined Eric Garrott Associates as a director of the company. At that time this was a relatively small agency, but under Garrott's dynamic leadership it quickly grew. In due course it took over Crawfords and Dorlands, eventually being itself absorbed by Saatchi and Saatchi. But some years before that happened I had, in 1973, left the company, finding it increasingly difficult to reconcile any form of executive role in business with parliamentary life. Since then my business activities have been restricted to part-time directorships and consultancies, which are less demanding and time-consuming.

But in 1959 my principal goal was to get into Parliament as soon as I could. That meant I would have to be chosen for a seat which was safe or at least promising for the Conservatives.

When Hailsham offered me the job of being his personal assistant I asked whether he would object to my fighting a hopeless seat at the general election (almost always a necessary first blooding). Hailsham generously said I could, as long as I did not leave him till the last possible moment after I had dealt with all the details of the election campaign programme and found a suitable replacement to accompany him on the actual campaign tour. Fortunately this I was able to do. Mark Colville (Lord Colville of Culross) stepped efficiently and effectively into the breach.

I had been on the approved list of candidates since 1955, and at some stage of our association Hailsham suggested that I should let my name go forward for winnable seats as well as unwinnable ones. This was because several candidates had been chosen whom he and Central Office considered inadequate. As it turned out I was nearly picked for two safe seats, but in the end only got a hopeless one – Blyth in Northumberland. In those days Blyth was an impregnable Labour stronghold, commanding a 25,000 majority and represented by a popular Member and former Cabinet Minister, Alf Robens. I duly fought Blyth in October 1959 and duly lost.

Not long after I found myself, instead of nursing a safe Tory seat, having to fight the unwinnable Blyth once again. Alf Robens was unexpectedly (for me at least) appointed Chairman of the Coal Board in June 1960, and made a Life Peer. A by-election had to be called, and as I was still nominally the Conservative candidate, I had to fight the seat a second time. I cannot pretend that I much welcomed the prospect of spending four winter weeks in Blyth at a time when I was busy trying to rebuild my credibility with Pritchard, Wood and Partners after two years' absence working with Hailsham. But although it was an expensive and time-consuming affair it turned out to be quite a rewarding one. I liked the officers of the association and got on well with them and with the loyal and devoted party workers. Moreover, by-elections, even in a hopeless seat, command some attention, and Central Office, through its splendid Northern Area Agent, Cyril Norton, gave me tremendous support. The Press, radio and even occasionally television were in attendance, which made canvassing less of a drudgery. My friends rallied round nobly. Both Peter Goldman and William Rees-Mogg spent several days canvassing on my behalf, and I still possess a wonderful picture of William addressing a bleak and almost deserted expanse of shore at Seaton Sluice. Undeterred by his surroundings he spoke learnedly about the economy and the importance of gold. (He himself had been the candidate for the nearby and equally hopeless constituency of Chester-le-Street at the general election.)

Peter Goldman performed the almost impossible task of making an effective last-minute appearance as understudy to a star. Hailsham had kindly volunteered to speak at my final meeting, and an unusually large crowd had gathered to hear him. As other commitments prevented him from leaving London in time to catch a train he had arranged to fly to Newcastle. But fog descended, flights were cancelled, and he could only telephone his regrets and apologies. Peter Goldman agreed to take his place. He was someone the audience had naturally never heard of, and their disappointment was obvious. But he quickly captured their attention and made one of the most brilliant impromptu speeches I have ever heard.

The Blyth by-election result saw the Labour candidate, Eddie Milne, who had inherited Alf Robens' mantle, safely returned with a reduced but more than adequate majority of 16,000. The smaller majority, largely accounted for by a reduced poll, gave me something I could boast about. That, and the fact that I had enjoyed a good Press during the campaign, enabled me to leave Blyth feeling reasonably confident that it should not be too long before the cards dropped my way and I was chosen for a Conservative seat.

In the event I was both short-listed and the runner-up in several seats including Mid-Bedfordshire, Colchester, and Dorking before being selected at Westbury in October 1962. The sitting member and Deputy Speaker, Sir Robert Grimston, who had represented the constituency since 1935, had announced in the summer that he would retire at the next general election, and at that time October 1963 and June 1964 were thought of as probable dates.

Westbury, a Wiltshire county constituency, although a traditional Tory seat, only had a Conservative majority of 5,800 in the 1959 election victory, which saw the Conservatives returned to Westminster with a majority of more than a hundred seats. Grimston, having been a much respected member for thirty-three years, was well dug in. The government was now in the defensive, so I would have to work hard to reassure my supporters that all would be well on the day. It was, and I was elected with a majority of 4,900. Considering that the Conservative majority in Parliament of one hundred was changed to a Labour majority of four, this was an excellent result and we were all delighted. The fact that my father became increasingly ill as polling day approached was my only real anxiety and sadness. I rushed back to London the day after the count and was able to spend a few hours with him before he died.

I have always enjoyed the best possible relations with my officers and association. There have been issues on which we have disagreed, but they have always been resolved in an open and friendly manner. They loyally supported me in 1967–68, when my views on the Middle East conflict were apparently so unorthodox. Now they happily remind me that I was right and that my views have become almost conventional. Capital punishment too has caused its problems, but this was a question on which my Executive was itself divided, and it has always treated my abolitionist views with courtesy and understanding.

It is now over twenty-six years that I have been in Westbury, first for two years as the adopted candidate and then as Member. In that time, if I omit a brief interlude which lasted less than a year, I have had only three agents, the third only recently appointed. Ian Thomson was with me from 1962 to 1975, when he retired (he sadly died in 1988), David Williams from 1975 to 1985 when he too retired, and then again in 1987 when he fortunately agreed to be agent for the general election. Both, in their different ways, were superb agents. I have been equally fortunate in the support I have secured from numerous party workers over the years and I have many good and loyal friends among them. Westbury has been and remains a happy scene.

The fight for the Tory leadership

ALTHOUGH my official association with Quintin Hailsham had ended in October 1959 when he ceased to be Chairman of the Conservative Party, we had kept in touch. So when in early June 1963 I was rung up by Christopher Herzig, his loyal and very able private secretary at the Ministry of Science, saying that Quintin would like me to come round for a talk as soon as I could manage it, my only reason for a slight feeling of surprise was that I had lunched with him at the Carlton Club not many days before. Wondering what could have come up in the interval to make another meeting so urgent, I arranged to go and see him the next morning.

When we met in his office at the Ministry of Science in Richmond Terrace Quintin came straight to the point, after first impressing on me the need for secrecy. He said Harold Macmillan had invited him round for a talk and raised the subject of succession to the leadership, which would arise if he decided to quit before the general election, due by October 1964 at the latest. This was at a time when many inside the Conservative Party thought that Macmillan should resign immediately. All that year things had been going badly for the government. In January de Gaulle had vetoed Britain's entry into the Common Market, and then there had been two sex scandals, the Vassall and Profumo cases, which had been badly mismanaged and led to the resignation of Ministers. The Press was almost unanimous that Macmillan's back was to the wall, or even that he was on his way out.

Macmillan had told Quintin that his original choice for a successor had been Alec Home, and that he had in fact asked him whether, if the situation arose, he would be willing to disclaim his earldom to make him eligible as a candidate for the leadership. Largely as a result of

Tony Benn's attempts to remain a Member of the House of Commons, when his father, Viscount Stansgate, died in 1960, a Peerage Bill enabling peers to renounce their titles had been introduced and was then on its way to the Statute Book. Apparently Home's response had been far from enthusiastic, and in any case, Macmillan added, he was no longer his first choice. He lacked the ambition and the steel necessary to get the job, as well as the economic expertise to compete with Harold Wilson, the new opposition leader, who at that time was at the height of his 'white heat of the technological revolution' phase.

Macmillan had therefore come to the conclusion that Quintin was the right man. He had a first-class intellect, was very popular with the party, was the right age, a national figure, and soon perhaps to become internationally known. (He was shortly to go to Moscow to assist in negotiating a test ban treaty.) Did he want the job?

Quintin's answer was that yes, of course he did. It was a position that anyone in the top rank of politics could not possibly refuse, if offered it. But it was an awesome task. Moreover, he didn't think that Macmillan should go before the general election, and meanwhile he was prepared to go on supporting him loyally and wholeheartedly, as he had always done. And then, what about Rab? Surely he was the most obvious successor. 'On no account,' said Macmillan. 'Rab simply doesn't have it in him to be Prime Minister.'

'What do you think about it all?' asked Quintin. 'You know very well what I think,' I said. 'I believe you would make a great Prime Minister, in spite of your temperament, and if there is anything I can do to help bring this about, I am entirely at your disposal. But it won't be easy. Harold Macmillan may well let you down when it comes to the point.' (In retrospect this was rather a prophetic warning, although of course I had not really thought it through at the time.) 'And only a minority of your colleagues in the Cabinet would support you. You simply must win round a few more if you are going to have a real chance.' I had often reproached Quintin for not taking more trouble about improving his relations with his colleagues, and had recently been hearing stories from Peter Goldman and others in a position to know, that he was making himself unpopular in Cabinet by talking too much and intervening in the affairs of other departments. I had also become increasingly aware, when talking to Iain Macleod (Leader of the House and Chairman of the party) and Reggie Maudling

(Chancellor of the Exchequer), that, though they were always very cordial to me personally, a slight chill would arise whenever Quintin's name came up in the conversation. They were themselves, of course, both potential candidates for the leadership.

I told Quintin I thought there were two essential things he should do: he should remain in as close contact with the Prime Minister as possible, and should concentrate on improving relations with his colleagues in the Cabinet – and I mentioned some specific names, including John Boyd-Carpenter, Christopher Soames, Reggie Dilhorne, Duncan Sandys, Ernest Marples and John Hare (later Lord Blakenham). He should make an effort to listen to them, and should on occasion entertain them socially. 'You're quite right, dear boy,' said Quintin, 'but that's out of the question. Mary wouldn't hear of it – and anyway, you can't teach an old dog new tricks.' 'I don't accept that,' I said. 'And if the old dog is planning to take over the circus it may have to pick up a new trick or two.' Quintin laughed uproariously, and we parted on the understanding that I would tactfully sound out a number of journalists and MPs and that we should keep in touch.

I left Quintin in a state of considerable elation. There appeared to be a real chance, if the cards dropped right, that he could succeed Macmillan. But I could also see innumerable hurdles ahead. I felt certain that the most important single factor was Macmillan – how far he could be trusted to back up and help Quintin all the way. It must also be right for Quintin to try to win round more colleagues, but knowing Quintin so well, and therefore knowing how utterly uncalculating and guileless he was in his personal conduct (one of his very captivating characteristics), I feared he would never take enough trouble to do this.

I did not go back to the office that day, but spent the afternoon trying to analyse the situation and to work out in my own mind how best to help. While realising of course that my contribution could at best be only peripheral, I became increasingly convinced that my analysis of the priorities for Quintin was right: one, Harold Macmillan; two, Cabinet colleagues.

I decided that my first step should be to speak to Lady Hailsham, and find out how she felt about it and how far she was willing to help. My relationship with Mary Hailsham was good, but we were slightly wary of each other. For two years as Quintin's personal assistant I had lived almost in his pocket, and had inevitably got to know her well. She was a splendid woman, attractive and determined. While devoted to Quintin, and utterly loyal to him, she was also insistent that she too had a life of her own to lead, with duties and obligations to fulfil, and these ought not to be sacrificed to Quintin's politics. The children must always come first – not necessarily before Quintin, but certainly before politics. During my time with Quintin I had on several occasions clashed with her over this question of priorities, and though sometimes I had won, more often she had. I knew that she was quite fond of me, and recognised my commitment to Quintin, but I knew also that she would never let me influence him against her wishes.

So I telephoned to Mary, telling her that I wanted to speak to her privately, without Quintin's knowing about it, and invited myself round to The Corner House, Heathview Gardens, Putney, since the sale of Carters Corner in Sussex their only home and generally known to Quintin's intimates as 'Putters'.

When I arrived Putters was in the sate of friendly chaos which I knew so well, and which was now accentuated by the presence of baby Catherine, the fifth Hailsham child, very much a trailer and only eight or nine months old. Her presence did not make my conversation with Mary any easier, but in spite of several noisy and prolonged outbursts I battled on and succeeded in saying my piece.

Mary's reaction was interesting and not quite what I had expected. Yes, she said, she did want Quintin to become Prime Minister, although personally she would hate it and dreaded the thought of it. She wanted it because she knew Quintin would make a superb Prime Minister. But she didn't trust Harold Macmillan one little bit.

As far as Quintin's entertaining his Cabinet colleagues went, my pleas fell on stony ground, and surveying the surrounding disorder, my ears assailed by baby Catherine's screams, I had to admit that my idea of quiet home entertainment at which selected colleagues would be gently influenced in the right direction, was a non-starter – might even prove counter-productive.

As a final rather desperate throw I suggested planning a few dinners in a London restaurant like Wilton's or Prunier's, both of which Quintin liked, though he seldom patronised them as he was a cautious spender. Mary firmly dismissed the idea on the grounds that they could not possibly afford the extravagance – and anyway, baby Catherine's nannying problems were also to be considered. Surely she could find a baby-sitter, I protested. 'It may be easy to find one in Chelsea,' said Mary (I then had a small house in Burnsall Street, off the King's Road, and two young children), 'but it's not as easy as you seem to think in Putney.' And that was that.

However, Mary showed herself genuinely concerned, and as I left assured me that she was a hundred per cent behind the attempt, was prepared to be fully supportive of it, and would telephone to me if there was anything she thought I should know or do. We parted with a display of considerable cordiality, but driving down Putney Hill I was very aware that my visit could not be summed up as 'mission accomplished', but rather as 'first hurdle not cleared'.

The only other person, apart from Mary Hailsham, in whom I decided to confide was Oliver Poole. He was, as I knew from having worked closely with him in the past, not only very shrewd, well informed and influential, but also a strong supporter of Quintin for the leadership. He told me Harold Macmillan had in fact recently spoken to him in precisely the same terms, and that he had passed the message on to Quintin. He had not hitherto been aware that Macmillan had also spoken directly to Quintin, but in the light of his own conversation with the Prime Minister this came as no surprise. He said he would discuss it all with Quintin when they next met. Later Toby Aldington was to confirm to me that Poole had also spoken to him at the same time about the June offer to Quintin.

Poole said he did not think Macmillan had yet made up his mind whether to go or stay, but probably would do so before Christmas. He agreed with my assessment, and in particular with the advice to Quintin about cultivating his Cabinet colleagues, but was not surprised that I had made so little headway over this either with Quintin or Mary. (I had told him in strict confidence about my visit to 'Putters'.)

I suggested to Poole that he might perhaps try to arrange some social encounters himself. John Hare in particular I knew was close to him, as indeed were several other members of the Cabinet. Poole said he was not very hopeful about this, on the grounds that trying to organise Quintin and Mary might prove too difficult. We agreed to keep in touch and to review the situation after the summer holidays.

During the summer speculation about the Prime Minister's intentions – would he go? would he stay? – continued unabated. He came badly out of a debate on the Profumo affair on 16 June, a former Tory Minister, Nigel Birch, calling on him to 'make way for a younger colleague', and quoting from Browning's 'The Lost Leader' to great effect. In the vote at the end of the debate there were twenty-seven Conservative abstentions. With this was now inevitably combined discussion of how a new leader of the party should be chosen. There was fairly general agreement, inside as well as outside Parliament, that it was no longer satisfactory to rely on the new leader simply 'emerging', as had happened in 1957, as a result of a process which essentially consisted of confidential discussions between a small number of elder statesmen. There was a strong feeling in the party that, while not necessarily wishing to imitate Labour where the leadership was then decided by a vote of MPs, the Parliamentary party should somehow be more actively brought into the process.

Hailsham went to Moscow on 14 July. 'He had', Macmillan was to write later, 'qualities of energy and imagination which might appeal to Khrushchev', and though Britain was inevitably a somewhat minor third party in the main negotiations between the two super-powers for a test ban treaty his contribution to the successful conclusion of the talks was by no means negligible. One observer described his interventions as 'distinctly refreshing compared with those seasoned negotiators, Harriman and Gromyko'.[1] However, when agreement was reached most of the credit accrued to the Prime Minister rather than to his emissary. 'A triumphant Macmillan comes to the House to announce the news from Moscow,' later wrote the *Times* political correspondent on 25 July, and a leading article commented that 'nobody could think of any statesman who had worked more laudably for a test ban agreement'.

Later that day Macmillan addressed a meeting of the Conservative 1922 Committee. This was a somewhat emotional occasion, in the

---

[1] Before leaving for Moscow Hailsham and his party were briefed by an MI5 official of the perils they would have to be on their guard against, particularly drink and sex. 'The most important thing about drink', said the official, 'is to be a good judge of your own capacity.' 'My dear chap,' said Hailsham, 'the difficulty is that the more I drink the less able I am to judge my capacity. But as for sex – since we'll probably only be away ten days I expect I'll manage.'

course of which he insisted that he cared nothing about himself, his only purpose being to serve the party and the nation and to make sure of victory at the next general election. On the question uppermost in everybody's minds, his own future, all he would say was that a decision would be made 'at the right time'. But when would that be? Rab Butler later wrote that when he came back from the Victoria Falls Conference on the future of the Central African Federation at the beginning of July he 'found it widely assumed among the back-benchers that in a matter of weeks or months Macmillan would have to make way for a new leader.'[1] Although the session seemed to be ending with a revival in Macmillan's fortunes this was against a background of an event which aroused much greater popular interest and which kept alive the seamier scandals which had so much damaged the government's reputation – the trial of Stephen Ward for living off the immoral earnings of Christine Keeler. Parliament rose on 2 August. Stephen Ward was found guilty on 31 July and committed suicide on 3 August.

There is some difficulty at this point in tracing the development of Macmillan's thought about his political future. According to his final volume of memoirs, *At the End of the Day*, it was after he and his wife had returned from a visit to Finland and Sweden that he was able, at home at Birch Grove, to find time to reflect on it. His diary for 16 August records his reflections:

The choice is between a) *resigning* in [the] week before Parliament meets – about 22 October or so; b) going on and fighting an election and saying so at the Conference. I don't particularly want a tiresome eight weeks from November to Christmas, with Party in House of Commons making trouble and then resigning at Christmas. Unless there is some great *international* prize the extra two months are not worth the trouble. So it is the choice between finishing my political life at the end of October, or going right through to and including the election.[2]

On the other hand he had earlier, on 10 April, taken the opportunity of the annual luncheon of the 1922 Committee at the Savoy 'to make it quite clear that I intended to lead the Party in the next election',[3]

[1] *The Art of the Possible*, p. 231.
[2] *At the End of the Day*. Macmillan, 1973, p. 491.
[3] Ibid, p. 405.

though this of course was before he risked, as he put it, being 'drowned by the flood of filth which had seeped up from the sewers of London'.

When I next met Quintin and Oliver Poole it was in September, separately but in the same week. Both told me that in their opinion Macmillan had decided to stay on as Prime Minister and fight the next election, although Oliver Poole added that it was not yet a final decision. That would be made at Christmas.

Surprisingly, Macmillan makes no mention in his memoirs of his June approach to Hailsham, nor of an even earlier approach to Rab Butler in January 1962: 'Either I shall decide to go before the election, in which case it [the leadership] all falls on you, or it will be a year or two after the Election, in which case it will not be so certain'.[1] What he does record is that on 5 September 'my mind is beginning to be clearer about my own position. I *must* stay to deal with Lord Denning's report [into the security aspects of the Profumo affair] on 1 October in Parliament – say early November. But I cannot go on to an early election and lead in it.' But the same day he wrote to the Queen that on the question of the leadership of the party and the life of the present Parliament he had not yet reached a decision.[2] On 11 September he saw Butler and 'was rather careful *not* to give him any idea about which of the several alternatives I would choose,' while a week later he reported Lord Home as being 'very distressed to think that I had any idea of retiring, but could well understand my reasons and thought them sound.' On 18 September he recorded in his diary: 'I still feel that my decision *not* to fight the next election is right.' Yet after 'a long discussion of the problem with my son, Maurice,' on 6 October, 'I am beginning to move (at the last minute) towards staying on – for another two or three years.'

When he came to write his memoirs Macmillan confessed 'on looking back at these two or three weeks of hesitation I am surprised and shocked by my vacillation,' and suggested that perhaps this 'curious lack of grip' was due to the onset of an ailment which was soon to lay him low. But in fact, as has been seen, the uncertainty regarding his intentions had been having an unsettling effect on his colleagues in the party for a matter of months, or even years, rather

[1] *Rab: The Life of R. A. Butler*, Anthony Howard. Cape, 1987, p. 290.
[2] *At the End of the Day*, pp. 492–3.

than weeks. So that when the blow fell party, Parliament and public were plunged into instant confusion.

On Tuesday 8 October Macmillan presided over a meeting of the Cabinet, at which he announced that he proposed to use the occasion of his winding-up speech at the Conservative Party Conference, due to begin in Blackpool the following day, to disclose his intentions. Convinced that he had the full support of the Cabinet to stay on and lead the party to the next election, he withdrew to allow a free discussion of his statement, and according to his account all Cabinet colleagues except one reacted to it favourably. But in the middle of the night Macmillan had found himself unable to pass water and had suffered 'excruciating pain' when he attempted to do so. His hopes that the doctors might be able to patch him up sufficiently to make the Blackpool speech possible proved illusory. Their unanimous verdict was that there must be an immediate operation to relieve the tumour (whether benign or malignant could not yet be known) which was responsible for the inflammation of his prostate gland, and that same evening he was taken to the King Edward VII Hospital for Officers. The news that the Prime Minister was in hospital and awaiting an operation was contained in a statement issued from 10 Downing Street shortly before 10 p.m.

For the next ten days 'the fight for the Tory leadership' was to be fought with great intensity in Blackpool and London. But before giving an account of the struggle there is one element in it which needs to be emphasised because at first sufficient weight was perhaps not attached to it, though it was to prove crucial to the outcome. This was Macmillan's determination that in no circumstances should Rab Butler be permitted to succeed him.

Why was this? It has been seen that nearly two years before Macmillan had spoken to Rab as his natural successor – from July 1962 he had in fact assumed the post, little known to constitutional lawyers, of Deputy Prime Minister and First Secretary of State, and had frequently taken charge in the Prime Minister's absence, as he had in the absence of Churchill and Eden. But Macmillan's attitude to this 'patient and unselfish political camel' (too many straws might break his back) was patronising, and in the opinion of Rab's biographer 'it is difficult to resist the conclusion that Macmillan, by the year 1962, had come to regard Rab as a trout he could tickle and play with at will.'[1] His theory was, ostensibly at any rate, that Butler would not be a good Prime Minister because he didn't really want the job. After his last interview with Butler before his illness Macmillan recorded in his diary: 'I saw Butler – who would clearly prefer me to go on, for – in his heart – he does not expect the succession *and* fears it.'[2]

But none of this really accounts for the degree of vindictiveness which Macmillan devoted to blocking the succession for a second time of the man he had defeated six years earlier, and who had since served him with exemplary loyalty and skill. When his turn came to write his memoirs (one volume against Macmillan's six) Butler reflected on his years as Under-Secretary at the Foreign Office in Neville Chamberlain's post: 'The fact that he [Macmillan] had spent much of his early life as a rebel while I was a member of the despised and declining "establishment" underlines a difference of temperament between us. It may also lie at the root of our future relationship.'[3]

It was more than temperament. Butler was sixteen when the 1914–18 war ended and had therefore not taken any part in it. Macmillan had served with distinction in the Grenadier Guards, being wounded three times, showing much gallantry, and the war and its slaughter of a whole generation had a profound effect on him, featuring prominently in nearly all his speeches. Part of this may have been theatre, but a great deal was obviously genuine. The comradeship in arms which the war continued to evoke for him could never be shared with Butler. The fact that Butler had not worn uniform in the 1939 war, whereas his principal rivals for the leadership – up to the emergence of Alec Home, that is – had all served honourably in the armed forces, may also have counted against him. Was there a trace of something approaching contempt on Macmillan's part for the only civilian among them?

Moreover, Butler was a Baldwin man, Macmillan a Churchill man. Butler's hero was Peel, Macmillan's Disraeli (and Disraeli had largely destroyed Peel). Butler was Cambridge and Impressionist paintings, Macmillan Oxford and Trollope. So the comparison between the two could continue. But was there perhaps an extra ingredient that added to the friction between these colleagues and rivals? On 27 May 1930 a

[1] *Rab*, p. 290.
[2] *At the End of the Day*, p. 499.
[3] *The Art of the Possible*, p. 144.

letter appeared in *The Times* from Harold Macmillan, who after five years as Member for Stockton-on-Tees had lost his seat at the 1929 general election. In it he referred to Sir Oswald Mosley's resignation from Ramsay MacDonald's Cabinet over the Labour government's failure to live up to its commitments on unemployment in the party's election manifesto. Macmillan supported the principle which prompted Mosley's resignation. Was it now to be accepted, he wrote, that political parties' programmes were never supposed to be carried out? 'I suspect that this is the real way the game ought to be played. Only, if these rules are to be permanently enforced, perhaps a good many of us will feel that it is hardly worth bothering to play.'

The next day a short answering letter appeared in *The Times*: 'Sir – We have read with interest and some surprise Mr Harold Macmillan's letter published in your issue of today. When a player starts complaining "It is hardly worth bothering to play" the game at all it is usually the player, and not the game, who is at fault. It is then usually advisable for the player to seek a new field for his recreation and a pastime more suited to his talents.' The letter was signed by four Conservative MPs, the last signatory being that of R. A. Butler, MP for Saffron Walden since the election in March 1929 which had left Macmillan out in the cold. If Macmillan assumed Butler to be the moving spirit behind this letter, as was almost certainly the case, it may have proved, as Butler's biographer wrote, 'one of those political "teases" that are never perhaps quite forgiven'.[1] Certainly Macmillan was quite prepared to show open ruthlessness towards his rival. There was, for example, the critical meeting of the 1922 Committee which they both addressed on 22 November 1956, the day on which 'the Conservative Party came as near to mutiny as it had done at any time during the whole Suez imbroglio'. 'From the perspective of his own ultimate Leadership prospects, this joint appearance turned out to be a highly expensive mistake. Rab spoke first – briefly, sombrely and somewhat flatly . . . Macmillan, by contrast, turned in a veritable political organ voluntary lasting thirty-five minutes – pulling out every stop and striking every majestic chord in his well-practised repertoire, including a *tremolo* on his own advancing years. According to Enoch Powell who, as a backbench Conservative MP, was present, "One of the most horrible

[1] *Rab*, p. 42.

things that I remember in politics was seeing the two of them at that 1922 Committee Meeting – seeing the way in which Harold Macmillan, with all the skill of the old actor-manager, succeeded in false-footing Rab. The sheer devilry of it verged upon the disgusting."[1] But Macmillan's success and Butler's second defeat were by no means assured.

Neither those who were satisfied with the old way of doing things nor those who wanted a change in the method of choosing a party leader can have contemplated the situation with which they were now confronted – the eclipse of the Prime Minister only a matter of hours before the annual party conference was to open. In describing the events of the next few days I quote as often as possible from diary notes made at the time.

On Tuesday morning, the day on which most of the party's top brass were to travel north in preparation for the conference, I received a telephone call from Mary Hailsham. She said she was having difficulty in finding someone to look after baby Catherine and so might not be able to accompany Quintin to Blackpool. She was therefore asking me to revert to my old role for a few days and generally look after him. But she said that if events seemed to make it necessary she would come to Blackpool, though in that case she might have to bring Catherine with her. I said that of course I would do what she asked, but urged her not to bring the baby to Blackpool. It would be distracting for Quintin and people would be liable, either deliberately or accidentally, to misinterpret her reasons for doing so.

The next day, Wednesday 9 October, was the first full day of the conference. The report of Macmillan's illness had reached the delegates late on the previous evening and they were now trying to digest it. There was little hard news but a great deal of gossip and speculation. I spent a lot of time with Quintin, who was due to speak that evening at a party rally in the Morecambe and Lonsdale constituency.

Others I spoke to at length included Peter Walker and Ian Gilmour. Peter Walker, MP for Worcester since 1961, had been a joint founder of Slater-Walker, the initially very successful investment bank, and the dynamic and highly accomplished Chairman of the Young Conservatives at the time when I was Quintin's personal assistant. We had seen

[1] *Rab*, p. 240.

a good deal of each other then and came to know each other well. Ian Gilmour had entered Parliament as Member for Central Norfolk at a by-election in November 1962. He had become proprietor of the *Spectator* in 1954 and from 1954 to 1959 was its editor. He had made an outstanding success of this, converting a rather old-fashioned and unadventurous magazine into perhaps the most exciting publication in the country. Young and little-known journalists like Bernard Levin, Henry Fairlie and Katharine Whitehorn became part of a team which, under Ian's direction, made the *Spectator* compulsory reading for everyone interested in politics and the arts. At Blackpool we were still only acquaintances, but were quickly to become and to remain the closest of friends.

In his speech at Morecambe, Quintin spoke with great affection of Macmillan: 'Some of us have been with Mr Macmillan since the beginning of his premiership in 1957. We love our political chief . . . we know that with your aid and modern medicine and surgery and with the help of Providence [what is wrong with him] can be cured. So now, Harold, get well quick.' But when the former Member for the constituency, the late Lord Fraser of Lonsdale, spoke of Quintin as 'one of three names on the short-list' to succeed Macmillan, he declined to speculate on his future.

His supporters were less inhibited. The following morning Peter Walker, Ian Gilmour and I were joined in our discussions by Tony Royle (now Lord Fanshaw of Richmond), who had been returned to Parliament as Member for Richmond at the 1959 general election after losing to the Liberal, Mark Bonham-Carter, at the Torrington by-election in March 1958 by only 219 votes – in this respect more fortunate than Peter Goldman. (It was after this victory that Bonham-Carter's mother, Lady Violet Bonham-Carter, declared that she 'had the strange feeling of being a member of an army of liberation entering occupied territory which for years had been ruled by quislings and collaborators'.) He had already proved himself an astute political tactician. The four of us decided to work closely together on behalf of Quintin and for the next momentous days we became in effect the inner group managing his bid for the leadership.

All of us knew Quintin well, though Ian and I were the closest to him personally, Ian having been in his chambers before leaving the Bar for journalism. Both of us had no doubt about our preference for Quintin as leader, who we also thought would be the most effective contestant in the forthcoming general election and therefore the most likely to win it. But we were quite clear that if this proved impossible Rab was our second choice. Peter Walker and Tony Royle, on the other hand, were fundamentally opposed to Rab.

Thursday October 10. Morning telephone call from Mary to say that she is coming to Blackpool after all and bringing baby Catherine with her. She asks me to speak to Felicity Yonge [for many years the Chairman's senior private secretary in Central Office] to see if she will baby-sit during the Conservative Political Centre meeting that evening, which Quintin is billed to address for the first time since the famous meeting at Brighton in 1957. If not, she hopes that the hotel will be able to find a reliable substitute. Felicity Yonge agrees to do so, and Quintin insists on going to Preston to meet Mary and the baby and drive them back to the hotel.

Soon after 5 o'clock Alec Home reads to the conference a message he has brought that day from Macmillan whom he saw in hospital. In this he informs the delegates that he has told the Queen that he cannot hope to 'fulfil the tasks of Prime Minister for any extended period' and further hopes 'that it will soon be possible for the customary processes of consultation to be carried on within the party about its future leadership.'

Meanwhile Quintin is back in the hotel from Preston with Mary and the baby. These go straight up to Room 194, Quintin staying behind briefly in the lobby where he talks to Humphry Berkeley [at that time Conservative MP for Lancaster] and Ian Gilmour. Then I go up with him to his room.

He says there are now three options open to him. He can disclaim his peerage immediately; or he can announce that he intends to remain in the House of Lords; or he can say nothing and wait to see how things develop. We agree that the third option, though superficially attractive, is ruled out for two reasons – first, all the media will be pressing him for a statement on his intentions, and he is not at his best when being evasive, and secondly, if he is to get the support of waverers he must establish overwhelming support in his own territory.

I then say that I take it he has put forward the second option for rhetorical reasons only, as I assume he has made up his mind that he will try to win the leadership. But I add that if he has changed his mind he should see Rab immediately, pledge his support to him and negotiate whatever position he aspires to in government.

Though I am certain Quintin has already decided what he is going to do he gives no direct answer but asks me how I would rate his chances. I say that, given he has not increased his support in Cabinet as much as I had hoped he would, I would estimate them at twenty-five to thirty per cent if he disclaims immediately, but virtually nil if he plays for time. He had to be a front runner because I couldn't see him being chosen as a compromise candidate. A note of farce creeps in as our conversation is repeatedly interrupted by baby Catherine crawling about on the floor and so we are driven to take refuge in the bathroom. Quintin sits on the loo and I sit on the edge of the bath.

Quintin asks me to speak to Oliver Poole and arrange a meeting in his room after he has changed. I call on Oliver Poole in Room 107. He thinks exactly as I do, and at 6.30 Quintin joins us. Oliver Poole is in favour of 'crossing the Rubicon at the first available opportunity', and suggests that the Conservative Political Centre meeting, which is bound to be an emotional occasion, would be the ideal setting. In fact Quintin has already decided to disclaim at the meeting, and we agree on the wording of the disclaimer to be made when he replies to the vote of thanks at the end of his speech.

At 7.15 Quintin telephones to Rab, who is perfectly friendly but advises Quintin to wait before taking any final step. There would, he said, be nothing to prevent him from doing so at the end of the Conference, should he so wish. Quintin is now considering how we should proceed.

At 7.30, as instructed by Quintin, I inform the Chairman of the CPC, Anthony Sumption, and Peter Goldman that Quintin intends to make an important statement in reply to the vote of thanks after his speech. I also agree with them that I'll be responsible for getting Quintin and Mary to the Baronial Hall in the Conference centre by 8.30.

At 7.45 Quintin retires to 'cogitate' in the bathroom. I talk to Mary, who is calm and sensible. Felicity Yonge is going to baby-sit. Just after 8 we drive to the Baronial Hall, Quintin in a very emotional state, talking about how precious his father's name has been, and still was, to him, and therefore now that he was about to relinquish it this really was for him a momentous step.

CPC meeting. The speech went well, but obviously the *pièce de résistance* was the disclaimer at the end of the vote of thanks. 'I felt,' Quintin told his audience, 'it would be contrary both to my duty as a colleague [of the Prime Minister] and my duty to the state to do any act which could be interpreted as an act calculated to undermine the authority of the Prime Minister of the day. But it must be obvious to you that that situation no longer exists. I shall continue to try to serve the country honourably but I wish to say tonight that it is my intention to disclaim my peerage.'

This was a highly charged and emotional moment. Quintin delivered his message to great effect and the applause and enthusiasm in the hall was indescribable – indeed, Ronald Butt of *The Times* later told me he thought it more like a Nuremberg rally. I watched the platform party closely to observe their reactions: Geoffrey Lloyd appeared livid; Keith Joseph embarrassed; Toby Aldington [as Toby Low until 1962 MP for Blackpool North], William Rees-Mogg and Peter Goldman all embarrassed; Peter Thorneycroft supportive; Martin Redmayne, Chief Whip, stony and prefectorial, clearly not best pleased; Michael Fraser rather embarrassed.

The meeting was followed by the CPC party, at which I had a long talk with Aldington. We agreed that it was going to be a very tough and not very agreeable week ahead. He was quite frank that he was firmly behind Rab. We discussed the whole matter amicably and agreed to remain in touch, should the occasion require it. Quintin then went on television, where he did well, and then to the Young Conservatives' Ball, where he was greeted with a storm of applause.

After the party, together with Ian and Peter Walker I start lobbying and speaking to the Press. William [Rees-Mogg] is strongly against what has been done, though he likes Quintin and would certainly see him as his second preference. He thinks Rab deserves to inherit, and should do so. This is also the opinion of Peter Goldman, Humphry Berkeley, Christopher Chataway, George Hutchinson and Ronald Butt. I also talk at some length to Clive Hewlett, Chairman of the North-Western Area and an old Cambridge acquaintance, who is solidly for Quintin. I also speak to Central Office people, Richard Webster and Gerald O'Brien.

Friday October 11. Early meeting with Ian and Peter Walker to discuss tactics. We divide responsibilities to some extent for the day – Ian and Peter to deal with MPs, and me to deal with the Area Chairmen and the party organisation. I still have good contacts with the Area officers, having got to know them well while I was working with Quintin in 1957–59. Several of them are still in their old positions, while in other cases their deputies, whom I'd also got to know, have taken over.

In the afternoon I see a number of Area Chairmen and officers. There appears to be overwhelming support among them for Quintin. Clive Hewlett is particularly helpful in arranging meetings for me and for the Area Chairmen to see Quintin if necessary. Various other meetings – two senior MPs, Douglas Glover, Gresham Cook. The three of us have a long talk with Julian Amery and Maurice Macmillan, both solidly for Quintin.

Later in the afternoon Randolph Churchill flies in from Washington. This fills Ian and me with some trepidation, because he's rather an unguided missile. We manage to get Ian to replace Gerald Nabarro on television, and that will make sure that Quintin's case is put as strongly as it can be. We are trying to get as many MPs as possible to commit themselves to Quintin while still at Blackpool, also Area Chairmen. I talk to Eric Chelmer, the Chairman of the National Executive, and other Area functionaries, Theo Constantine and John Howard.

We agree in a talk with Quintin that, though we should be doing everything to obtain as much support as possible as quickly as possible, he should not seek any further publicity. Unfortunately the presence of Catherine has, as I feared, been played up by the Press, and many interpretations put on it. Of course she came just because Mary couldn't arrange for someone suitable to look after her in Putney but they assume she's here to attract support for Quintin as a devoted family man.

Telegrams and letters are pouring in, and I'm dividing them into ones which are important because of the people who sent them, and those which are less important but help to indicate feeling in the constituencies. I have lunch with Quintin, and we discuss his views on government, and whether he should give any indications as a bait to colleagues about future Cabinet appointments. We agree that this would be a mistake, and could be used against him.

With Ian speak to Tony Lewis [*New York Times* correspondent] about a new rumour which is circulating about Alec Home being put forward as a possible compromise candidate. Both Ian and I take this very seriously, though Tony Royle and Peter Walker are inclined to dismiss it. Tony Lewis remarks that anybody who had seen a reluctant candidate in American elections would agree that Alec Home this morning appeared to fit the part to perfection.

Lord Home's own account of the probable origin of this rumour is that after he had read Macmillan's message to the conference he had 'walked back with Quintin who knew by then that he was Macmillan's selection, and I told him that the idea had my support. Had I known that he intended to throw his claim to the leadership into the ring within a matter of hours, I would have tried to dissuade him from it, for people never like being bounced.' It was after what he calls 'this débâcle' that 'a number of Conservatives came and told me I ought to consider coming forward . . . It was the last thing I had anticipated and the last thing I sought.' His visitors included John Hare, Selwyn Lloyd, Reggie Dilhorne and Bill Anstruther-Gray. 'They recognised that I had not looked for it and did not want the leadership, but the well-being of the Party must be put first.'

Much more significant than the soliciting of these distinguished politicians was the fact, of which we were then unaware, that Macmillan was probably in the process of switching his backing from

Hailsham to Home. That the leadership was really the last thing Lord Home had anticipated can hardly be taken literally, since Macmillan had sounded him out about it earlier in the year, as Macmillan had told Quintin in June, and the possibility that he might succeed had been canvassed in the Press. One backbencher, Dr Donald Johnson, Conservative Member for Carlisle, had in June expressed the wish in a speech that if, as he hoped, Macmillan retired in August, Home should become caretaker Prime Minister.

At this stage the talk about Home was still widely discounted. He had wound up the foreign affairs debate in the conference that Friday morning in what was acknowledged to be a very effective speech, but even before that Iain Macleod, now Chairman of the party and another possible contestant for the leadership, had heard of rumours that Home 'might be drafted'. 'Don't be so bloody ridiculous,' had been his reaction. 'Alec told us in Cabinet he wasn't a runner.'[1]

Quintin's response when Ian and I warned him of the rumoured Home emergence was very much the same. 'I simply don't believe it,' he said. 'Alec has told me that he is not a candidate, and we have agreed that we could not possibly both leave the House of Lords simultaneously.' Alec Home has given his own version of the episode in his autobiography. He explains that after Macmillan had left the Cabinet meeting of October 8, and it had become clear that it was most unlikely he would be able to go to Blackpool and that the leadership question would then come up, there was a short discussion in his absence. 'The Lord Chancellor (Viscount Dilhorne) said that, as he was not himself a candidate for the leadership, if anyone wished to have any private talk he would be available. I said the same applied to me. Enoch Powell later cited this indication as a kind of pledge which, when events turned out as they did, I should have had the whole Cabinet's leave formally to withdraw. It was, however, nothing so dramatic or pompous – merely a statement revealing that at that time the question of my succession to Macmillan had simply not crossed my mind.'[2]

Toby Aldington recalls that he spoke to Alec Home before he told the conference of Macmillan's decision to stand down and asked him

[1] *Iain Macleod*, Nigel Fisher, p. 237.
[2] *The Way the Wind Blows*, p. 180.

whether he was going to be a candidate for the leadership. Aldington said he wanted to know this because he had some private information from Central Office and government sources which he felt he could not pass on to anyone who was a candidate. Alec Home confirmed that he was definitely not in the running. Two days later Aldington and Home were at a lunch attended by other members of the Cabinet. Home said he wanted a private word with Aldington and suggested that they should walk back to the hotel together. Home said he owed Aldington a most profound apology for having misled him. 'I did tell you I was definitely not a candidate,' he said, 'but now I've been persuaded to let myself be considered. I'm consulting my doctor.' Aldington's comment is: 'Alec apologised in such an honest and charming manner it was impossible to hold it against him.' He adds he is convinced that Alec Home was telling the absolute truth on both occasions and that no improper use was made of the information thus obtained. Anyone who knows Alec Home would wholeheartedly endorse this.

A long leader published in *The Times* that Friday morning, assessing the qualifications of the possible successors to Macmillan, only said of Lord Home that since he had not declared his intentions it was fruitless to speculate on them. Turning to Quintin it concluded that, in spite of his great qualities, 'he has not the record to show that he would be a successful Prime Minister in what must be decisive years for the country's history.' Rather surprisingly the article came down in the end, if somewhat lukewarmly, in favour of a very long odds outsider: 'If Mr Heath is too young – after all, he is a mere year older than President Kennedy – then Mr Butler is the best choice. But that "if" needs to be questioned. Sooner or later the reins of Conservatism will have to be placed in the hands of a new generation. There is much to be said for it being done now.'

I have a word with John Morrison.[1] He is clearly for Home, as indeed is Nigel Birch,[2] whom I also speak to. Ian and I begin to suspect that there is behind the scenes a conspiracy to bring Home in, and we discuss whether Macmillan will remain staunch for Quintin in these circumstances – or, indeed, whether

[1] MP for Salisbury. Chairman of 1922 Committee. First Lord Margadale of Islay.
[2] MP for West Flint. Resigned as Economic Secretary to the Treasury in January 1958 together with the Chancellor of the Exchequer, Peter Thorneycroft, and the Financial Secretary to the Treasury, Enoch Powell.

he is part of the conspiracy, though this seems improbable as he has only just had his operation and Maurice Macmillan continues to be a hundred per cent for Quintin.

At the adopted candidates' party which I attend [having been adopted for Westbury a year before] Ted Heath comes up and remarks rather icily: 'I see the campaign managers are busy.'[1] I also notice that later he has a long talk with John Morrison, and they seem to be getting on famously. I wonder whether he is not party of the conspiracy. The rest of the candidates at the party are very strongly in favour of Quintin.

Saturday October 12. I have further long talks with William Rees-Mogg, Ronald Butt, George Hutchinson and other journalists, emphasising Quintin's honesty, integrity, intellectual capacity etc. and the fact that all the publicity, which has been enormous, was really forced on him. I explain that if he was going to compete – and it was perfectly reasonable that he should – then he had no alternative but to disclaim and to announce it immediately. The publicity simply followed. I also try to explain that baby Catherine's presence had nothing to do with publicity seeking.

With Ian and others discuss the possibility of Quintin's arriving at the Conference and getting on to the platform, and then, when the storm of applause develops, as it certainly would, getting Maurice Macmillan to ask the delegates for a vote as to whether Quintin is their choice for leader. Maurice Macmillan quite favours this idea. Ian and I are very doubtful and Oliver Poole strongly against any Conference demonstration. He points out that it would not decide the issue and would further alienate Quintin's Cabinet colleagues. Ian and I agree. Peter Walker would on the whole go for the demonstration.

In the afternoon Rab, standing in for Macmillan, addresses the Conference. Randolph Churchill, who had arrived from America with a mass of badges simply bearing the letter 'Q', proposed to disrupt the occasion by scattering these around. Ian and I strongly urge him not do to this as we think it would be wholly counter-productive, but he shouts at us that we are 'wet' and decides to go ahead. When the meeting starts we keep as far away from him as possible so that no one should think that those of us who are by now well known to be operating on Quintin's behalf should get involved. The same is true of Peter Walker and Tony Royle. Randolph's antic turns out to be a damp squib, though naturally the Press plays it up for all its worth.

Rab's speech is good, but not up to the challenge. [Reporting from

[1] Frederick Erroll (now Lord Erroll of Hale) was later to confirm that in his opinion at this juncture three of the most active supporters of Alec Home were Ted Heath, John Morrison and Selwyn Lloyd.

Blackpool the day before, the *Times* political correspondent had written: 'Mr Butler needs to make the speech of his life here tomorrow afternoon if he is to strengthen his hopes of winning the leadership of the Party.' It certainly was not that.] No doubt it was very difficult for him, but the response was friendly though totally lacking in enthusiasm. There is no doubt that Quintin has the heart of the Party.

Return to London by car. Anthony Sumption agrees that he should write a letter to *The Times*, as Chairman of the CPC at the Thursday meeting, explaining why Quintin had no alternative but to make a statement at the meeting.

Sunday October 13. Visit Quintin at Putney, and give him the letters I'd received and divided. We agree on the ones he should answer immediately – i.e. those from MPs, Area Chairmen, and party organisation notables. The others can be dealt with in due course. Lunch at Ferry House with Ian. Johnny Dalkeith[1] there too. He is willing to help in Scotland; is going there the next day and will try to arrange for Scottish MPs and the Scottish Party Area to come out in favour of Quintin.

In the afternoon we have a meeting at Tony Royle's – Peter Walker, Ian, Tony and myself. We draw up lists of MPs and start telephoning them and canvassing their support. Though there are some of these I know well, it is obviously for the others to do most of this. I will continue to concentrate on the party organisation. (This process continues through Monday, Tuesday and Wednesday, with frequent meetings at my home in Burnsall Street or at Tony Royle's or at White's with Ian and Peter Walker, to co-ordinate progress.)

Quintin is scheduled to speak at the Motor Show. Christopher Herzig, who is always very co-operative, shows me the speech he is to make and we discuss whether there should not be some new pieces included in it in view of the current situation. Should there also be an injection of '*gravitas*'? There was also a suggestion – I'm not sure who from – that Quintin should speak to Lord Salisbury.

Further meetings with John Howard, Theo Constantine, Richard Webster, to rally National Union support. Peter Walker would do something to counter Nick Scott, Chairman of the Young Conservatives, and solidly in favour of Rab.

Ian and I continue urging on Quintin the need to talk to Rab and find out what he is thinking about things. In particular, what he thinks of the growing suspicion that a Home bandwagon is being engineered behind the scenes.

[1] Ian's brother-in-law and now Duke of Buccleuch

Wednesday, October 16. Long talk with Daphne Poole, who is a hundred per cent solid for Quintin. But we are definitely facing a crisis over Home, and it's difficult to get accurate information. I telephone to Randolph – perhaps for the first time in exchange for the innumerable times he has telephoned to me. He is clearly of the opinion that Home is a very serious challenge and that Macmillan is coming out in his favour. I report this immediately to Quintin, who blames Selwyn Lloyd. Ian and Peter Walker come round to Burnsall Street. We make further attempts with Press contacts of Ian's to confirm Randolph's story, but not very successfully.

Thursday October 17. Speak to Quintin at the Ministry of Science. Oliver Poole suggests – more than suggests – that I must cancel my constituency visit on Friday, which I do. I have a long talk with Ian at White's in the morning, followed by a meeting with Ian, Peter Walker and Tony Royle, and then a long talk with Maurice Macmillan, which is very interesting. He is still solidly for Quintin. He speaks about Quintin's loyalty, and I think these are more or less his exact words: 'People fail to realise that when he has got angry it is because he has felt strongly about somebody else. It is his loyalty to my father which made him lose his temper over Jack Profumo on television.'[1] I urge him to speak to the Prime Minister, and he promises to do so. He asks me to ring back at Chelwood Gate at half-past three, but when I do so he has already left for Oxford. In view of our conversation I find this surprising. I wonder whether he did speak to the Prime Minister, and if he did whether the conversation is one he didn't think it possible to tell me about.

In the afternoon I have a message from Randolph to say that the Home succession is more or less arranged. I immediately telephone Ian and we agree that we must go and speak to Quintin. Telephone Quintin, who tells us to come and that he would expect us. I agree to meet Ian at the bottom of Putney Hill.

We arrive at Quintin's, who greets us with a cry of 'Taper and Tadpole! How nice to see you!' He quickly proceeds to say that the Home thing is simply not on. 'It must be stopped.' We have a brief talk, and then Quintin insists on telephoning to Home to find out whether the news is true or not.

[1] On 13 June, interviewed on the BBC programme 'Gallery', Quintin had gone over the top in his denunciation of the fallen Minister. 'It is intolerable for him in his position to have behaved in this way, and a tragedy that he should not have been found out, that he should have lied, and lied, and lied – lied to his friends, lied to his solicitor, lied to the House of Commons . . . A great party is not to be brought down because of a scandal by a woman of easy virtue and a proved liar.' Quintin's outburst was much criticised, though obviously what Profumo had done was damaging to Macmillan, not to him.

'Surely we are entitled to know,' he says. This is not easy for Home is at an official dinner, but Quintin insists that he must be brought out of it. From what can be heard it is clear that Home is confirming the truth of the story. 'This is disastrous,' says Quintin. 'The most awful thing I have ever heard.' And a lot more in that line.

'I hope you will have some time for me after what I've just said,' Quintin remarks before putting down the telephone. He tells us the story is true, that Alec Home thinks he will now succeed and that he has got the necessary support. We discuss this, but can't see it being possible, bearing in mind the number of people who are supporting Rab and the level of support which we know there is for Quintin in the House of Commons and at least among some members of the Cabinet.

Oliver Poole rings up and asks Quintin if he is on his own. Quintin replies, 'Dennis Walters and Ian Gilmour, who as you know are very staunch, are here,' and he tells him about his battle with Alec Home. Oliver Poole asks him to make us swear that we know nothing about this talk. 'It can only do you harm in the long run,' he says.

Julian Amery telephones to say he is on his way and wants to talk urgently. Quintin decides that he should get in touch with some of the Ministers who are backing Rab and try to find out how strong their opposition is. He first telephones to Enoch Powell. He starts the conversation: 'Aristides! Themistocles here!' Apparently Enoch is passionately against the Home candidacy and remains strongly for Rab.

Julian Amery arrives, obviously after a very good dinner, with a large cigar. Until a few days ago he had been a strong Quintin supporter. He nods at Ian and me, but after exchanging a few words says that he wants to talk to Quintin alone on privy councillor terms. A pantomime scene follows in which Ian and I are taken by Mary along a passage behind the kitchen where we can listen through a partition to the conversation taking place in the sitting-room. Julian Amery is trying to persuade Quintin to accept Alec Home as the successor. He thinks there is no alternative and that it would be good for Quintin and essential for him to remain in the Cabinet.

I then telephone Michael Fraser and Toby Aldington. Soon afterwards Peter Thorneycroft, who has been consistently steadfast throughout and very sensible in his advice, also arrives. Again we go through the farce of the corridor. Peter Thorneycroft argues very logically and honestly about the situation. He tells Quintin that he does not think he can now get the leadership, and that, although it may still be possible for Rab to block the Home succession, he doubts it. Quintin's position is therefore very important. 'We need you in the Cabinet and it would be a mistake on your part to join with Rab in a blocking move. I don't believe that

Rab could now lead a united party, and I believe that he is aware of this himself.'

John Junor [*Sunday Express*] telephones to say that Rab is willing to talk to Quintin. I ring the St Ermin's Hotel and get Mollie [Butler] on the telephone. I immediately pass her over to Quintin, who speaks to her briefly and then to Rab. Apparently his opening remark was 'I was just dozing off.' This brought forth a barrage from Quintin: 'This is no time to sleep! Don your armour, dear Rab! You must fight, dear Rab! There is still time.' Apparently this brought the response, 'I take note of your remarks, but now I really must doze off.'

There followed telephone conversations with Toby Aldington, Michael Fraser and others. Toby is at Enoch Powell's house. Also there Reggie Maudling, Iain Macleod and Freddie Erroll, all a hundred per cent opposed to the Home solution and still strongly in favour of Rab – as is Edward Boyle. It is possible that Reggie Maudling and Iain Macleod still look on themselves as better compromise candidates than Home. I explain again to Toby that Quintin would prefer Rab to Home but that Rab really must ring Quintin and speak to him. After all, Quintin has made various attempts to speak to Rab, not very satisfactorily, and the last conversation with him at St Ermin's had been pretty negative. Toby says that he will see that Rab rings in the morning, and impress on him that he must respond favourably.

Thursday 17 October was what Macmillan in his memoirs was to describe as 'the decisive day'. In the morning, pursuing what he regarded as 'the customary processes of consultation', he had seen at his hospital bedside the Lord Chancellor, who was to report on opinion in the Cabinet; the Chief Whip and John Morrison to report on opinion in the House; the Chief Whip in the Lords; Oliver Poole and other party officials. As a result he dictated a memorandum to the Queen in which he said: 'The remarkable and to me unexpected result of all these four groups of people asked to give their views was (contrary to what I expected) a *preponderant first* choice for Lord Home ... in Cabinet, ten for Home; three for Butler; four for Maudling; two for Hailsham. Among three hundred MPs consulted, the largest group (not by much, but significant) was *pro*-Home. But, again, no one against. In the Lords, two to one for Home. The constituencies were about sixty per cent for Hailsham; forty per cent for Butler, with *strong* opposition feelings to both. Mrs S[hepherd] and Lord C[helmer] were certain that everyone would rally round Home.'

During the night I have a number of conversations with Toby Aldington in regard to Michael Adeane [the Queen's Private Secretary] at the Palace. There was a suggestion that there should be a conference of the four other contestants – Rab, Quintin, Reggie Maudling, Iain Macleod – and that the Queen should be informed of its outcome before she proceeds to invite Alec Home to the Palace.

Randolph Churchill in his lively paperback *The Fight for the Tory Leadership* described the activities on Thursday night and Friday morning of what he called 'the five Caballeros' who still wanted to stop the Home succession – Powell, Macleod, Maudling, Aldington and Frederick Erroll, President of the Board of Trade (p. 136): 'It is strange that they should have sought so late in the day – too late for effective action – to arrest the inevitable march of events; unwittingly they had been overtaken by them. Be that as it may, they persuaded the Chief Whip, Redmayne, to join them so that their collective view might be passed on to the Prime Minister before it was too late. It was too late – much too late, even though it is believed that one Caballero in desperation telephoned to the Queen's Private Secretary, Sir Michael Adeane.'

Rab in his memoirs says of the Thursday evening meeting in Enoch Powell's house: 'This was a meeting of revolt against the choice of Home . . . One presumes and hopes that the Chief Whip informed the Prime Minister, as he was requested to do, that seven or eight members of the Cabinet were opposed to the choice of Home. What is certain is that Macmillan decided to ignore this powerful objection.'[1]

Frederick Erroll recalls a meeting he had had with the Chief Whip the day before (Wednesday) at which he had expressed his view on the succession. It would, he thought, be better if a generation was skipped and the leadership went to Reggie Maudling. Martin Redmayne had told him it was too late: 'It's all arranged – it's going to Alec Home.' Erroll immediately went to see Maudling and Iain Macleod, who had still heard nothing officially about this, and then the three of them went round to Rab, to tell him that he could count on their support if he chose to fight. 'Alec can't possibly form a government without you,' they said. But Rab refused to commit himself.

[1] *The Art of the Possible*, p. 247.

Friday October 18. In the morning I telephone to Michael Adeane and tell him that it would be unwise for the Queen to call Home without knowing how the other four stand. This is what we are now seeking to arrange. Quintin is calling at Oliver Poole's at 10.15 and suggests that I should meet him there. I ring Oliver Poole and we talk, and he seems a little uncertain about the next step. But I express the view most urgently that if anything is to be done it should be done immediately, before Home goes to the Palace. He too asks me to come round at 10.15.

Telephone Ian, who comes to Burnsall Street and gives me a lift to Oliver Poole's flat in Eaton Square, and on the way we discuss the situation. We agree that the idea of the Queen holding a conference with the four is absurd, and that any blocking operation must be carried out immediately.

Meeting at Oliver Poole's. Quintin limping about on a stick, his foot hurting him. We agree that Rab must be spoken to at once, and that he should contact Reggie Maudling for a meeting of the four. Oliver Poole leaves to telephone Rab, and fixes an appointment with him at St Ermin's Hotel. Quintin and I go to the Ministry of Science, where Oliver Poole will telephone when he's made the necessary arrangements with Rab.

One of his political colleagues comes in, well-meaning, but unhelpful. Talking of Edward Boyle Quintin remarks, 'I'm always a bit suspicious of fat men who are not interested in women.' He looks at my face, which must have fallen slightly, and adds hastily to the visitor, 'I hope you don't think that was a personal remark aimed at you?' Not the most tactful of apologies.

I ring Ian and ask him to come round as soon as possible. Ian arrives and we wait in Quintin's office. We agree that we should try to telephone to Maurice Macmillan. In fact Maurice Macmillan telephones Quintin. I'm not clear about exactly what was said, but I think Maurice Macmillan has said something like: 'We need you. You are the only man in the party who can go round the country and make speeches that will create excitement and influence people. You have the vision to look ahead. You will be Prime Minister one day.' But what he is saying in effect is that, though still a supporter of Quintin, he thinks that it is better for him to serve in a Home government. The bit about being Prime Minister one day cannot be taken too seriously.

Oliver Poole telephones and Quintin then makes off to the Home Office to see Rab. Ian and I hang about waiting to hear the outcome, but Quintin does not report because he has to go straight off to a lunch date. Apparently Rab had refused to do anything decisive, and Reggie Maudling, who was also at the meeting, remained uncertain.

It would seem that Home has gone off to the Palace. I go with Ian to White's for lunch and we talk, among others, to Peter Rawlinson[1] and David Price[2] who are as confused as anyone else. Telephone Oliver Poole, who is out but due back at three. With Ian to the Ministry of Science. Quintin talks of the formula which has apparently been arranged. It would seem that though Home has gone to the Palace he is not Prime Minister yet. He has had his interview and reserved his position, depending on whether he can get enough support. Home has told Quintin that, should he become Prime Minister, he doesn't intend to press him to stay in the Lords.

Peter Thorneycroft comes round. Ian has to leave for Norfolk, but we agree that I should telephone him at 7.15. Mary Hailsham arrives, plus Catherine. Then Oliver telephones and asks me to go round to Central Office. Toby Aldington also present for most of our talk. Toby thinks it is not yet over and that Rab still has some fight left in him. Oliver conveys to me by a glance that he doesn't believe this to be true.

We discuss Quintin's disclaimer, and I am very firm that he should stick to this, to which they both agree. We then talk about constituencies for him. Oliver mentions Worthing and St Marylebone. He thinks that Morecambe and Lonsdale is too far away, inconvenient for Quintin. Toby Aldington leaves, and I have a quick private talk with Oliver. He is convinced that Home will now get it and that from Quintin's point of view better to row in. He is shocked by Rab's weakness.

Return to the Ministry of Science and have a long talk with Mary. She is very good, and absolutely firm that Quintin should continue with his decision to disclaim. She then goes home, and I keep Quintin company. We agree that I should go round late in the evening and meanwhile try to find out what is happening in the Alec Home camp. Before doing so I speak to Michael Fraser who is still of the opinion that all is not lost, and also call on Peter Goldman. I then ring Peter Walker, who is at Granada television. He clearly considers it is all over; much prefers Alec Home to Rab and thinks Quintin's telephone conversation with Alec Home a great pity. He suggests that Quintin should move in with Alec as quickly as possible. Obviously Peter has left the Quintin camp and is now, together with Selwyn Lloyd, who always has been, firmly with Home.

I take Peter Goldman home and ring Peter Thorneycroft, who asks me to call on him at once at the Ministry of Defence. He is impressively objective regarding Quintin. He thinks that Alec Home will definitely get the premiership, that Rab will eventually join the government, and that it would therefore be foolish for Quintin to stay out on a limb. In the unlikely event of

[1] MP for Epsom. Solicitor General.
[2] MP for Eastleigh. Parliamentary Under-Secretary, Board of Trade.

Rab's getting it, he thinks Quintin's position would be very similar. We both agree that there is no longer any chance of Quintin's getting it himself.

Telephone Ian in Norfolk. I go to Putney at 8.45 p.m. Henry Brooke has just rung to say he has supported Alec Home all along (I find this most surprising) and urging Quintin to do so now and do so quickly. Quintin has just been summoned to Number Ten where Alec Home is seeing people. He insists on going alone in his car. He asks me to look after Mary, and says he will come back immediately after the meeting and will bring Oliver Poole and Peter Thorneycroft with him. He thinks Julian Amery will want to come too.

I am offered food – eggs and bacon – very welcome by this time of night. I talk to the doctor, who is a little concerned about Quintin. He must, he says, look after his foot and take the medicines prescribed, but apparently is doing neither. A very nice man. I watch television with Mary and the girls – Nigel Birch, Humphry Berkeley, Henry Fairlie, Peregrine Worsthorne, Humphry Berkeley good; Henry Fairlie outraged by everything that appears to be happening.

I telephone Number Ten and speak to Christopher Herzig. The meeting is almost over, and Quintin has decided to go to Peter Thorneycroft's flat instead of coming home. Mary rings Peter Thorneycroft's and speaks to Carla, arranging that she and I should go round there instead. I drive her to Eaton Square. She talks about the Macleods.

Carla lets us in. Oliver Poole, Peter Thorneycroft, Quintin in a corner looking rather ill, Julian Amery, Carla, Mary, and myself. Quintin starts off: 'I'd better repeat the story to you. The essence is that I will serve under Alec – he is now Prime Minister – if Rab and Reggie Maudling do. I shall continue as Minister of Science, with the Arts thrown in. Also there is a Cabinet reform job which Alec would like me to do – getting the Plowden Report on higher education through. I'm not seeking a great position and am contented that it is not on offer. It would look as if I had been bought.'

Mary clearly not too satisfied about the job. Neither am I, who have a strong feeling that the situation is highly unsatisfactory for him as well as generally – bad for the party and for the future. However, there is strong approval from the others. General condemnation of Rab. Oliver Poole thinks that when it came down to it Rab didn't really want the job because he felt he couldn't do it. I wonder. Oliver also expresses the view that if Alec Home could not form a government the party would split: 'You are the only one that matters,' he tells Quintin. 'He can form a government without the others, but not without you.' Oliver and Peter Thorneycroft are clearly very anxious to commit Quintin fully to the new government.

Quintin notices that I'm not joining in the general chorus of pleasure and asks me what I think. I tell him I'd like to think about it, but that there are two points that strike me immediately. First, that he should stick by his disclaimer, and that if he has agreed to serve if Rab and Reggie Maudling also agree there is nothing much more to be said about it. But to hell with the theory of being bought. After all he has done and been through he must get an important and satisfying job. Everybody knows he is not the kind of person who could be bought.

We break up. Toby Aldington and Michael Fraser telephone, full of fight, but too late I think, and their general doesn't seem to be fighting at all. Michael Fraser especially thinks the Alec Home solution crippling in the long run for the party. I pass on, without saying who made it, Oliver's comment that if Alec Home came back and said that he could not form a government it would be disastrous for the party now, which could even split. Michael replies: 'I don't think it would split. Anyway, better a near disaster now than a catastrophe later.'

Telephone Ian later that evening to bring him up to date on developments. We both agree that the situation could not be gloomier.

Saturday October 19. Toby Aldington and Michael Fraser ring. They report that Macleod, Powell and Boyle will not serve, but that Rab is still wavering. Reggie Maudling also is still wavering, but is under strong pressure from Macleod to stay out. Oliver rings me. He is clearly very anxious that in the present crisis, with so many still either out or undecided, Quintin should not change his mind. I tell him the information I've just had. Rab will go in, he says, and in any event a Rab solution would now be worse than an Alec Home one: I've got a great affection for Rab, Dennis, as you know. He was very good to me as a young man, etcetera, etcetera. But I tell you, Dennis, if you had seen him yesterday morning, dithering about in a gutless sort of way, you would not want him to be Prime Minister of this country. I was quite appalled; quite disgusted.'

Ian arrives. We ring Quintin to tell him what we have heard. Damn Powell, Boyle, Macleod etc. It's all too late. 'Tell Edward Boyle to ring me if you can get hold of him,' says Quintin. 'It's too late now. Rab is joining. It's better for the party to serve under Alec Home, although he's not the right man for the job.' He concludes by saying, 'Thank you both. I don't know what I would have done without you. In fact, I couldn't have gone through it without you.' He is very emotional and his voice seems to be breaking.

That Saturday the Court Circular reported: 'The Queen this morning received in audience the Earl of Home who kissed hands upon his appointment as Prime Minister and First Lord of the Treasury.' Rab Butler had been effectively blocked, and the candidate to whom

Macmillan had belatedly transferred his blessing had duly come out on top. From the hospital bed where he had over the past week shown such mastery of events Macmillan contemplated the unsuccessful efforts of others to thwart his design. In his diary for the day before, Friday 18 October, the last day of his seven-year premiership, Macmillan wrote: 'It seems that the news that the general choice favoured Home got out last night (leaked by someone). Meetings were organised . . . the idea was an organised revolt of all the *unsuccessful* candidates – Butler, Hailsham, Maudling and Macleod – against Home. Considering this intense rivalry with each other during recent weeks, there was something rather eighteenth-century about this . . . and somewhat distasteful.'

What is unquestionable is that the way Macmillan, either by design or because his judgement was impaired by illness, handled events between May and October 1963 was not merely somewhat but highly distasteful. Maudling's version of the 'famous Thursday evening meeting in Enoch Powell's house' should be recorded: 'Rab did not come, though we were in touch with him by phone. The Chief Whip came round and joined us. We made it clear that in our view the choice was a mistake from the party point of view. I know that Harold Macmillan has said that in his view there was something rather unseemly about our behaviour, but for once I cannot agree with him. We all had a strong and genuine feeling: we all thought a mistake was being made. It was not only our right but our duty to say this in the most effective way we could.'[1]

Given Macmillan's eventual determination that Alec Home was to succeed him, could there have been any other outcome to the contest? This is a question to which there can be no certain answer. Much depends on establishing the point at which Macmillan switched his support from Hailsham to Home, and that is something which on the published evidence cannot be done. In his memoirs Macmillan himself is far from specific. He records that on the Wednesday 9 October, the day before his operation, he 'got a lot of work done' in hospital. This included 'some general plans about the date of my retirement and successor taking over. If Hailsham is to be a competitor, he must at once give up his peerage and find a constituency.' 'If he is to be a

---

[1] *Memoirs*, Reginald Maudling. London 1978, p. 129.

competitor' is hardly the endorsement that might have been expected from one who had told Hailsham in June that in the event of his deciding to retire before the next general election he would like Hailsham to be his successor, and who, a few days before, when his resolve was not to resign until early in 1964, had favoured Hailsham or Macleod, 'preferably the former', as his successor, both of them being, in his view, 'the men of real genius in the Party, who were the true inheritors of the Disraelian tradition of Tory Radicalism.'[1] On the other hand, at this stage Hailsham was widely regarded as 'the Macmillan family candidate', and Maurice Macmillan, who was probably as close to his father's councils as anyone, remained a staunch supporter of Hailsham, at any rate until the morning of Thursday 17 October. Perhaps it was after speaking to his father later that day that Maurice Macmillan realised that Alec Home, not Hailsham, was to be regarded as the heir apparent. This would perhaps account for his failure to answer my telephone call, as arranged.

Macmillan being a man of many devices, another explanation suggests itself. Why urge Hailsham to hurry up about disclaiming his peerage and not give the same advice to Home? Was he at that stage not considering Home as a competitor? That seems improbable. Perhaps the explanation he would have offered is to be found in the episode described by Lord Home's biographer:

Next day, Wednesday, 9 October, Home was summoned in the afternoon to the King Edward VII Hospital for Officers in London where Macmillan was being prepared for his operation. The Prime Minister, speaking under considerable strain, confirmed that he intended to resign. He talked of possible successors and to Home's astonishment indicated that he regarded Home as a real possibility.

This, Home recalled, was 'the first time I heard any suggestion that I might succeed Harold. I told Macmillan that it was impossible. I was a peer and it was useless to think about it. I simply dismissed the idea and left it like that so that it played no part in my thinking.'[2]

But did Macmillan take that rejection as final? This was not, in fact, the first time Macmillan had broached the possibility of Home's

[1] *At the End of the Day*, p. 496.
[2] *Sir Alec Douglas-Home*, Kenneth Young, Dent, 1970, p. 164.

succeeding him. Though neither of them mentions this, it had come up some time earlier in the year (as Macmillan had reported to Hailsham in June), when Home's response had been 'far from enthusiastic'. But not so unenthusiastic as to prevent Macmillan from putting the idea forward a second time. And if twice, why not a third time – as was in fact to happen?

Is it conceivable that Macmillan, having already shifted his choice, though without telling anyone, to Home, foresaw the criticism Hailsham would incur of being over-eager to get into the fray by his disclaimer at the CPC meeting on the Thursday evening? It was only that morning that Macmillan had been successfully operated on, and to some observers there must have been a sharp contrast between Alec Home, the statesman arriving at the conference with an inspiring message from the stricken leader, and the effervescent contender trying on the crown amid scenes 'reminiscent of a Nuremberg rally'. 'His evident eagerness for the Premiership nauseated many who would at least have tolerated him before.'[1]

As recorded in my diary notes, Oliver Poole and I had that same day been urging Hailsham that he should disclaim his peerage, and that this must be done quickly. Ian Gilmour, Peter Walker, Tony Royle and, perhaps most important of all, Mary, his wife, were of the same view. Even then, I rated his chances at only twenty-five to thirty per cent, as against nil if he did not disclaim. There was nothing dishonourable, let alone distasteful, in wanting to be leader of the party, and the sooner the succession was settled the better. Owing to Macmillan's vacillation the party had been plunged into the same state of damaging uncertainty that had plagued it between 1952 and 1954 through Churchill's failure to make up his mind when to retire.

With hindsight it is easy to say that Hailsham may have been unduly encouraged by the enthusiasm of his constituency supporters. It was, after all, not the constituencies which decided who was to lead the party. More cultivation of MPs, and above all of his Cabinet colleagues, would have greatly improved his chances. But this sort of canvassing was not in his nature – 'Rather than fool it so, let the high office and the honour go to one that would do thus.' There was a lot of the ancient Roman in him.

[1] Ibid., p. 164.

But what about the other candidates? Reggie Maudling had been strongly tipped to succeed in the summer when pressure on Macmillan to quit was at its height. John Morrison, according to Rab (A. Howard, p. 302), reported just before Parliament rose for the summer recess 'the strong inclination of the younger back-benchers to get someone of their own age group' – i.e. Maudling. On 19 June the political correspondent of the *Financial Times* (reported in Randolph Churchill's book) wrote: 'Increasingly, as one canvasses backbench opinion, it seems plain that if a straight vote were taken at this moment Mr Reginald Maudling would succeed Mr Macmillan.' But by September 'the Maudling bubble' had burst, though he and Macleod remained very much on stage at Blackpool, ready to step forward should there be any need to look afresh for a compromise candidate.

Rab Butler was an altogether different proposition. There can be no doubt that in 1963, as in 1957, he hoped to become Prime Minister and was bitterly disappointed when he failed. Macmillan's diary suggestion on the eve of the Blackpool Conference that Rab 'would clearly prefer me to go on, for – in his heart – he does not expect the succession *and* fears it' looks like a piece of self-justification for the shabby way he had treated his rival and the still shabbier treatment he was even then contemplating. He probably knew little of what went on in Rab's heart. It is true that Rab would have preferred Macmillan to continue as Prime Minister even after he had been put out of action, but this was because 'it would have been better for him and for everyone else if the decision had been taken at a less preposterous time.'[1]

It is also true that Rab could have blocked Alec Home's succession. If he had declined to serve under him Hailsham and Maudling would have stood out too, and Alec Home would have had to give up his attempt to form a government. But it might by then almost certainly have been too late for Rab to be the alternative choice. Could he have been that earlier? Again, almost certainly – but only if he had shown himself a more determined, even ruthless, fighter than he was by nature. 'It wasn't according to my nature,' he told Kenneth Harris in an interview later, 'to force myself if I was not chosen by a majority.'

[1] *The Art of the Possible*, p. 242.

'Force' and 'majority' are words that can be interpreted in many ways. Doing a bit more telephoning instead of 'dozing off' would hardly constitute *force majeure*. Rab explained his willingness to serve under Home: 'In my talk with Alec I had put the need for unity first and it seemed to me that the most unselfish way of achieving unity was to serve with a friend rather than force the issue the other way.' 'Force' again – and unselfishness is not a quality that wins battles. Describing the scene at St Ermin's Hotel in the small hours of 18 October his widow sums it up in a note of exasperated admiration: 'I felt he was putting loyalty to his party above loyalty to his country, but I was wrong. I think to him the two were synonymous'[1].

What about 'majority'? There were twenty members of the Cabinet – Macmillan, Butler, Home, Hailsham, Maudling, Brooke, Sandys, Macleod, Thorneycroft, Hare, Heath, Soames, Erroll, Boyd-Carpenter, Noble, Powell, Boyle, Joseph, Deedes, Dilhorne. Macmillan (or Dilhorne) assessed their preferences (presumably omitting himself) as Home ten; Butler three; Maudling four; Hailsham two.

Macmillan says he ordered the sounding to be made 'on Monday night' (14th) and results to reach him on Thursday (17th). So these figures represent opinion on 15/16th. Macmillan meanwhile had seen Butler, Home, Macleod, Heath, Maudling, Hailsham, Thorneycroft, Boyle, Soames, Selwyn Lloyd (but not in the Cabinet any longer), Hare, Brooke, Joseph, Sandys – i.e. all except Powell, Erroll, Boyd-Carpenter, Noble, Deedes. 'The general impression that I received was that, though there was a good deal of division of opinion about who would succeed me, practically all of these Ministers, whether Hoggites or Butlerites or Maudlingites, agreed that if Lord Home would undertake the task of P.M. the whole Cabinet and the whole Party would cheerfully unite under him.' (Macmillan, diary for 16 October.) So his general impression happily anticipated the more precise calculations of Dilhorne.

The Annual Register for 1963, a typical example of 'received opinion', says that 'a majority in the Cabinet vetoed Butler'. From the views I heard, either expressed to me or reported at the time by others in a position to know, I believe this statement to be false, as also do Toby Aldington, Frederick Erroll and Enoch Powell.

[1] *August and Rab* by Mollie Butler, Weidenfeld and Nicolson, 1987, p. 82.

As a footnote to the affair two quotations are of interest. The first is from the Macmillan memoirs, *At the End of the Day*, p. 494:

When the Foreign Secretary came to see me [18 September 1963] I had a talk with him about my own position. Lord Home was very distressed to think that I had any idea of retiring, but could well understand my reasons and thought them sound . . . He fears that there will be complete disunity in the Party and that great troubles will follow. I may be forced to stay. I replied 'In that case I shall be "drafted" – not a "limpet". I don't want it to be thought that I am just clinging on.'

The second comes from the biography, *Sir Alec Douglas-Home*, written by Kenneth Young with the collaboration of the subject, p. 59 (the passages in inverted commas are direct quotations from tape-recordings):

One September evening Home, invited to dinner at Chequers, broached the subject – 'reluctantly' because he greatly enjoyed working with Macmillan. Nevertheless he was quite firm. The party had had 'terrible luck' with the Profumo affair, and he had come to the conclusion that Macmillan 'had lost too much ground to recover his winning form.' This opinion was shared by other colleagues, was gaining currency in the Party, and Macmillan should know about it.

'There was most emphatically no plot to oust him,' he emphasised. Nor was he bringing 'pressure' to bear. To stay or go was entirely a matter for Macmillan to decide: 'I didn't seek to influence him at all, and said that whatever his decision it would be supported.'

But the bowed dispirited Macmillan of June and July had vanished completely . . . 'After that evening at Chequers, I knew he had decided to go on, providing his health allowed.'

Can they be reporting the same occasion?

The surprise emergence of Alec Home had far-reaching consequences for the Conservative Party and for the future of British politics. Inevitably the conclusions which follow cannot be proved. I myself believe them to be well-founded, but *ex-post-facto* theorisings can be a rich breeding ground for controversy. They are certainly not intended as an attack on Alec Home. Having been returned as Member for Westbury in the 1964 general election, I was elected not long after joint secretary of the backbench Foreign Affairs Committee. Alec Home, after losing the leadership of the party to Ted Heath in 1965, soon became, as Shadow Foreign Secretary, its chairman, and for the next four years in opposition I worked under him and closely with him. I could not imagine a more considerate, fair and civilised person to serve. My respect for him grew with the passage of time, and history will, I believe, confirm the reputation he holds of having been a wise and distinguished Foreign Secretary.

That said, I remain firmly of the opinion that he should not have become Prime Minister and Leader of the party in 1963. I believe that his selection was the result of a complex intrigue, master-minded by Harold Macmillan with the connivance of a number of players of varying importance, all of them impelled by different and often conflicting motives.

Arguably, any of the other potential successors to Harold Macmillan – Rab Butler, Quintin Hailsham, Reggie Maudling, Ted Heath or Iain Macleod – would have won the 1964 election. Alec Home rightly commanded respect and affection within the Conservative Party, but, even discounting the play the popular Press made with his 'matchstick economics and grouse-moor' image, he was no competitor for the then convincingly dynamic Harold Wilson in trying to hold the middle ground in politics. Yet to do so was essential for a Conservative government aiming at a political miracle. It failed, and hence the narrow defeat of October 1964. The prizes of victory at that juncture were immense. A fourth general election defeat in a row would almost certainly have precipitated a split in the Labour Party, which in the event did not take place until 1982 with the breakaway of the Social Democrats. A split in 1964 would have been more decisive, and so brought in its wake a genuine and fundamental political realignment.

The artificially contrived selection of Alec Home for the leadership also had a significant effect on the future of the Conservative Party. One-nation Toryism never recovered from it, although admittedly in 1973, towards the end of the Heath government, there were signs that its revival was round the corner. This opportunity, however, was finally killed off by the badly judged general election of February 1974, followed by the second election defeat in October of the same year, combined with the violent industrial confrontation of that period.

The Conservative Party, goaded and frustrated by irresponsible trade union blackmail and bullying, veered firmly to the right. As Keith Joseph was not willing to challenge for the leadership, Margaret Thatcher, who suffered from fewer inhibitions, did so, thus inheriting the mantle and the crown. A new Conservative Party emerged – a courageous but more doctrinaire party, possessing many positive features which were needed to meet the requirements of the eighties, but remote from the historic vision and grandeur of Winston Churchill and the compassionate wisdom and understanding of Rab Butler, Quintin Hailsham and Iain Macleod.

Another and unarguable result of the fight for the Tory leadership was that Quintin Hailsham would never be Prime Minister. My own feelings about this are perfectly summed up by one sentence in a thank-you note sent to my wife Bridgett and me by Harold Acton in 1983, after he had dined with us in Tuscany at a time when Quintin had also been a guest: 'What a Prime Minister we have missed!' he wrote.

PART III

Politics and the Middle East

B Y 1966, after eighteen months in Parliament, my prospects
looked reasonably promising. I was joint secretary of the
backbench Foreign Affairs Committee, a post which allowed
one greater scope than when one's own party was in government.
Moreover, before the setting up of select committees these were the
only forums where MPs could debate and influence policy in different
and specialist fields.

The same year saw me selected as one of the two Conservative
representatives of an all-party delegation to the General Assembly of
the United Nations led by Maurice Edelman. The other Tory member
was Robin Balniel, subsequently Minister of State for Defence and
Foreign Affairs and now Earl of Crawford. This kept us in New York
for about a month.

Not long afterwards, early in 1967, the *Sunday Times* conducted a
'spot the future Prime Minister' quiz. It picked out twenty 'promising'
young politicians, ten Conservative and ten Labour, and asked
Ladbrokes to quote the odds against their reaching Number Ten
Downing Street. At 200 to 1 against, my odds did not compare favourably with those of Peter Walker, 10 to 1, or Jim Prior, 33 to 1, but
I did considerably better than Margaret Thatcher, 1000 to 1 against.

At 5 to 1 Dick Marsh headed the Labour field, closely followed by
Peter Shore, Bill Rodgers and Dick Taverne, all 10 to 1, Roy Hattersley
scoring 100 to 1 and Shirley Williams trailing at 500 to 1. Of these
Labour entrants only Peter Shore and Roy Hattersley still belong to the
Labour Party. Two of the others were among the original SDP Gang of
Four, while Dick Taverne and Dick Marsh quitted the party even
earlier.

I was not foolish enough to take any of this seriously, for becoming Prime Minister had never been among the objectives I had at any stage of my life considered remotely attainable or even desirable. Reaching the Cabinet, on the other hand, did not seem beyond the bounds of possibility and achieving ministerial office rather probable. I certainly did not then envisage that I would spend the whole of my parliamentary life on the back benches.

Although soon forgotten, the *Sunday Times* quiz caused a fair amount of comment at the time and an even greater amount of irritation among some of these who resented not being included among the starters. But however insignificant this innocuous journalistic game may have been, if nothing else it did confirm that my political prospects appeared to be set relatively fair.

As I was the most junior officer in the Foreign Affairs Committee, I had last choice when areas of responsibility were allocated; the world was carved up between us in a very amateur fashion, and when it came to my turn, the only area still remaining happened to be the Middle East. Anglo-American relations, the Soviet Union, Europe and the Far East, all appeared then more interesting and had been taken up by my seniors. Though Aden was simmering, the Middle East – even the Arab/Israel dispute – seemed at that particular moment to be for a brief spell fairly quiet.

To understand the area one was supposed to be specialising in it was obviously necessary to visit it. This was not easy to arrange in those days except as a member of an occasional parliamentary delegation, never a very satisfactory solution. There were no funds in opposition for travelling, except for Alec Douglas-Home as shadow Foreign Secretary. The rest of us had to pay for ourselves or get some grant. Without this we simply could not go. Fortunately an old friend of mine, Geoffrey Keating, came to the rescue. Geoffrey was a remarkable individual. He had had a first-class war record, largely in the Middle East, and had an apparently endless network of contacts throughout the world, particularly in Europe, America and many Arab countries. Some of his activities were rather mysterious, but among other things he acted as trouble-shooter and special adviser to Sir Maurice Bridgeman, Chairman of BP. In that capacity he was able to help politicians who for one reason or another were interested in the Middle East to visit the area. If they got to know and understand its problems they would be better able to protect British interests there – and no doubt incidentally BP's interests as well, where these coincided with Britain's. Nothing was expected in return. What was provided was a first-class ticket to any country one wanted, hotel accommodation and introductions to local politicians. Normal introductions to ambassadors and so on I could of course arrange for myself through the Foreign Office.

Thanks to Geoffrey Keating I visited Beirut on a couple of occasions, and this gave me a chance to talk once again to Palestinians. Since 1948 I had completely lost touch with Musa Alami and Palestinians in general. Now I was able to talk to people like Walid Khalidi and Yusuf Sayigh, who brought me up to date on their problems. I thus began to get a new perspective on the issue. In particular it became apparent to me through talking to them and others that the Israelis were plotting a new war. Israeli raids on Jordan were acts of provocation designed to make it more difficult for Hussein to keep out of war when it came, and the so-called 'surprise war' of June 1967 was already well prepared. The most destructive of these raids was that on Samu on 13 November 1966 in which, as U Thant, Secretary General of the United Nations reported, one hundred and twenty-five houses, in other words virtually the whole village, were destroyed. The Israelis said only forty. Eighteen Jordanians were killed. The Security Council, by fourteen votes to nil, passed a resolution censuring Israel, but of course nothing else happened. Warnings that Israel was not only preparing for another war but was determined if possible to provoke one were looked on at that time, even by averagely well-informed people in this country, as absolute rubbish. Thus by giving such warnings I was already beginning to move slightly out on a limb.

True, these views were shared by many diplomats, though not all, as a clear view of our national priorities in the area was confused by the phenomenon of Abdel Nasser. For some people there was the strong legacy of prejudice left by Suez, but equally there can be no doubt that Nasser was then pursuing policies in the Gulf which were hostile to British interests, as well as playing a highly controversial role in the Yemen war. So the Foreign Office, though certainly not pro-Israel, was on the one hand critical of Israel because of the injustice done to the Palestinians which left a dangerously intractable situation in the area, and on the other hand harboured genuine fears about what President Nasser was up to in the Gulf.

In 1966 and early 1967, thanks again to Geoffrey Keating, I visited several Gulf states, including Kuwait, Bahrain and Saudi Arabia, Oman and the Trucial States (now the United Arab Emirates). In Saudi Arabia where I had a long meeting with King Feisal I found considerable suspicion of Nasser's Egypt and hostility towards it, based on understandable fears that the Arab nationalism he had unleashed was aimed at bringing about the downfall of all kings, sheikhs and princes everywhere.

Ascetic, gracious and aristocratic in manner, subtle and persuasive in argument, King Feisal made a lasting impression on me at my first talk with him in April 1967. The King was obviously much troubled by Abdel Nasser's activities, especially in the Yemen, while at the same time sharing his concern at the divisions in the Arab world and the impotence which they engendered.

On Jerusalem King Feisal was eloquent and uncompromising. As the Defender of Holy Places he could not envisage any settlement which left Israel in control of the Old City. So here again there was much argument about where British interests lay. It has to be remembered that at that time our involvement on the ground was much greater than it is now. Britain was still in *de facto* control of the Gulf from Kuwait to Oman, and then as now the Middle East was an area of great political, strategic and economic interest for all Western Europe as well as America. That at least has not altered, even though the British presence is no longer what it was.

1967 was also the year of the Six-Day War – a misnomer, because its outcome was in fact decided in the first few hours of 5 June with the destruction on the ground of almost the entire Egyptian Air Force. Israeli forces rapidly overran the Sinai peninsula and the Gaza Strip, as well as occupying the rump of Palestine (the West Bank) and East Jerusalem, which had been since 1950 incorporated in the Hashemite Kingdom of Jordan. This provoked the flight of another wave of Palestinian refugees.

In the aftermath of the war a host of visitors – reporters, politicians, analysts, and simple tourists – descended on Israel and the territories it had occupied to applaud its successes and prophesy great things for its future. A small group of MPs was invited to have a look at the other side, at the defeated Arabs, to see what had happened to them. Ian Gilmour and I went from the Conservative Party, Colin Jackson and Robert MacLennan from the Labour Party. Although Ian and I also visited Cairo, we concentrated our attention on the fate of the Palestinians, many thousands of whom had been driven across the Jordan River into a second exile on a scale comparable in misery, if not in numbers, to the mass uprooting following the war of 1948. Much of what we saw profoundly disturbed all of us.

Ian and I wrote an article which appeared in *The Times* on Thursday 27 July under the heading 'The Fate of the Arab Refugees: there is a great deal of talk about peace, but none about justice'. In it we described some of the makeshift camps on the East Bank, in Jordan, where conditions 'vary only from the appalling to the impossible'. We explained some of the pressures – physical, psychological, economic – which Israelis had used to encourage the Palestinians to leave their homes and the obstacles that were being put in the way of those trying to return. We suggested that the reason why Israel was behaving in this way was that 'the most likely next territorial claim for Israel is the Israeli-occupied West Bank', and that what the Israeli Foreign Minister, Abba Eban, had called 'the conflict between Israel's demographic and her territorial interests' would be resolved 'if the Arabs were removed from the West Bank in sufficient numbers'. We wrote about the sights we had seen at the Allenby Bridge, where the refugees carrying their few pitiful possessions were harassed by officious Israeli soldiers and watched by applauding American Jewish tourists in bermuda shorts who seemed to treat the whole spectacle as if it was part of a zoo.

In the light of what has happened in the last twenty years these criticisms and prognostications have a prophetic accuracy, so that the furious reaction which they provoked seems today quite extraordinary. I certainly was unprepared for the storm which broke over our heads, and there were, I think, two main reasons for this. First, I had innocently supposed that my indignation at what I had seen on both banks of the Jordan – an indignation fully shared by my three colleagues – would be echoed by the majority of people in England when they were told about it. Secondly, I failed to appreciate the strength of the Zionist lobby which, though mercifully not as powerful as in America, permeated virtually every layer of society and every walk of life, except the Foreign Office and the Treasury, where British interests remained paramount. Ironically enough, the Foreign Office is often depicted in obtuse right-wing circles, particularly in parts of the media, as 'the Ministry for Foreigners'. They fail to understand that the protection and furtherance of British interests requires some historic vision and diplomatic finesse. Also, that chauvinism is a blunt and counter-productive instrument.

The Zionist lobby was particularly strong in the media and had effectively conditioned public opinion. Books and films like *Exodus*, innumerable newspaper and magazine articles and the almost unanimous editorial attitude of the British Press had built up a picture of gallant little Israel surrounded by hordes of bloodthirsty, marauding, aggressive Arabs waiting to drive these wretched, defenceless people into the sea. This picture, and the euphoria created by the June war in which brave little David crushed boastful Goliath with a few perfectly aimed shots from his sling, could not be dented by one article – or even by a series of articles, had any newspapers been prepared to print more, which they were not.

As for the Palestinians, who remembered or cared about them? There might as well have never been an indigenous population in Palestine as far as the West was concerned. The only Palestinian to impinge at all on Western consciousness was the loud-mouthed and ineffectual Ahmed Shukeiri, their spokesman at the UN in New York. His disastrous rantings were of course fully publicised by the Israelis. I recall Harold Beeley, later to be Ambassador in Cairo but then one of Britain's permanent representatives at the UN, telling me how, after a particularly violent and flatulent speech by Shukeiri, a beaming Abba Eban came up to him: 'Wasn't it marvellous! If he didn't exist we would have had to invent him!'

It did not help the presentation of the Arab case in London that for much of this time some of the most important Arab countries, Egypt for instance, did not have full diplomatic relations with Britain. Several withdrew their ambassadors in protest over alleged Western collusion with the Israeli air strike of 5 June 1967; others had been withdrawn earlier for different reasons but, as is almost always the case, the Arabs' over-reaction was counter-productive. Those ambassadors who remained did their best in an unfavourable political climate, and in particular the ambassador of Kuwait, Sheikh Salem al-Sabah, was indefatigable in his efforts. Also from the moment he returned to London and for many years afterwards the support and advice of Nadim Dimechkie, the ambassador of Lebanon, an exceptionally intelligent and well-informed observer of the international scene who became a close personal friend and subsequently Dean of the Diplomatic Corps, was both wise and unsparing.

On top of all this there was 'Colonel' Nasser, as Eden and others used to refer to him with contemptuous emphasis, since Suez profoundly unpopular in Britain where his recent defeat had been a cause of rejoicing. His name, and even more his image, still provoked near-apoplexy in some right-wing circles, which managed at the same time to combine strong pro-Israel sympathies, anti-Semitism, and a detestation of Nasser and all 'gyppos' in a repellent and contradictory cocktail of prejudices. On the Left, for different reasons, the situation was also heavily slanted against the Arabs, the presence of many Jewish MPs in the Parliamentary Labour Party, most of them keen and active Zionists, making an even-handed approach to the problems of the Middle East impossible. There were, of course, honourable exceptions, both among the ordinary public and in academic and literary circles, but they were a small minority, mostly people who knew the Middle East through the universities, diplomacy and commerce. Their weakness was that they were isolated and uncoordinated and had no outlet in which to express their civilised protest.

The Times came under such fierce public attack and private pressure that the Editor felt it necessary to call on two MPs, Philip Goodhart and Eric Heffer, both prominent in their respective parties and both sympathetic to Israel, from where they had just returned. They were expected to counter what we had written. This they endeavoured to do in two articles which appeared in *The Times* on 29 July, but being fair-minded individuals as well as pro-Israeli their rebuttals were not quite powerful and convincing enough to satisfy Israel's more vehement supporters. In any event enough damage had been done to enrage and astonish the Zionist establishment. For many days the correspondence columns of *The Times* were flooded with letters, and on the same day as the Goodhart/Heffer articles there appeared a magisterial editorial leader. This, entitled 'Over the Jordan', conceded that 'there is a sharp conflict of evidence', and concluded: 'There are certain specific things that should be done. Those who fled should be allowed a longer time by the Israeli authorities to put in their applications for return, and given more help with them . . . Above all, the rest of the world, which has been quick to show practical sympathy, should realise that whatever happens in the political field the plight of the refugees is going to be an enduring one, and that winter is going to make it far worse than it has been in the past two months.' That, at any rate, turned out to be absolutely correct.

More denunciation of our article followed swiftly. One quotation will suffice. *The Jewish Observer and Middle East Review* described it in an editorial as 'one of the most one-sided and mischievous pieces of writing ever to appear in that august newspaper'. This sort of criticism was no doubt to be expected. What I had not been prepared for was the personal abuse and opprobrium which I came in for.

On the evening of the day on which the *Times* article appeared I had been invited to dinner at the house in Hyde Park Gate of Nigel and Vanessa Lawson. On arrival it was apparent that the party was to be a large one, a buffet supper. Vanessa Lawson, Jewish herself, always delightful, amusing and tolerant, someone I counted as a dear friend and who proved to be one at that difficult time, greeted me with the remark: 'You'd better have a drink immediately, before they go for your blood. What a pity your partner in crime [Ian Gilmour] couldn't come – at least he would have deflected some of the flak from you.' I took this to be a joke, but quickly discovered my mistake. A journalist whom I knew came up, rather the worse for drink, and abused me aggressively. Then, as I went down towards the garden, two complete strangers, both, it seemed, Jewish, rounded on me with the most offensive personal attack, accusing me of being anti-Semitic, a neo-Fascist and so on. Naturally this made me very angry, and I found myself involved in a series of extremely sharp and disagreeable arguments. What I had looked forward to as a pleasant evening turned into a most unpleasant one. I began to understand what I had let myself in for.

A few days later I went to another evening party at which there were present several members of the Marks and Spencer families. I was then still married to the daughter of Archie McIndoe (Sir Archibald McIndoe) who had died in 1960 and for whom I felt great affection.

Simon Marks, Israel Sieff and Simon Marks' sister Elaine, married to Neville Blond, had all been close friends of Archie's and the Blonds were neighbours of his in Sussex. They had been, and their families continue to be, generous supporters of the Burns Unit at East Grinstead Hospital which he had made internationally as well as nationally famous for the wonderful work it did for the burns victims of war. (Seeing the wounded in Jordan suffering from the effects of napalm bombing I had devoutly wished that the treatment at East Grinstead had been available for them.) So I had got to know the family well and had an easy and friendly relationship with them, having some years earlier even been for a few days a guest on a yacht Simon Marks had chartered to cruise in the Mediterranean. They must have known that any suspicion of anti-Semitism was as remote from me as from my wife or my late father-in-law.

As I came into the room I saw Elaine and went up to greet her in the usual way. To my astonishment, she turned on her heel and walked in the opposite direction. A few minutes later I received practically the same greeting — or rather lack of greeting — from another member of the family. Catching sight of Marcus Sieff (later Lord Sieff of Brimpton) I went up to talk to him. He did not actually walk away, but was extremely cold, and another unpleasant argument followed. The whole atmosphere was so disagreeable that I went away. Anthony Blond, Elaine Blond's stepson, the enterprising publisher, not long after and to his great credit, took a very independent line about Israel's policies and was highly critical both of it and of the injustices perpetrated on the Palestinians.

Another swift and hostile reaction to the article came from one of my closest friends, Peter Goldman. There was of course no question of his accusing me of anti-Semitism or breaking off relations, but he did claim that Ian and I had allowed ourselves to be bamboozled by Jordanian propaganda. I remember being struck at the time by the extraordinary paradox of how anyone who spoke up for the Arabs was swiftly and inevitably accused of having become the victim of propaganda while those who visited Israel and repeated Israeli arguments were simply relating objective facts. This curious paradox has continued to recur, although much less extensively, and indeed, since the beginning of the *intifadeh*, visitors to the West Bank and Gaza have returned enraged at what they have seen and heard of Israeli brutality.

Part of the explanation for it lay in the vigour and tenacity with which Israeli and Zionist supporters had successfully propagated a number of attractive myths. For example, there was the myth that the refugees fled from Palestine in 1948 because they were ordered to do so through broadcasts from their leaders. In spite of the most exhaustive investigations no evidence of any such broadcast has ever been produced. This particular myth was demolished in an article in the *Spectator* of 12 May 1961 by Erskine Childers. 'There was', he wrote, 'not a single order, or appeal, or suggestion about evacuation from Palestine from any Arab radio station, inside or outside Palestine, in 1948. There are repeated monitored records of Arab appeals, even flat orders, to the civilians of Palestine to *stay put* . . . Even Jewish broadcasts (in *Hebrew*) mentioned such Arab appeals to stay put. Zionist newspapers in Palestine reported the same: none so much as hinted at any Arab evacuation orders.' Broadcasts which did prompt Arabs to flee came from Jewish, not Arab, radios. Thus on 27 March, four days before the big Haganah offensive against Arab centres, the radio of the terrorist Irgun (headed by Menachem Begin) put out a warning in Arabic to 'Arabs in urban agglomerations' that typhus, cholera and similar diseases would break out 'heavily among them in April and May'. The myth has persisted because it is a comforting way of shuffling off from Israeli shoulders responsibility for all the suffering that was caused. There are many honourable exceptions, and Childers quoted from one of them, Nathan Chofshi: 'We came and turned the native Arabs into tragic refugees. And still we dare to slander and malign them, to besmirch their name. Instead of being deeply ashamed of what we did and trying to undo some of the evil we committed . . . we justify our terrible acts and even attempt to glorify them.'

And more recently it has been Israeli historians who have done most to destroy the myth that the Palestinians fled their country under orders from their leaders. Dr Benny Morris, in an article published in 1986 based on a report of the Israeli Defence Forces Intelligence Branch, points out that this report 'goes out of its way to stress that the exodus was contrary to the political-strategic desires of both the Arab Higher Committee and the governments of the neighbouring Arab states . . . The Arab Higher Committee decided to impose restrictions, and issued threats, punishment and propaganda in the radio and press to curb emigration.' The report cites the three major causes of this 'emigration' as, first, direct hostile Jewish operations against Arab settlements; second, the effect of such operations on nearby Arab settlements; and thirdly, operations by the 'dissidents' (Irgun and Stern Gang – the Deir Yassin massacre and so on). Among 'minor causes' of the exodus the report lists psychological warfare 'aimed at frightening away Arab inhabitants', and 'ultimate expulsion orders' by the Jewish armies. 'What a beautiful view,' Ben-Gurion said to a friend as he watched the expulsion of Arabs from Haifa. At the time, however, the myth was overwhelmingly accepted as fact, even by those who should have known better, and Ian and I were engaged in constant battles when arguing against the popularised version of what had happened in Palestine.

In spite of all the subsequent unpleasantness I had no regrets for what we had written. Indeed, the more the attacks the more committed I became to the position which I had adopted. The whole business seemed to me completely unfair, and I was shocked at how energetically and effectively the point of view of 'the other side' was suppressed. Some of those who were at first prepared to join us in speaking out found it embarrassing or risky to do so, and gave up. This also made me more determined to keep on, and so I became involved in what was emerging as an embryo 'Arab lobby', which at that time was pathetically ill-equipped in human and financial resources compared with the well-established Zionist lobby. The skill and dedication of people like John Reddaway and Michael Adams did, however, make up to some extent for the imbalance.

Although much strengthened over the years – for instance the Conservative Middle East Council of which I am chairman has a membership of over sixty from both Houses of Parliament – the so-called Arab lobby still cannot compete in numbers, finance and organisational discipline with the Zionists. In reality, of course, there is no mystery about this much maligned 'lobby'. It consists of people who put British not Israeli interests first and who consider that the Palestinians have been, and continue to be, abominably treated. They are also aware that continuing Israeli intransigence poses a serious threat to peace and stability in a crucial strategic area of the world.

One of the disadvantages of there being so few of us at the outset was that we inevitably became a sort of stage army, to be wheeled in on every occasion. If the subject cropped up in the House, either in a debate or at Question Time, there were only Ian and myself and occasionally Tufton Beamish (later Lord Chelwood) on the Conservative side and a few Labour Members, in particular Christopher Mayhew and Colin Jackson, who were prepared to come forward. It was the same when it came to writing letters to the newspapers or appearing on radio or television programmes. Because there were no others willing to speak up we were accused of being fanatics and obsessed with the Arabs. But this was not so. It was simply that there was no one else. When it was the case of a controversial but respectable issue, such as whether or not we should join the European Community, Conservative and Labour MPs were queueing up to be heard, confident that it would be good for their image. But the cause of Palestinians served nobody's image.

For some time the pressures to which I was subjected were almost entirely social and political, but quite unpleasant enough. Even what was supposed to be friendly advice proved not always palatable. Thus two or three senior colleagues in the House, with whom I had established a good relationship, gave me a quiet warning that I should drop the Palestine issue if I wanted to have a successful political career, or that at any rate I should make it a secondary interest and not a main one. Sound advice, no doubt, but for the reasons already explained – the smallness of our numbers and the difficulty of recruiting others – not advice I felt I could follow.

Then a business angle cropped up. I was at this time a director of two companies, Eric Garrott Associates, which has already been mentioned, and Specialised Travel Limited. One of the biggest accounts held by Eric Garrott was the internationally famous cosmetic firm, Helena Rubinstein. Some time towards the end of 1967 or beginning of 1968 Eric Garrott asked me to lunch with him at Tiberio's Restaurant. He then told me that he had been approached by somebody very high up in the Helena Rubinstein empire, whom he refused to identify by name, who had discreetly hinted that if I was not silenced or sacked it would be very difficult for the company to continue with the agency.

Eric Garrott, a workaholic and a brilliant advertising man, was fair but tough, and not much concerned with the niceties of foreign affairs, and I could see that he was not at all happy about the dilemma in which he had been placed. I told him I sympathised with his problem, but had no intention of being silenced; should he decide to sack me I would explain the reasons for it in a speech in Parliament. Moreover, I reminded him that my presence was of some value to the agency when dealing with the account of Middle East Airlines, also handled by Eric Garrott Associates, and which Sheikh Najib Alamuddin had built up into one of the finest small airlines in the world. MEA was not as lucrative for the agency as Helena Rubinstein but in its own way almost as prestigious. Eric Garrott laughed and told me he had no intention of sacking me, but had just felt that I ought to know what had happened. In the event Helena Rubinstein did not leave the agency, and probably Eric Garrott would have resisted the pressure if there had been more of it, but the episode inevitably weakened my standing and damaged my relations with him. Indeed, had it not been for the fortuitous MEA connection I think my position would have become impossible. This partly accounted for my great devotion to MEA, which I made constant use of in my flights to and from, and within, the Middle East. It remained a marvellous airline, until a large part of its fleet was destroyed on the ground at Beirut International Airport by a piratical Israeli attack.

My experience with Specialised Travel was on similar but happily slightly different lines. The chairman and main owner of the firm was a great friend of mine from Cambridge days, Michael Battsek; the joint managing director was Harry Baum, and Michael's wife was another director, all of them Jewish. Michael had started up the business soon after leaving Cambridge. It combined being a straightforward travel agency with a special side which laid on tours linked to some cultural event in Europe, mainly for the benefit of teachers and students from America. It did the same for occasions of a political nature, such as conferences, and I had been brought in as a director, at £100 a year, plus expenses, to advise on this aspect.

Michael was a very civilised and moderate Zionist, and although we sometimes argued about the Middle East it was always in a perfectly rational manner. I now heard that some of the Jewish firms that used his services had let it be known that they thought it intolerable that I should remain on the board of the company. So on this occasion, unlike with EGA, it was I who broached the subject. Obviously if I resigned, as I offered to, it was not going to be a financial disaster, but Michael told me he could not dream of letting me do this. He said he was ashamed of the pressures that had been put on him. Although he disagreed with many of my views he regarded them as perfectly legitimate and knew there was not a vestige of anti-Semitism in them. He said he would be extremely hurt if I insisted on resigning. So I did not. But his attitude was very much the exception rather than the rule.

When the Palestinian uprising started in December 1987 it seems to have taken some people by surprise. It should not have done so. The evidence of Israeli behaviour in the Occupied Territories was there for all to see and reported by many. As early as November 1967 a long dispatch by David Holden in the *Sunday Times* recorded that the Palestinians 'can still feel pride because they can still feel hate, and unhappily the Israelis – like most conquerors – give them plenty of reasons for doing so.' Holden had heard exactly the same language from official Israeli spokesmen which was regularly dished out to journalists reporting on the *intifadeh* (uprising) in 1988: 'If you know the Arab mentality you know this toughness is probably good. I don't think they really understand any other language.' All the by now familiar techniques were already in operation: 'Houses are blown up and men arrested with remarkable expedition ... No figures were made available to me for the number of Arab houses thus destroyed in the occupied area but they must by now run into four figures. A total of 350 alleged "al Fatah" men have been arrested and another 600 men are officially admitted to be in prison on various charges ... Night searches, threats, and police beatings have been alleged to me by many Arabs. Even when the more lurid descriptions are discounted, I am left with the impression that there is some tough, and at times deliberate, intimidation by the Israelis ... Israeli officials themselves admit they make mistakes. Disarmingly, they say, "we are not supermen", and they point out that military occupations are apt to be nasty for the occupied. But to the Arabs, inevitably, every act of violence or intimidation seems part of a Zionist master plan to drive still more of them out of their homeland.' All this was after only five months of occupation, not twenty years.

Sixteen months later Gavin Young gave an illuminating account of how occupation was creating the new breed of Palestinians which the world has seen in action in the uprising: 'Almost two years of occupation and under-employment have driven Palestinians on the West Bank to a frenzy of self-education and debate. In homes and restaurants, night and day, the past, the nightmare present and the impenetrable future are ceaselessly analysed . . . True stories of Israeli arrests, beatings or the blowing up of houses mix with rumours of torture and death and fedayeen exploits to feed the high fires of Palestinian nationalism . . . But at the same time, the occupation is deepening the generation gap. It is the younger people, including women and girls, who are the most daringly active thorns in the flesh of the Israeli occupation or at least the most bitterly passive.' And so it went on. But so went on also the flood of articles and speeches proving that the Israelis were the most benevolent and misunderstood of conquerors and any trouble the work of a few misguided terrorists.

That particular line was put a stop to by the uprising which began in December 1987 and is still continuing. When the Minister of Defence instructs the soldiers that they should aim to wound demonstrators rather than arrest them, and when well over three hundred men, women and children had been shot dead in less than a year, benevolence is not something that even Israel's staunchest apologists would lay claim to. More and more attention has been focused on the corrupting effect the occupation and the suppression of the Palestinians has had on the Israelis themselves. The persecuted have become the great persecutors. The extent to which this corruption has spread was shown, for example, in a dispatch in the *Daily Telegraph* of 17 May 1988 from its correspondent in Tel Aviv:

Unrepentant Israeli schoolboys yesterday gave a chilling account of how they 'tore into' defenceless Palestinian detainees at a para-military base on the occupied West Bank.

According to several reports, at least three out of 60 pupils from the southern village of Yeroham took part in the beatings while on a training visit to the Ofer base, near Ramallah, north of Jerusalem.

One of the three, Yuval Apallo, 16, told the newspaper *Hadashot* that on the way to the base they passed a group of Arab detainees who were blindfolded and bound hand and foot. 'We asked if we were free to beat them, and he (the group leader, a sergeant) said "Why not?" In the evening after supper, when everybody went to their rooms, we returned to the same place. I easily identified the detainee I saw in the morning. I removed his blindfold and smashed my fist in his face. He started bleeding, begging not to be hit, but I grabbed a truncheon and cracked him one in the face.'

Another prisoner began screaming, Yuval said, and that drove him to further violence. 'I took an iron fence post and beat the hell out of him. He looked like pulp, a heap of flesh and bones. Hell, I punched all of them with blows. Later I heard that he was put in a plaster cast and that he is still in hospital.'

Yuval said that two other pupils who were with him looked on as he attacked the defenceless Palestinians. 'As I was beating them I had a great feeling. I had a great need to hit them. I'm telling you, if I had a machine-gun then, I would have killed him. Not because of what he did or said to me, but because of what those Arabs are doing to my country.'

Osnat Suissa, 15, said she later heard the students bragging to their classmates: 'Soldiers let us beat up a trussed-up Arab.' She said: 'The three were exhilarated. They told us how they tore into the Arabs with blows. I was not particularly interested in their story. I couldn't care less. Nobody at the base made any stink about it. I'm amazed that anyone at all is now troubled by it.'

Looking back, and in justice to politicians in my own party, I should record that many of them, deeply worried by the implications of what was going on, did try to grapple with the problem. Thus at the beginning of August 1967 Reggie Maudling, then Deputy Leader of the Opposition, had talks with leaders of ten Arab countries, at the end of which he proposed a five-point plan: Israeli withdrawal from the territories occupied in the recent war; in exchange for withdrawal 'effective guarantees against future aggression'; a 'resolute effort' to solve the refugee problem; 'appropriate recognition of the unique religious status of Jerusalem'; special attention to the needs of Jordan.

Nor was this sort of language used only when we were in opposition. When the Conservatives came back again after the 1970 election Alec Douglas-Home, once more Foreign Secretary, lost little time in taking up a clear position on the Middle East conflict. Speaking to a Conservative audience in Harrogate on 31 October he described the Arab/Israel problem as 'the most difficult and dangerous of all those with which your government is faced in foreign affairs.' 'Both sides', he said, 'believe they are right. Both sides believe that force is legitimate and necessary for them to achieve their goals.' So what was needed was some sort of equilibrium in the area which both sides would be prepared to accept, and he suggested that this could only be reached if 'two fundamental principles' were acknowledged: 'the inadmissibility of the acquisition of territory by war, and the need for a just and lasting peace in which every state in the area could live in security.' Such a settlement must 'take account of the legitimate aspirations of the Palestinians'. Needless to say, this eminently sensible proposal was regarded by the Israelis as outrageous.

Ian Gilmour and I made several more visits to the Middle East together, and on our return, if we felt that what we had seen was of sufficient general interest, we would turn it into an article, and usually *The Times* would publish it. But, as we had already discovered, writing about the area not from an Israeli point of view could be a tricky business. The impression we received was that this was considered in rather doubtful taste and something that had to be quickly disowned, or, better still, suppressed.

There was, for example, the curious story of an article which we wrote in April 1968 after one of these visits in which we had seen, among others, President Nasser and King Hussein. This article described, I think for the first time in England, the creation of much more sophisticated Palestinian resistance movements, and particularly of Fatah 'which seeks to defeat Zionism but not to drive out all the Jews'. By any normal journalistic standards this had real news value, and was accepted by the *Sunday Times* and set up in type. But for some reason it never appeared in the paper.

Another example of the obstacles besetting any attempt to get a non-Israeli point of view published came a year later. On 29 June 1969 the Arab League paid for a four-page supplement on Palestine inserted in *The Times*, to which half a dozen well-qualified writers, including Ian but not myself, contributed articles. This was made to appear with an ear-piece: 'These four pages are a political advertisement sponsored by the London Office of the League of Arab States. *The Times* has accepted it for publication in accordance with its traditional policy, but does not vouch for any of the facts or opinions expressed.' A top leading article contained a much longer disclaimer, ending up: 'Most of the articles in [the supplement] have been written by people in Britain who strongly sympathise with the Arab cause in general and with the misfortunes of the Palestinian Arabs in particular. It has long been a principle of *The Times* that any group or lobby has the right to put in print what they believe in, provided it is not libellous or a direct incitement to violence or hatred. The Arab League advertisement does not come into that category. It is extremely partisan (and of course there are plenty of partisan statements on the other side). It is certainly not the sort of publication that is helpful. It is not calculated to bring a settlement any nearer.' The next day a letter signed by some of the contributors was printed which pointed out, *inter alia*, 'You recently published a comparable supplement on Israel on your own initiative. The contributors to it were equally "partisan", although few of them could be described as authorities on the politics of the Middle East. Yet you saw no reason to comment in any way on their right to express their views or on the "helpfulness" of their contributions.' Those who had contributed to the supplement were put on a sort of editorial black list, and nothing from their pens was allowed to appear for the next two years.

Four months later the Foreign Editor of *The Times*, Teddy Hodgkin, a friend of mine, who had lived for over five years in the Middle East, half of the time in Palestine, came back from a visit to the land he knew well, shocked by what he had found. An article by him called 'Grim Reports of Repression in Israel-occupied Lands' appeared in the paper on 29 October. This was followed by a flood of letters, approving and disapproving, and some intemperate accusations in the House of Commons in which I became involved. Three days later a leading article called 'To be Fair to Both' appeared. This, which was almost certainly written by the Editor, William Rees-Mogg, is worth quoting from:

Mr Hodgkin's own record as a student of Middle Eastern affairs and as a conciliator rather than a propagandist needs no defence. Yet we have the extraordinary attack on Mr Hodgkin and on *The Times* made by Mr Snow in the House of Commons on Thursday night. Mr Snow said: 'I am personally not surprised that the newspaper which was friendly to the Nazi Government and its sinister and terrible anti-Semitism should now see fit to publish an article like that.' This was followed by an attack on Mr Dennis Walters by Mr Shinwell, who also accused Mr Walters of anti-Semitism.

There are a number of things to be said about this response. In the first place it is obviously hysterical. If a calmly argued report of the conditions of the Arab people in the occupied territories is equated with the anti-Semitism of the Nazis, then nobody except an avowed Israeli propagandist can be allowed to discuss the state of Israel at all. Mr Shinwell has always used ridiculously exaggerated and unjust language and his language as an old man is no more defamatory than was his language when he was young. But unfortunately Mr Shinwell and Mr Snow do represent a reaction which anyone has to face who publishes any grave and substantial criticisms of any part of the Israeli position.

I have no doubt that William Rees-Mogg came under enormous pressure from the Zionist lobby to do something much more positive than try 'to be fair to both'. At any rate, whether coincidentally or not, early in 1970 he paid his first visit to Israel. After five days there he came back and wrote three articles of the same length as Hodgkin's under the general heading 'What Israel Thinks'. These were in many ways excellent, carefully balanced, recording what he saw as the shortcomings as well as the achievements of the new state. But inevitably this meant that the Israeli angle received considerably more coverage.

I have gone into the matter of *The Times*'s coverage of the subject at some length because William Rees-Mogg, besides being, as I have explained earlier, an old and close friend of mine, is one of the most fair-minded and humane men I know. Showing the difficulties which so just a man came up against helps to explain why many other editors hardly bothered to make even an attempt at fairness.

One other follow-up of Hodgkin's article is worth recording. On the day it appeared he was asked by the BBC to take part in 'The World at One'. He was asked questions arising out of the article, and his replies were pre-recorded. When he heard them played back after the one o'clock news he was astonished to find that each of his remarks was followed by a comment from the Israeli ambassador. This bit of editorial spatchcocking had been done without telling him, and the result gave the impression that the two of them had been engaged in a studio debate in which naturally the ambassador had always had the last word. Was this the result of timidity or bias, or a mixture of both? It is always difficult to tell.

The sort of pressures to which ITV, just as much as the BBC, could be exposed were described in an article in the *Listener* of 9 March 1970 by the very experienced broadcaster, Bryan Magee:

Unfortunately we in this country tended to look at the [Arab/Israel] conflict very much from one side, the Israeli side, until quite recently. And we were infected by the one-sidedness, the fanaticism almost. For instance, our television and newspapers reported the Six-Day War of 1967 almost entirely from the Israeli point of view, without much audible protest from anyone, so far as I can remember. Yet when it was all over I presented a programme on ITV which raised the questions, how did the Arabs feel now, what are their first reactions to defeat, how do they see their immediate future, and before the programme had even finished the switchboard at Television House was jammed with telephone calls protesting about British television being given over to the Arab point of view. There were shoals of letters afterwards, the Directors of the Company received personal complaints, there was a reference to the programme in the House of Commons. When I forced people to make their complaints specific they usually fell back on saying that I had had only Arabs in the programme and I ought to have had some Israelis too. But the purpose of the programme was to find out how Arabs felt. In any case, in the previous week literally dozens of programmes had been put on embodying the Israeli point of view, with Israeli spokesmen and no Arab spokesmen, and there were no sacks of mail, no criticisms in Parliament.

The question why it has almost always in the West been acceptable, and indeed at times almost obligatory, to support Israel but regarded as eccentric or even wicked to speak up for the Arabs is one that still puzzles me. Of course, immediately after the last war the full realisation of what the Nazis had done to the Jews of Europe gripped the conscience of us all. There was a peculiar horror about the gas chambers which pushed aside thoughts of the millions who had died on the battlefields, or who had been killed by bombing, starvation, disease, forced exile, and all the other scourges which engulfed almost the whole of Europe and large parts of Asia. Palestine, we were told, was the only asylum for the survivors of the holocaust, so the creation of Israel was no more than a belated act of justice, and no doubt the Jews, being essentially humane and liberal people, would see to it that their Arab cousins were well treated.

But there must have been more to it than this. I suppose the fact is that everyone thinks in stereotypes. The stereotype of a Jew was the grey-haired Central European professor, the violinist of genius, the sturdy and benevolent matriarch. The stereotype of an Arab was a man on a camel, or a full-bellied pasha sitting on a sofa fanned by odalisques, while for the millions of Allied troops who passed through Egypt and North Africa during the war he was the man who tried to sell them dirty postcards or who cheated them over a droshky drive. Jews were Western, spoke all the civilised languages perfectly, knew all about Shakespeare and Tolstoy, played and enjoyed classical music. Arabs were orientals who ate with their fingers and could actually listen to the caterwauling of singers like Om Kathoum with pleasure. There was no difficulty in choosing between them.

The new State of Israel did nothing to discourage these stereotypes. Once established in the heart of the Arab world it did all it could to distance itself from its surroundings – or rather, it was only prepared to meet its neighbours on a missionary basis; it would be glad to teach them all about agriculture and industry, health and art, if only they were not so pigheaded as to reject this patronage. Though the Levant was where the Israelis now were, in no circumstances were they to be called Levantines. They belonged to the West, not to the Middle East. They entered the Eurovision Song Contest and played bridge and football as part of Europe, and had some European governments not been so obstructive they would have joined the North Atlantic Treaty Organisation (North Atlantic?). The Arabs, on the other hand, spent their time quarrelling among themselves, and having, more's the pity, come into possession of a lot of oil, squandered the proceeds on Cadillacs, women, gambling, and making vulgar scenes in the most expensive restaurants in London, New York and Cannes.

Admittedly, things have changed quite a bit in recent years. It is becoming more generally understood that half the population of Israel is now oriental in its origins, not European. Begin, Shamir and Sharon are not such cosy characters as Weizmann and Einstein – to be more precise, all three have been closely involved in terrorist activities. Menachem Begin was head of the Irgun Zvai Leumi, one of the terrorist organisations which arose from the breakaway Revisionist wing of Zionism. Its best known achievement was the blowing up in July 1946 of a part of the King David Hotel in Jerusalem which contained the British military and civilian headquarters with the loss of 91 British, Arab and Jewish lives. It had earlier made an unsuccessful attempt to murder the British High Commissioner, Sir Harold MacMichael, but it did manage to murder two British sergeants, whose bodies were booby-trapped. It also resorted to kidnapping as an adjunct to blackmail, a technique which was to be copied all too often in the Middle East. The smaller but no less violent Lehi (Stern Gang), of which

Yitzhak Shamir was a leading member, murdered the British Minister of State, Lord Moyne, a year before the end of the war, and the UN mediator in Palestine, Count Bernadotte, a year after the war had ended.

Ariel Sharon is best known for his successful counter-attack against the Egyptian army in the 1973 war and for organising Israel's invasion of Lebanon in 1982. Horror, both inside Israel and in the rest of the world, at the consequent massacres in the Palestine refugee camps of Sabra and Shatilla forced his resignation as Minister of Defence. Earlier he had commanded the raid on the Jordanian village of Qibya in October 1953 in the course of which forty-two civilians were killed. As commander of the semi-secret Unit 101 he conducted more or less uncontrolled his own war against Palestinians and Jordanians. 'Major Sharon may be a good officer,' said Ben-Gurion, 'but we must get him out of the habit of telling untruths.' Not surprisingly, with men like these in charge of the government, the behaviour of their armies and police towards Palestinians and Lebanese reflected the mentality of a master race not of a persecuted minority. The Palestinians, meanwhile, have shown themselves to be a real people, with a real grievance, and with real courage. All the same, Israel continues to claim, as a right, the unqualified support of the West and, thanks to the indefatigable activity of a very powerful, rich and ruthless pressure group which keeps alive a combination of lingering feelings of guilt, apathy and the old residual stereotypes, until very recently continued to get it.

If a hundredth part of the moral indignation poured out over South Africa was diverted to what goes on in the Arab lands occupied by Israel, there might be greater hope for a change. But as I said once in the House after watching Jo Grimond on television speak with enthusiasm about Israel and then hearing him denounce South Africa: 'I cannot for one moment see why it should be acceptable to treat Arabs as second-class citizens in Israel, but morally repugnant to treat Bantus as second-class citizens in South Africa. I disapprove of both those policies.'

Although my intense involvement in the affairs of the Middle East was a handicap to political advancement, it provided some notable and fascinating compensations. My visits became more frequent, sometimes undertaken on my own initiative and sometimes, as will be seen, in a semi-official capacity. It became possible for me to meet most of the significant Middle Eastern leaders, not just on some fleeting parliamentary or PR occasion but in prolonged and repeated private talks. That would certainly not have been the case if I had pursued a more conventional approach to the problems of the area.

The next time Ian Gilmour and I went to the Middle East, early in 1968, our first stop was once again in Jordan, a country still distracted by the consequences of the Six-Day War. In addition to the flood of Palestinian refugees in the camps there were bands of more active armed young Palestinian men and women stopping cars on the main roads, demanding to see passes and extracting cash contributions – behaving, in fact, almost as a state within a state. Nemesis came for them two and a half years later when, in 'Black September', the Jordan Army's tanks and artillery moved against guerrilla positions in and around Amman, crushing them with heavy loss of life.

This was one of the many difficult – and often perilous – decisions which King Hussein has had to take. When the seventeen-year-old grandson of King Abdullah was abruptly called on to rule in 1952 there can have been few anywhere sanguine enough to believe that nearly forty years later he would still be on the throne, and indeed one of the respected elder statesmen of the world. He has never held strong cards, but in spite of this, through sheer determination and the strength of his personality, he has succeeded in keeping Jordan as a powerful influence in the affairs of the Middle East. Also, by skilful diplomacy, he has retained the ear both of the West and the Soviet Union. I have had many meetings with him, and have always found his comments forthright and relevant.

On this occasion, as well as seeing King Hussein, we took the opportunity to arrange a meeting with Yasser Arafat, then in the process of consolidating his control of the PLO though still little known in the outside world. He received us in an underground bunker, rather like a dugout in one of the 1914 war trenches, some way out of Amman towards the Jordan River. Spartanly furnished, this was now his operational headquarters, though even then he frequently changed his place of residence, a necessary precaution.

Arafat undoubtedly possessed star quality. Ebullient and enthusiastic, he tried gamely to speak to us in English, though his command of the language was inadequate and he often had to have recourse to an interpreter. He also spent some time telling us about the background of the Palestine problem and Zionism, which we knew as well as he did (a process I have had to endure many times from other Arab leaders) and, not surprisingly, showed a good deal of naïvety about international affairs.

Arafat maintained that the Palestine struggle was now unstoppable. It might take two years or fifty years, but eventually the whole of Palestine would be recovered. This did not mean, he was quick to add, that the PLO wanted to throw the Israelis into the sea, but that they were moving towards a binational state in which Jews and Arabs would have equal rights. We are like the Vietcong, he told us, and like the Vietcong in the end we shall be the victors. I pointed out to him that Vietnam and the Jordan valley were totally different in size and geographical structure, and that though it might be legitimate for him to talk in terms of a fifty-year struggle this was not something that could be welcomed or even contemplated by people living on the West Bank and watching the daily tide of Israeli annexations. To recover at least part of the territory would be better, I suggested, and therefore instead of talking all the time about the ultimate goal he should concentrate on regaining the West Bank as quickly as possible, even if this meant some sort of compromise. Half a loaf was better than no bread and a two state solution the only realistic outcome. Ian warned him against expecting American policy to change, either in the short or long term, and gave him an exposé of the Zionist lobby in America which has proved depressingly accurate. Arafat listened attentively, and seemed quite interested, but did not want to become involved in an argument. The overall impression was of his sincerity and dedication, as well as of his obvious intelligence and agility of mind.

In the years to come he was to need all the agility he could muster. Because of internal Zionist pressure the might of the US was to remain firmly aligned on the side of Israel, regardless of Western interests and irrespective of international law, justice and morality. Then, to keep his disparate forces aligned under the PLO banner in some form of unison while maintaining good relations with the sharply contrasting regimes and personalities of the Arab world, called for the wisdom of Solomon and the patience of Job. Arafat's qualities did not measure up to those of his illustious Semitic ancestors, but, given the obstacles he encountered and the enemies he has had to contend with, he has not been unsuccessful and has consistently shown himself brave, determined and resilient. The compromises needed in order to survive have inevitably created an impression of indecisiveness, but this is only partly justified and the true facts are more complicated and more complimentary to Arafat. The way he handled his own supporters and world political opinion at Algiers in October 1988 over the PNC declaration, which proclaimed an independent state of Palestine while renouncing violence and formally accepting UN resolutions 242 and 338, was masterly. Equally skilful was Arafat's performance a little later, after George Shultz had inexcusably prevented him from addressing the UN in New York. He surprised many by his surefootedness, but not those who knew him better and had over the years come to recognise and value his qualities.

Ian and I saw Arafat a couple of times more in Jordan before he was forced to flee following 'Black September'. On one of these occasions we raised the argument often heard in the West, that the Palestinians always reject any new offer put to them, only to take it up again later when it is no longer on the table. He admitted that there was something in this, but pointed out that he had to keep in step with the people he represented. Why was it accepted, he asked, that all the others involved – Americans, Israelis, British and so on – had to watch their constituencies, whereas he was always the one expected to show only statesmanship and responsibility? He had his constituency to watch too. There was much truth in this, though of course as a people without a country or a government the Palestinians were in a weaker position than any of the others.

The same argument about 'constituencies' applied to his appearance. There can be no doubt that the unshaven face and twisted kaffir make up an image that does him no good in the West. A clean chin, a neat suit and tie, would make him much more presentable in the corridors of Western power, which is where the fate of the Palestinians is most likely to be decided. But would such a sanitised Arafat continue to command support in the camps?

I suppose the most significant of my meetings with Arafat was one which took place in the late summer of 1981. This was a semi-official mission carried out on behalf of the Foreign Secretary, Lord

Carrington, though no doubt if news of it had leaked out it could always have been maintained that I was acting for nobody but myself. There had in fact been fairly regular contacts during the previous year between John Moberly, an assistant under-secretary in the Foreign Office (later Sir John Moberly, ambassador to Jordan and Iraq), and a representative of the PLO, Ahmed Sidqi Dajani, but these had got bogged down and the Foreign Secretary thought that, as I had established good personal relations with Arafat, I might be able to help in getting them moving again.

This was important because he felt there was now a real prospect of progress towards a Middle East settlement, and that of course would not be possible without the cooperation of the PLO. There had been a number of promising signs recently. The EEC summit at Venice in June the year before had unanimously recommended conditions for a settlement, which included conceding the Palestinians' right to self-determination, asserting the necessary involvement of the PLO, and condemning the establishment of Israeli settlements in the Occupied Territories as illegal.

The joint statement by the American and Russian governments on 1 October 1978 – which had met with a frosty reception in Israel and provoked frantic lobbying by the Zionist pressure groups in America – and Brezhnev's speech in February 1981 had both called for the recognition of the legitimate rights of the Palestinian people and for an Israeli withdrawal from the Occupied Territories, as well as for 'the security and sovereignty of all states in the region', including Israel. Then in August Crown Prince Fahd, the Saudi Prime Minister, now the King, had put forward an eight-point plan which, by advocating a return to the status quo ante the 1967 war, had been taken as indicating that his government was prepared to give implicit recognition of Israel's right to exist.

It was suggested that I should try to encourage Arafat to build on the Fahd statement and show readiness 'to advance on Venice lines'. The statement Lord Carrington was seeking from Arafat had become known as 'the conditional IF'. Arafat should say categorically that the PLO was prepared to recognise the State of Israel within its 1967 borders if Israel at the same time agreed to the creation of a Palestinian State on the West Bank and in Gaza. An Arab summit was due to meet shortly in Fez. If Arafat could be persuaded to issue a statement along these lines, also endorsing Fahd and proclaiming the PLO's preference for negotiations rather than the military option, there seemed a real chance that the Arab League, or at any rate a majority of its members, might be ready to move in the same direction.

So I set out for Beirut via Rome, where the embassy was to be my link with the Foreign Office. Bridgett had gallantly insisted on coming with me in spite of the fact that Beirut, after six years of civil war, was a place of continual tension and not a little danger. We were met at the airport by representatives of the PLO and two heavily armed guards and driven to a rather sleazy PLO hotel. There it appeared that we were involved in one of the usual Middle East muddles – though all the preliminary arrangements had been quite explicit, something had still gone wrong and apparently Arafat thought that I was arriving the following day, and was now in Damascus. I pointed out that we were due back in Rome the next day, so urgent messages were sent off while we had dinner in the basement; there was a curfew at the time and quite a lot of shooting. Eventually we were told that it had been possible to contact Arafat and that he was on his way back and would be in Beirut around midnight. As midnight approached we piled into a car and were driven through the deserted town at breakneck speed, stopping only for the frequent checkpoints, which were manned by Syrians as well as the PLO. One of them our driver missed, but spotting in the car mirror a rifle pointed at him he abruptly reversed at about sixty miles an hour, fortunately before any shots had been fired.

We had not long to wait at PLO headquarters before Arafat turned up, and our discussions started immediately – poor Bridgett having to wait in an anteroom drinking coffee with the guards for the three and a half hours they lasted. He was accompanied by Shafiq Hout (journalist and writer, formerly an executive member of the PLO and today head of the PLO mission in Lebanon), Abu Walid (Saad Sayel, at that time Chief of Staff of the Palestine Liberation Army, killed in action in 1982), and his private secretary and personal interpreter, Mahmoud Labadi. Arafat was in an ebullient mood. He said he was definitely in favour of building on the Fahd initiative. Not only had he spoken favourably of it in public – and by expressing his willingness to set up a state in part of Palestine he had implicitly accepted that the other part would be Israel – but he had said yes to the Russo-American statement, yes to Brezhnev's speech, yes to UN Resolution 242, if linked to the other relevant UN resolutions – all this without getting anything in return. What more was he expected to do? He pointed out again, as he had at earlier meetings, that he had to carry his own people with him; moreover, he lived in a minefield of his Arab neighbours, and was permanently squeezed by the super-powers. By making the sort of statement we wanted he would be taking a big risk, without any guarantee that he would benefit from it. If the only inducement being held out was for more talks with the Americans, that was too high a price to pay. He recalled the contacts he had had with the Americans in Morocco and the thanks Kissinger had sent him when he intervened to help the American embassy in Beirut. When they thought the PLO could be useful, said Arafat, the Americans were always eager to make use of it, but the rest of the time the PLO was dismissed as nothing but a bunch of terrorists.

At this precise moment all the lights suddenly went out, and although some very powerful torches were swiftly produced for us Bridgett, sitting in the dark with the guards who twiddled their guns and did not speak English, had no idea what was happening. But they were most friendly, and after coffee pressed her to drink Coca-Cola, not one of her – or indeed my – favourite beverages. I could not stop myself from enquiring whether this was a Beirut electricity hazard or the prelude to an Israeli commando attack. Arafat was perfectly confident that it was the former, so I carried on and said that the sort of statement the British government was looking for could have a dramatic effect on public opinion in the West, and would rob the Israelis of one of their main propaganda themes; any formula put forward would be conditional on progress being made, so there was really nothing to lose. Arafat was not convinced. He started talking about Mrs Thatcher. Could she not, he said, repeat in the Middle East the success she had had in settling the Rhodesian problem, which was surely more difficult because of feelings in Britain and in her own party and because of the white settlers?

Arafat several times stressed the importance he attached to a meeting with Lord Carrington, who was at that time President of the European Council of Ministers. He had met previous Presidents, notably Thorn and van der Klauw, and now he had seen Cheysson. He very much wanted to work something out with Lord Carrington before he gave up the presidency. If he had something concrete to show the Palestine National Council he was confident he could carry it with him, but if he came to it empty-handed nothing could be done. He refused to be drawn on what would constitute 'something concrete', but hinted that perhaps formal recognition of the PLO by the European Commission would do. I told him I was sure that Lord Carrington genuinely wanted to get things moving, which was why he was pressing for a statement from Arafat that he could use a springboard. Arafat asked if we could answer for the Americans. I said that of course we couldn't, but that if nothing was said by him he could be certain that the Americans would remain immobile. That unfortunately remained true until Shultz's recantation on 14 December 1988 when direct talks with the PLO were at last authorised.

It was not until after 4 a.m. that Bridgett was rescued and we both received the warm and bristly embrace of the Chairman. The next morning I discussed our meeting with Walid Khalidi at the Institute for Palestine Studies, where I was told that Arafat would like to make it up to Bridgett for her boring wait by inviting us to lunch at a house outside Beirut. But our plane left at four, so the offer of a 'jolly' had to be declined. Back in Rome I passed a report on the meeting to the Foreign Secretary through the embassy, and when I got back to London a few days later I went to see him. He thanked me for going, said that there had obviously been some progress, and thought everything Arafat had said was reasonable – 'but he didn't in fact agree to say the one thing we wanted him to say.'

I argued Arafat's case for him a bit, pointing out that we were asking for something from him that it was far from easy for him to give, whereas the Israelis were never asked to give up anything and continued to get away, literally, with murder. Carrington, essentially a pragmatist, did not disagree, but emphasised the difficulties he faced, particularly in regard to America. He was too tactful and loyal to mention another equally formidable difficulty – the attitude of the Prime Minister. Mrs Thatcher harboured a deep suspicion of the PLO and of Arafat in particular, though she had never met him. Her main circle at the time was strongly Zionist, as was her Finchley constituency with one of the largest concentration of Jewish voters in Britain. Marcus Sieff, Paul Johnson and Patrick Cosgrave, among others, were always at hand to ensure that Israel's views were vigorously presented and the PLO and its leader dismissed. In fairness to the Prime Minister it should also be said that her sympathies never extended to include Messrs Begin and Shamir, both of whom she heartily disliked, and that King Hussein remained a steady favourite.

One of the many misfortunes of the Palestinians was that they never made proper use of the one among them who had a wide and subtle understanding of politics and politicians in the West, particularly in Britain. I have already spoken to Musa Alami as one of the two Arabs who were responsible for interesting me in the affairs of the Middle East while I was still at Cambridge. I used later to see him regularly, either in London, Jerusalem or Jericho, until his death in 1984. After the 1948 catastrophe he ceased to be actively concerned in politics, but he still loved talking about them, and nobody talked about them better. Fortunately, today much greater use is made of Palestinians with degrees in Western universities, of which there are many thousands in every discipline. Intellectuals like Edward Said and diplomats like Bassam Abu Sharif have shown themselves able to hold their own in negotiations with anyone anywhere. Similarly, when Walid Khalidi visited London in March 1983 as a member of an Arab League delegation he greatly impressed the Prime Minister.

Much the most significant figure on the post-war Middle Eastern scene was, of course, Gamal Abdel Nasser, and I met him four times, always at his house in Mashiet el-Bakr on the outskirts of Cairo. This was where he had made his home while still a serving officer in the Army, and although naturally additions had been made to it after he became President it was still a modest structure – and a well-guarded one, the road in which it stood being blocked off to the public.

I recall in particular one of these occasions, early in 1970, not long before his death. Nasser as always had been captivating and at ease, and after a long tête-à-tête discussion of international affairs (his English although not perfect was good enough for him to dispense with the services of an interpreter and he did not bother with aides in attendance as witnesses), when the atmosphere had become agreeably relaxed, I said something about all political leaders making mistakes. 'Do you think I have made mistakes?' he asked. 'Which ones?' 'With the greatest possible respect,' I said, 'certainly at least two. First, I think you miscalculated the dire consequences for Egypt of the June war in 1967, and secondly, I can't see that being bogged down in Yemen has done you or your image any good.'

He took this well, and started to explain. He said that yes, certainly in retrospect the June war had been a great mistake. But he had never intended that there should be a war. What he had felt at the time was that Israel's provocations against Syria and Jordan could not be left unchallenged; if they were, then Israel would unleash even more and bigger raids against its Arab neighbours. So he had to do something. But he had been assured that the Americans and Russians had reached an understanding, and that just as the Russians would not allow him to make a pre-emptive strike, in the same way the Americans would restrain the Israelis from doing so. Admittedly the war of words in the summer of 1967 had reached an alarming level, but it was never meant to escalate into a shooting war. So he was forced to conclude that either the Americans had broken the pledge they had given to the Russians (and he implied this was what the Russians had passed on to him), or they had been unable to control their satellite. Then had come the catastrophe of the destruction of the entire Egyptian Air Force on the ground and the consequent defeat of the Army in Sinai. After all that he had felt obliged to offer his resignation, but the way in which he had been called back by the Egyptian people had persuaded him that he still had a contribution to make on their behalf.

As regards Yemen, he said it might look as if Egypt's involvement there had been a mistake. 'But,' he said, 'when I come down to breakfast and see my family . . .' And here he broke off into a parenthesis about not seeing enough of his family, about how he worked too hard and how his only chance to relax was when he could get a day at the farm of Mohamed Heikal or Anwar Sadat, about how his health was suffering and his attempts to cut down on his smoking. 'When I come down to breakfast,' he went on, 'my children say to me, "You are supposed to be leader of the Arab world, so how can you allow the sort of things that go on in Yemen?" Could I just do nothing? Let me put it like this. In your United Kingdom all parts are equally civilised. But suppose there was one part of it – Scotland, say, or Yorkshire – where there were no hospitals, no schools, no proper roads, and where people were living in thirteenth-century conditions. Could you tolerate that? And not only is that how things were in Yemen, but I knew that there were many people there who wanted me to come and help them to enjoy the advantages of the modern world. I felt I had a responsibility there, and that is how we got involved.' This was perhaps not a wholly convincing argument but it was presented in a very attractive manner.[1]

I saw Nasser's successor Anwar Sadat on numerous occasions, the first being soon after he had been catapulted into power owing to the fact that less than a year before he had almost casually been made Vice-President, not, it was generally agreed, with any intention that this was to mark him as Nasser's heir. However now, as the Cairo wits put it, 'the little donkey had suddenly become a great horse.'

Sadat received me at the pleasant house he owned near Alexandria. Later I was to see him at some of the other residences he had accumulated – at the Barrage outside Cairo, at his house in Giza by the Nile, and at Aswan. He was always a natty dresser, on this occasion wearing a long white linen shirt and white trousers. Later his wardrobe was to become more costly, his suits designed by Balmain and Cardin, and his uniforms, as a field-marshal and commander-in-chief of the armed forces, verging on the fantastic.

But to begin with he was courteous, affable and unaffected. And I should add that as far as I was concerned he remained both courteous and affable whenever I met him, but no longer unaffected, especially when later he had moved into the stratosphere. I brought him a personal message from Alec Douglas-Home, for which he expressed his warm thanks. But rather surprisingly one of the main impressions which I gained at this first encounter was that Sadat was a considerable snob, and that what seemed to intrigue him most were the intricacies of high society in Britain. He said he couldn't understand how it was that Sir Alex (as he always called him) could serve under Mr Heath. Sir Alex was an English aristocrat, wasn't he? 'Well, Scottish,' I corrected, 'but an aristocrat certainly.' 'And Mr Heath, as I am told, is of humble origin. Is that so?' I confirmed that yes, Mr Heath's background was relatively humble. Sadat remained puzzled. I told him the joke about the fourteenth Earl of Home and the fourteenth Mr Wilson, and that amused him, and I tried to explain to him that though the British class system was still fairly potent it was no longer all that relevant when it

[1] 'Politically and diplomatically, as well as militarily, nothing did more than his [Nasser's] Yemeni adventure to create the conditions for Israel's pre-emptive strike of 5 June 1967 and those lightning conquests which the Arabs remember as a catastrophe second only to the original loss of Palestine.' *Sadat* by David Hirst and Irene Beeston. London, 1981, p. 98.

was a question of power. But Sadat went back to the matter of Alec Douglas-Home's peerage. 'It must have been very difficult for him to give it up,' he said. 'But I suppose he can get it back whenever he wants.' I said that was probably true, but for the time being he preferred to be Foreign Secretary – and what a good one he was. President Sadat wholeheartedly agreed.

I saw Sadat twice in Aswan, where he liked to spend part of the winter. The first occasion was after the 1973 war but before the 1977 Camp David agreements, when I flew down from Cairo with Amintore Fanfani, then President of the Italian Senate and many times Prime Minister. He was going to have a talk with Sadat and had brought as a gift two of his own paintings, which he kindly unwrapped to show me; they proved to be rather good.

The next time we met there was a few years later, in the course of another of the Middle East tours I made with Ian Gilmour, and we found ourselves talking to somebody very different from the man I had first known nearly ten years ago. Still perfectly courteous, Sadat was now one of the best-known actors on the international stage, the man who had caught the attention and won the admiration of the world (apart from the Arabs) by the boldness of his 1977 pilgrimage to Jerusalem, whose signature of the Camp David accord with the Israeli Prime Minister, Menachem Begin, had won them both the Nobel Peace Prize – an award which, in the case of Begin, had the effect of permanently depreciating its value and significance – whose face had been on the cover of *Time* magazine as its Man of the Year and in hundreds of other magazines and newspapers: a great man, in fact and obviously relishing every minute of his new-found glory. (If the world had a tendency to overestimate Sadat, there may have been an equally misleading tendency to underestimate his successor, President Hosni Mubarak, who, as I know from personal experience, is a shrewd observer of events.) He no longer started the conversation by asking after 'Sir Alex', but after 'my friend, Sir Alex', and from there moved on to reminisce about 'my friend, Jimmy [Carter]', 'my friend, Henry [Kissinger]', 'my friend, the Shah', and all his other distinguished coequals. He mentioned a meeting he was shortly to have with the Israelis, and 'my friend, Menachem' hovered on his lips until, perhaps remembering the audience he was addressing, he deftly changed it to 'Mr Begin'.

Sadat spoke very critically of the other Arab states, which had ostracised him since Camp David; they did nothing but talk, whereas Egypt was the only country which had actually done any fighting. We put in a word for Syria, which had after all in the 1973 war almost achieved a breakthrough (and, it could have been argued, though we did not, had subsequently been let down by Sadat's first unilateral disengagement), but he brushed it aside. He claimed that, as he was still negotiating with the Israelis about a proper implementation of Camp David, which meant eventual Israeli withdrawal from the West Bank and Gaza, he was really the only hope for the Palestinians. He had, he said, made considerable progress with 'my friend, Ezra [Ezer Weizman]'.

By then Egypt had become ineluctably more or less a prisoner of America, which alone was keeping its precarious economy going after the rich Arab governments had withdrawn their subsidies. Certainly, Sadat had some cause for complaint on that score. At an earlier meeting, when he was about to set out on a journey which was at least partly fund-raising, he had banged his fist on the arm of his chair. 'I shall go,' he told me, 'but I shall not ask them for aid. I am not a beggar.' I had said I did not think there was any question of his being a beggar: 'You are not asking for money for yourself, but for the upkeep of the Egyptian Army and Air Force. You aren't asking for cash to use in a casino but because you and Syria are the only countries that can maintain the necessary pressure on Israel.' 'You are very kind,' he said. 'It may be as you say. But I am *not a beggar* and I am not prepared to let anyone accuse me of being one.'

In the spring of 1971 a friend and neighbour of mine in Wiltshire, Bill Luce, said he thought it might be a good idea if I went to Tehran and saw the Shah. Although not the last British Political Resident in the Gulf – there were two after him – Sir William Luce had been the last in the pro-consular mould – the most outstanding of whom I suppose was Sir Percy Cox in the First World War – who had maintained the imperial presence there by a combination of naval might and personal authority. Bill Luce, whose knowledge and experience of the area were second to none, was a man of absolute integrity whose entire life had been devoted to the service of his country. Once a policy of withdrawal from the Gulf had been decided on he was recalled by Sir Alec Douglas-Home to act as his personal representative for

Gulf affairs. He told me that if withdrawal was to be carried out in an orderly fashion there were two matters which ought to be cleared up with Iran first, and could only be achieved by reaching an understanding with the Shah. These were Bahrain and the islands of Abu Musa and the Tunbs in the western approaches to the Straits of Hormuz.

Iran's claims to sovereignty over Bahrain had often in the past been vigorously pressed, an empty seat in the Majlis for the member from Bahrain acting as a permanent reminder, but were now more or less dormant. On the other hand it was obvious that if the United Arab Emirates, then in process of formation, began life by handing over the islands, which zealous nationalists in other parts of the Arab world would represent as sacred Arab soil, there could well be trouble. Bill Luce suggested it might be helpful if this point was made to the Shah not only at formal diplomatic level but also by someone known as a politician sympathetic to the aspirations of governments and communities in the area. So he asked me to go.

A meeting with the Shah had been arranged by the Iranian ambassador in London, Khosrow Afshar, and took place a day or two after I arrived in Tehran. It went on for a much longer time than I had been told to expect. The Shah was extremely courteous, very well informed and with a good understanding of the nuances of politics in Britain, America and the countries closer to him. For example, he told me he thought the West was underestimating the problems facing Pakistan, that East Pakistan would be certain to break away from West Pakistan, and that though this might cause a temporary crisis it would not in the longer run have much effect on the balance of power in the Indian sub-continent. This was an accurate prophecy which found little support at the time. On the specific problem I had come to raise he said he recognised that the small sheikhdoms in the Gulf should be helped to make a success of their new independence, but emphasised that far and away the most important political and military presence in the area would always be Iran – not quite how things were to turn out some years later. In fact it was the rulers of the Arabian shore of the Gulf who were to be most severely tested by the fall of the Shah and the outbreak of the long war between Iraq and Iran, which brought new political and military perils upon them. That they weathered these is a tribute to their courage and resilience, qualities which have been shown by nobody more than the Ruler of Kuwait, Sheikh Jaber al-Ahmed al-Sabah, who is undoubtedly one of the most impressive and dignified of the Arab leaders I have met. Quietly spoken and extremely well-informed, he personifies all that is best in the Bedouin tradition of paternalist government. His influence is felt far beyond the borders of Kuwait.

In the event Iran did gain possession of the disputed islands, as a result of a tacit understanding between the Shah and the British government that this should be done discreetly and a cash payment made to one of the sheikhs most closely involved. The new State of the United Arab Emirates was proclaimed on 2 December 1971, Bahrain and Qatar becoming formally independent at the same time. Unfortunately an Iranian unit jumped the gun and landed on the Greater Tunb on 30 November, where they were opposed by a police detachment from Ras el-Kheimeh (whose ruler was the only one who had up to then declined to join the federation), and one policeman was killed.

The most vigorous reaction to this minor incident was to come not in the Gulf but 3000 miles away. Colonel Gadaffi was listening to an Arabic news bulletin which reported the death of the policeman, and as zealous custodian of pan-Arab honour promptly cancelled all BP's concessions in Libya and seized its assets. Now that the process of our withdrawal from the Gulf was complete Bill Luce's function as special adviser to the Foreign Secretary was really at an end, but at the beginning of 1972 he was engaged in trying to find a way out of the Libyan impasse, which was regarded very seriously in Whitehall. In retrospect there can be little doubt that if the Tunbs affair had never happened Gadaffi would have found plenty of alternative excuses for acting against BP; he was already in conflict with most of the other oil companies operating in Libya.

Yet at the time it was still legitimate to be hopeful, and Bill Luce told me of a scheme which had been worked out and which it was thought might conceivably provide the basis for a settlement. This was for BP's confiscated properties to be transferred to a Spanish company which was in fact a subsidiary of BP. By this means, it was hoped, Gadaffi's face and BP's profits would both be saved. Bill Luce thought I might possibly be of assistance. Our ambassador in Tripoli had failed to gain access to Gadaffi; perhaps with my Arab contacts I might be more successful.

So in July 1972 I set out for Tripoli, and while waiting for an interview took the chance to see Leptis Magna and some of the other splendid Roman monuments in the barren land which was once the granary of Rome. After a few days the summons came and I was received by Gadaffi in the upstairs barrack room which served him as an office. His attitude was at first arrogant and far from cordial, and he launched straightaway into a monologue on the evils of Zionism and the rights of the Palestinians. After about twenty minutes of this I felt I had to make a choice – either to allow the ranting to go on indefinitely and possibly never get to the point, or to break in at the risk of giving offence and bring the interview to an abrupt close. When Gadaffi got on to the Protocols of the Elders of Zion I decided that I would interrupt. I told Gaddaffi through the interpreter – he had occasionally put in a few words of English, but of course the harangue was in Arabic – that, as Chairman of the Council for the Advancement of Arab-British Understanding and in various other capacities I spent a great deal of my time trying to explain to people the malevolent influence Zionism exerted on Western policies, and reminding them of the sufferings of the Palestinians, so that what he had been saying to me was really rather a waste of time. I added that I would exhort him, if he wanted to persuade others from the West who came to see him, never to bring in the Protocols, which had been proved to be forgeries and discredited anyone who used them as an argument. There was a lot of much better material he could use and it was a mistake to make a stand on the wrong ground.

To my great relief this interjection seemed to have a good effect. Gadaffi smiled broadly. He said he would like me to tell him more about what I thought were the best ways to influence policy in the West. I told him he should try to beat the Zionists at their own game, particularly in America. There the Zionist pressure groups helped members of Congress and Congressional candidates with money and in many other ways. He and his friends ought to set up an organisation called, say, the Committee for Justice in the Middle East, which would target certain key politicians, and without trying to dictate policy to them make sure that they were fully informed about the case for the Arabs. They should mount a really professional public relations operation to get this view across and perhaps even assist financially.

Gadaffi said he thought this an excellent idea. He would like to look into it further, and asked me to put my ideas on paper and come back in a few months' time for further discussions. Then we moved on to the main purpose of my visit, the BP problem. Gadaffi listened attentively to what I had to say, but argued that, though he did not wish to be unhelpful, it would be very difficult for him to go back on what he had done. He asked me to leave with him the two-page memorandum on the subject I had brought with me.

The meeting lasted quite a long time, and when it was ended Gadaffi escorted me down the stairs and shook hands warmly as I got into my car, which seemed to surprise his bodyguards and the embassy chauffeur about equally. Just before I drove away he asked me when I was going back to England. I told him that now I had had the honour of seeing him I would return as soon as possible, and would hope to be on the British Caledonian flight that same evening. When I got to the airport a posse of senior Libyan officials was there to greet me. One of them presented me with a carpet and another with three boxes containing dates, sweets and embroideries, together with a note expressing Gadaffi's appreciation and good wishes.

On my return to London I prepared the memorandum Gadaffi had asked for and waited for a summons, but in spite of my enquiries at the Libyan embassy and by the British ambassador in Tripoli not a word more was ever heard about it. The compromise over BP made a bit of progress at a lower level, but then collapsed. I came to the conclusion that Gadaffi was like a schoolboy, capable of sudden enthusiasms but not of any sustained interest. I also felt that he combined a certain mesmeric quality, with which he was able to bamboozle some other Arab leaders, with a streak of near-madness – perhaps not quite a Caligula but very definitely not another Nasser.

An Arab leader who is often bracketed politically with Gadaffi but who is very different from him in temperament, is President Asad of Syria. Syria was the Arab country which, in the early years of its post-war independence, gained an unenviable reputation for having more violent changes of regime than any other. These *coups d'état*, often dignified as 'revolutions', usually originated in the Army, and it was from the armed forces, in this case the Air Force, that emerged the man who has confounded this reputation by staying in power almost as long as Nasser did in Egypt.

Hafez el-Asad took over in 1970, and at the time when I am writing (1989) appears to be still firmly in the saddle. He has made both himself and his country factors which cannot be ignored in the Middle East equation, though the British government tried hard to behave as if he did not exist. It is ironic that, while successive British governments have lectured Third World governments on the folly of being too quick on the draw to break off diplomatic relations, explaining that the existence of such relations between two countries should have little or nothing to do with mutual approval or disapproval, the Thatcher government should have broken this rule in its dealings with Damascus.

My first meeting with Hafez el-Asad was connected with this same problem. Diplomatic relations with Britain had been broken off at the time of the 1967 war, but tentative moves had been made to get them restored. It was thought in London that a parliamentary mission to Damascus might be a useful first step, and I was asked to go on what amounted to a preliminary reconnaissance.

On this occasion I only met Asad very briefly, as he was just about to leave Damascus, but I had a long talk with the Prime Minister, General Klefawi, and other members of his government, and a month or two afterwards a parliamentary delegation, led by Tufton Beamish, did arrive and diplomatic relations between the two countries were duly re-established on 28 May 1973.

The next time I saw President Asad was in the summer of 1975. I described him then as 'calm, intelligent, and humorous', and as holding 'strong and well-defined views on Europe'. What in fact most impressed me was how extraordinarily well-informed he seemed to be about details of the political situation in Western Europe and America. Considering that he had hardly ever travelled outside Syria, he must have chosen his informants well and proved an exceptionally good listener. There was a sophistication in his questions and comments unusual in leading Arab politicians. Sadat, for example, in spite of all his travelling and meetings with the great and not so great, had what I called a 'visionary approach to the world', in which detailed facts played a small part.

Though he spoke a little English, Asad always enjoyed the services of excellent interpreters, and I found discussions with him satisfying and productive. He had an easy manner and an engaging smile, which made it quite difficult to remember that, even if he had not exactly waded through slaughter to a throne, he had at least had a tough climb from being a member of the Alawite minority to the top and was running a pretty ruthless police state.

At that time the Middle East was still trying to come to terms with the fallout from the 1973 war. Asad himself had drawn two clear conclusions from the war: first, that if the Arab countries acted in unison they could be more than a match for the Israelis; and, second, that the United States was totally committed, militarily as well as economically, to Israel. It was the American airlift which had saved the Israeli armies in the field, and it was American diplomacy which had rescued Israel politically afterwards. It was Nixon and Kissinger who had converted an Arab triumph into an Israeli recovery. Asad's disillusion had, of course, been compounded by Sadat's breaking off the battle without consulting his ally, but, though the sense of betrayal was unmistakable, Asad never accused Sadat to me in so many words.

I saw Asad a number of times after this, sometimes with Ian Gilmour and sometimes alone. On one occasion, after he had met Jimmy Carter in Geneva in May 1977, he spoke of the President quite warmly, as he did earlier of President Ford. He thought they were both probably honest in their endeavours to find some just solution to the Arab/Israeli impasse, but he had no confidence at all in their ability to pull one off; Zionist pressures on them would always prove too strong. He said it was foolish for the Arabs to imagine that any of the so-called 'peace initiatives' could have a satisfactory conclusion. All the same, after this Carter meeting he told me that he would like to send a personal message to Carter through Dr Brzezinski, his National Security Adviser, to the effect that he was interested in what the President had told him, but would like the general sentiments expressed in Geneva to be followed up by specific proposals. I was due to go to Washington soon after this, and told Brzezinski that Asad was looking for something on paper. Brzezinski said he would like me to assure Asad that the intention was to follow up the Geneva exchanges. When I reported this to Asad he complained that this verbal message did not take matters any further: 'I haven't seen any action or received anything in writing,' he said. Carter or Brzezinski may have sent a message later through another channel, but I doubt it.

Old Hansards are not exactly compulsive reading, even for those who took part in the debates they record. But when I started writing this chapter I did refresh my memory of what had been said by myself and other Members of the House of Commons in those early years when the Middle East had become my main political interest and when, as I have explained, because there were so few prepared to put the Arab case, I had to intervene rather often.

I think that in almost all my speeches I urged the need for Israel to be accepted as a part of the political geography of the area and for her borders to be secure. 'International morality rightly calls for [Israel's] protection,' was the way I put it the first time I had an opportunity of speaking on the subject after my original visit in July 1967. (This was in the debate on the Address on 2 November – appropriately enough, the anniversary of the Balfour Declaration.) But I added: 'International morality also calls for the protection of the rights of the Palestinian Arabs and of the refugees who are in the camps on the East Bank of the Jordan.' This dual obligation – which, after all, does no more than reflect the dual obligation enshrined in the Balfour Declaration – was something I repeated time after time. I do not recall any of Israel's many supporters in the House expressing equally even-handed sentiments, or indeed showing any concern for what happened to the Palestinians.

I hope readers will bear with me if I offer one more extract, this from a speech I made in the Foreign Affairs debate of 24 June 1968, because sadly it remains wholly apposite today and glaringly highlights how little has changed in the Occupied Territories after more than twenty years. It is hardly surprising in the circumstances that the Palestinians have reached the conclusion that a continuing uprising is the only hope of shaming world opinion into some kind of action.

After quoting from an *Economist* report describing Israeli repression on the West Bank and Gaza and the conditions in the Palestinian camps in Jordan I went on to say:

It is quite obvious from all this that the situation on the West Bank is deplorable, just as the conditions of the refugees on the East Bank are an intolerable outcome of the June war. In contrast to the awful reality of the conditions of the refugees and of life on the West Bank, with houses being demolished, villages bulldozed and Arabs arrested and deported, the following advertisement appeared in the *Observer* on Sunday. It was for Israeli Airlines and says: 'You can add your little bit to the gaiety of nations by joining in a folk sing-up.' It then goes on: 'You can bring to life biblical place-names, Jericho, Jerusalem, Bethlehem, Hebron and Nazareth.' It ends by saying: 'You can get to Israel in four hours.'

What possible right, except the right of blatant force, does Israel have to claim Jericho, Bethlehem, Hebron and indeed, Jerusalem, as parts of Israel? If this is an indication of the callous attitude of the Israeli authorities to the sufferings of the Palestinians I despair of a settlement being reached. Yet I believe that there is still a chance if both sides are prepared to compromise. If the Israeli moderates will only assert themselves while the Arab leaders are pursuing a moderate and realistic policy there is still hope, but I believe that time is running out for the chance of achieving a just settlement and a lasting peace.

As I have said, in those early days anyone who, like myself, plugged away at the unpopular theme of Arab or Palestinian rights was regarded as at best eccentric, a bit of a bore and a bit of a pariah; at worst as revealing the cloven hoof of anti-Semitism. How could anyone be so critical of Israel without implying criticism of the Jewish people who, as everyone knew, had suffered so appallingly? Blind endorsement of Israel and all its works was the only acceptable posture.

Israel's supporters in the House in those days were very cock-a-hoop and pleased with themselves. Their interruptions when I and others like me spoke were numerous and aggressive. But now, twenty years later, the position has changed markedly. It could almost be said that roles have been reversed; it is now Israel's supporters who are on the defensive. The 1982 invasion of Lebanon; the bombardment of Beirut by land, sea and air; the massacres in Sabra and Shatilla camps; and, more recently, the daily shooting, maiming, gassing, and detention without charge or trial of Palestinians of both sexes and all ages who are seeking only a minimum of respect and justice, have opened many eyes. Some of the most truculent of the Zionist MPs, like Shinwell, Snow, Paul Rose, Raphael Tuck and Ian Mikardo, have either left this world or the House of Commons; their successors tend to be rather more circumspect. The process of education has not yet gone as far as it should, but there has definitely been a change for the better.

This change has been reflected in Question Time. There are questions to the Foreign Secretary every three weeks, and I have always religiously put down the same one – to ask the Secretary of State if he can make a statement about progress to peace in the Middle East. This, if called, usually receives an anodyne reply but provides the opportunity for useful supplementaries. Twenty years ago about ninety per cent of the questions relating to the Arab/Israel problems had a pro-Israeli slant; today their share is down to about thirty per cent or less.

Being vindicated after twenty years gives some satisfaction. The secret of success, however, unless you are a Winston Churchill, is to keep a straight course and to be only a few inches ahead of the majority view. But twenty years is a long time in politics.

Sour grapes grow in many politicians' gardens, but I have tried to keep them out of mine. All the same, I think it is a legitimate part of this narrative to record that more than once I had good reason to believe that I would be made a junior Minister at the Foreign Office, or possibly Defence. Each time the fates (perhaps not quite the right word) decreed otherwise. At first it was my alleged Arab obsession. Then an election lost not won. In December 1973 at the height of the oil crisis which followed the October war it was hinted to me on the grapevine that in the next reshuffle my name would be put forward for a ministerial job at the Foreign Office. The lost elections in 1974 put paid to that.

Again before the 1979 General Election the Chief Whip, Humphrey Atkins, informed me that he would strongly recommend me for a Foreign Office post, and both Lord Carrington and Francis Pym, who became shadow Foreign Secretary after the death of John Davies, told me that they would like me with them should they become Foreign Secretary. In the period of opposition between 1974 and 1979 I had worked closely with both. It had always been looked upon as possible that Peter Carrington would get the Foreign Office although in those opposition years the position of shadow Foreign Secretary had been held in turn by Reggie Maudling, John Davies and Francis Pym.

When however in 1979 the election was won, Ian Gilmour rather unexpectedly became Deputy Foreign Secretary instead of Secretary of State for Defence, the department he had shadowed in opposition. Because the Foreign Secretary, Lord Carrington, was in the House of Lords his deputy was a good deal more than just a number two. He was Lord Privy Seal, a member of the Cabinet and the principal Government spokesman on foreign affairs in the House of

Commons. As has been abundantly shown in these pages Ian is not only one of my most intimate friends but my closest ally in politics. His appointment was richly deserved and he carried it out with great skill and wisdom, especially over the Rhodesian negotiations, but quite understandably it was too much to expect Mrs Thatcher to allow two such well known Arab sympathisers in the Foreign Office. An alternative job in a kindred ministry was not on offer.

However, when the select committees were formed, thanks to no small extent to the energies of the Leader of the House, Norman St John Stevas, another friend from Cambridge days, it seemed reasonable to assume that I would find a place in the Foreign Affairs Select Committee. I had, after all, been either joint secretary or joint vice-chairman of the Conservative backbench Foreign Affairs Committee almost continuously between 1965 and 1978, when I was ousted by a right-wing pro-Smith Rhodesia coup, and I had carried out some quite delicate missions on behalf of the Foreign Office, a number of which I have described.

So it was with some confidence that I forwarded a request to the chairman of the selection committee that my name be considered for inclusion, a request which was supported by the Foreign Secretary, his Deputy, and the Leader of the House. But when the names were announced mine was not among them. For the first time that I can remember, because I have never taken much for granted in politics, I was not only surprised but angry. I asked the Chief Whip, Michael Jopling, and Norman St John Stevas for an explanation. Was there a black mark against me of which I was not aware? If there was, I ought to know about it so that I could repudiate it. Absolutely not, quite the contrary, said Michael Jopling, looking rather sheepish and proffering some wholly implausible reason. Norman was more forthcoming but asked me to keep what he was telling me confidential. Now that ten years have passed and he has retired from active politics to the House of Lords I feel no longer bound by this restraint. My name, he said, had been included on the original list for the committee but Mrs Thatcher had struck it out and substituted another. It came as a disappointment and a surprise that the Prime Minister should have done so, and even more of a surprise that she should have been involved at all when the post at issue was such an insignificant one. Fate again?

Showing sympathy for Palestinians has not been helpful to a career in the Labour Party either. Christopher Mayhew had been a member of an official Labour Party delegation which visited Israel in 1963, and become 'shocked by the Israeli leaders' self-righteous indifference to the sufferings of the Palestinian refugees, and found [himself] speaking up warmly for the Arabs in their presence.' Complaints about his attitude were made by prominent Israelis to Harold Wilson, and a year later, when Wilson became Prime Minister, Mayhew, though in opposition he had been deputy spokesman on foreign affairs, was not given any Foreign Office post in the government. Wilson denied that the Israeli complaints had anything to do with his being passed over, but a leading Israeli newspaper, *Ma'ariv*, reported: 'Gordon Walker, appointed Foreign Minister, apparently wanted Mayhew as his deputy. But Mayhew did not get the post. Why? In London, there are rumours that the leaders of the Jewish community in Britain, or Israeli friends of Wilson, brought to the Prime Minister's attention the dangerous misunderstandings that might arise from such a nomination. How can a pro-Arab be put in charge of Middle East affairs, while Wilson claims to treat Israel with friendship?'

The Labour Party has repeatedly shown itself almost as readily responsive to Zionist pressures as the main American parties. It was the party's 1944 conference which passed the extraordinary resolution on Palestine: 'Let the Arabs be encouraged to move out as the Jews move in', and when Ernest Bevin, as Foreign Secretary, showed greater realism, he was widely accused (naturally) of being anti-Semitic. Indeed, he aroused such paranoia in Israel that Ben-Gurion, when on a visit to England, sought out Bevin's grave to stamp on it. It is interesting that a recent work by an Israeli scholar, Dr Avi Shlaim, should come to the conclusion that Bevin, 'who is usually portrayed in Zionist accounts as the great ogre who unleashed the Arab armies to strangle the Jewish state at birth, emerges from the documents as the guardian angel of the infant state' (*Collusion Across the Jordan: Abdullah, the Zionist Movement and the Partition of Palestine*).

Harold Wilson never made any secret of the fact that all his sympathies were with Israel, or, as he put it to the Foreign Affairs Committee of the Knesset in 1972, 'the Labour Party supports in principle Israel's views on the Middle East.' His visits to Israel were frequent, but except for a few days in Tunisia he never went to any Arab country, and when a group of businessmen, including the

President and Director General of the Middle East Association, concerned for British trade in the area and worried by the one-sided approach of the Wilson government, asked to see the Prime Minister, he refused to meet them.

However, perhaps the most extraordinary example of the way in which some Labour Members have put their devotion to Israel above any other loyalties comes from the early days of Attlee's government. The story is contained in the biography of John Strachey, then (October 1945) Under-Secretary for Air, later to be Minister for War (*John Strachey* by Hugh Thomas, London, 1973):

One day [Richard] Crossman, now in the House of Commons, came to see Strachey. The former was devoting his efforts to the Zionist cause. He had heard from his friends in the Jewish Agency that they were contemplating an act of sabotage, not only for its own purpose but to demonstrate to the world their capacities. Should this be done or should it not? Few would be killed. But would it help the Jews? Crossman asked Strachey for his advice, and Strachey, a member of the Defence Committee of the Cabinet, undertook to find out. The next day in the Smoking Room of the House of Commons, Strachey gave his approval to Crossman. The Haganah went ahead and blew up all the bridges over the Jordan. No one was killed, but the British Army in Palestine were cut off from their lines of supply with Jordan. A few days later, the Foreign Office broke the Jewish Agency code. Crossman was for several days alarmed lest he and Strachey might be discovered.

In fact this was an operation in which the Irgun and Stern Gang as well as the Haganah took part, and as well as the bridges the railway was cut in fifty places, naval craft sunk, and the Haifa oil refinery attacked. This was an operation to which a Labour Government Minister and another future Cabinet Minister gave the green light, and it was only by great good luck that a 'few' British soldiers were not killed. It should here be acknowledged that in spite of all the many things which the Labour Party has got wrong in recent years its policy on the Middle East has become much more even-handed and sensible. Gerald Kaufman, the Labour shadow Foreign Secretary, spoke out courageously when he visited the West Bank and Gaza in the spring of 1988 and, like everyone else, was shocked by what he saw. He has continued to take a balanced and constructive line on the Arab/Israel problem.

I was particularly struck by the speech of another Labour MP in the foreign affairs debate in November 1988. Eric Heffer, whom I have already referred to as a good friend of Israel in the context of *The Times* articles of July 1967, followed me in the debate. After recalling that time, after the Six-Day War, he went on:

The Israelis said that the area would be in their hands for only a short time and they would use it as a bargaining factor for peace. Twenty-one years later matters are worse, with area after area having been taken over by the Israelis, new settlements established and new reactionary concepts developed. There are people in Israel who are sick of what is happening and who want peace. Some of the early pioneers and their children want peace. The current state is not what they thought would happen and they are concerned about it. We must encourage the state of Israel to reconsider its future and we must help it in every possible way.

He said he agreed with the contributions Ian and I had made to the debate, that he agreed with the PNC Algiers declaration which proclaimed the independent state of Palestine, and that he hoped the Labout Party would invite the PLO to send a delegate to its annual conference. That is a very far cry from the Wilson/Shinwell/Mikardo days of Labour.

To a large extent the change of opinion in the House reflects, I believe, a change of opinion in the public, and even to a certain extent in the media. There have been some excellent programmes about Palestine on television, though many more about Israel, and the overall bias on both the BBC and ITV remains pro-Israel but no longer outrageously so. There has also been an improvement in press coverage which, with a few notable exceptions, is now rather more even-handed.

The same shift in opinion can be seen in other European countries, notably in Italy, where for long guilty feelings about what the Fascist regime did to the Jews meant that the political parties and the press were almost unanimously and uncritically supportive of Israel; but no longer. Germany, for obvious reasons, cannot initiate criticism of Israel, but will follow the lead of others, as the Venice declaration demonstrated. The voice of criticism has even been heard in the Jewish as well as the gentile community in America, though the Zionist lobby remains extremely powerful in Congress. Unlike President Reagan and

Mr Shultz, President Bush and Mr Baker are not committed to the Zionist cause and are obviously concerned about Israel's violations of human rights as well as its continuing arrogance and intransigence. In the circumstances their initial moves have been disappointingly slow, though this may no doubt be at least in part accounted for by the appointment of well-known Zionist sympathisers to many important posts in Government.

Epilogue

UNLIKE some others who have been fringe participants in historical events and who, writing about them afterwards, have gloomily contrasted the present situation with their earlier hopes, I would describe the world at the time when I write, towards the end of 1988, as in slightly better shape than it was in 1939. Not only are Hitler, Mussolini and Stalin dead, but even their own fellow countrymen have for the most part long been heartily ashamed of them. And in spite of the ever-present threat of nuclear destruction the sense of impending doom is much less strong than it was immediately before the war, or at the height of the Cold War in the late 1940s and early 1950s. In fact anyone who was somehow transported from the Europe of 1939, or even from the Europe of 1945 and 1946 immediately after the end of the war, to the Europe of today would find it completely unrecognisable. There have been difficult and even dangerous moments in all the major countries – Britain, France, Italy, West Germany – but all have been weathered, and they now enjoy not just prosperous economies but also established parliamentary democracies, as Britain has been fortunate to do for much longer than the others. These work reasonably well because they are accepted by a majority of their citizens as the best available way of running things in an imperfect world.

When I recall the way in which totalitarianism spread like a blight across almost the whole of Europe before the war I am greatly relieved at the failure in recent times of its simplistic and, to many, superficially attractive solutions to take a real hold anywhere. What is more, the dictatorships which survived the war in Spain and Portugal have given place to democracies which have every appearance of being there

197

to stay, and the regime of the Colonels in Greece lasted only seven years. But the outstanding example of a people turning away from totalitarianism is, of course, in Gorbachev's Russia.

This may be too sanguine a view, but I trust not. The European Union – another phenomenon which would make the eyes of a Rip van Winkle start out of his head – is, I think, in spite of all its imperfections, another check against backsliding. A completely federal Europe I would not regard as practicable, but I believe a confederation to be a realistic goal.

Though 'in Europe' since 1972 the United Kingdom remains in many ways a case apart. One of only a small handful of countries in Western Europe to escape the humiliating nightmare of occupation we were, partly for that reason, late-comers to the Union and so missed our chance of helping to frame its rules. It is our fault that these were drawn up largely to suit the needs of France and Germany rather than us. In spite of the passion for continental holidays which possesses almost every family in the country we remain an essentially insular race.

I see this insularity, or at any rate a much reduced interest in foreign affairs, reflected in the House of Commons. When I was first elected in 1964 foreign affairs debates were still considerable occasions, and the wind-up speakers could be sure of addressing a House in which there would probably be a couple of hundred members present. Nowadays, though there is no shortage of people wanting to speak there is a marked decrease in the number prepared to listen. The wind-up speakers will be lucky if they have an audience of thirty or forty, and many of these will be there for reasons of duty rather than interest. This change is no doubt largely due to Britain's diminishing role in the world, but it is certainly a far cry from the great foreign affairs debates in the years immediately preceding the war when the House was often so crowded that many members were unable to find seats and when they provided the dramatic highlights of parliamentary sessions.

Comparing the House of Commons as I first knew it a quarter of a century ago with the House as it is today, I find it hard to decide how much my impressions should be attributed to changes in the House and how much to my own change of attitude. There can be no doubt that the sheer drudgery of parliamentary business has greatly increased. Too many of the debates are repetitive and unnecessarily time-consuming and more use of the guillotine would be salutory. Three-line whips when a Member's attendance to vote is wellnigh compulsory are too frequent and as a result their significance has been greatly diminished.

There is perhaps an inevitable loss of vitality when one party has been in power so long and when the opposition has been so feeble. But the Tories had won three consecutive elections in the 1950s and Macmillan's leadership was never so concentrated as the one that has evolved under Mrs Thatcher. It is both unfortunate and disappointing that in recent years there has been nobody comparable to Rab Butler, Maudling and Macleod with the necessary experience to provide more balance. Although Quintin Hailsham survived in Cabinet until 1987, as Lord Chancellor he was largely confined to the law and its improvement. Moreover, in those days the rank and file of the party was less triumphalist and rather more capable of showing a healthy nonconformity than it is today. The prolonged standing ovation at the end of Conservative Party conferences is in danger of becoming as much a meaningless ritual as is the singing of the Red Flag at the close of those of the Labour Party.

It would be foolish to try and predict the way the political scene in Britain is going to develop. It should not be forgotten that the Conservatives lost three elections in a row in the 1900s, and it is conceivable that the Labour Party will pull itself together and become capable of government again. A really serious economic crisis could have unpredictable consequences, and if the prophets of doom in America are right this should not be ruled out.

One of the main reasons for being uneasy about the future, apart from uncertainty over the outcome of Gorbachev's attempts to transform the Soviet Union, is that the United States is saddled with a constitution wholly unsuited to its role as the most powerful nation in the world. This enables policies to be controlled by a number of lavishly funded groups which can even buy their representatives into Congress. In several areas of the world American policy is dominated by these groups. The China lobby, headed by Senator Knowland, used to be one of the most effective, but its influence was a shadow compared with that wielded by the Zionist/Israel lobby over the years. It has often looked as though the American government was happy to pay a small country, whose true interests are diametrically opposed to its own, three billion dollars a year to run its foreign policy for it. This was surely not what the founding fathers intended – or what their descendants should put up with. Their admirable concept of a perfect democracy buttressed by infinite checks and balances and almost continuous elections of one kind or another was meant to suit the needs of a young, idealistic and isolationist country, relatively small in population although vast in area, recently emerged from the tutelage of London. They could not have envisaged then that their beautifully constructed system would, in wholly different circumstances, become an ideal vehicle for use by the unscrupulous. As I look around me, although in a negative way I feel relieved that things are not much worse, I am frequently dismayed by the lack of vision and states-manship which I see.

Although Part II of this book is wholly devoted to British politics, and in particular records the remarkable contribution made to them in the late fifties and sixties by Lord Hailsham, I suppose in the end it is mainly about justice – or rather injustice. To begin with, the mon-strous injustices of Fascism and Nazism, which had finally to be fought and conquered, and later the persistent and cruel injustice to the Palestinians, which has been inexcusably tolerated for reasons which I have tried to explain and expose.

As I conclude, however, there are visible signs of hope about Palestine. At long last it would seem that both the injustice and the long-term danger to peace which goes with it are being recognised where it matters most – in the real corridors of power. Some serious attempt to find a solution may not be too far away, though as often before the Bush Administration seems reluctant to put any real pressure on the Israelis to mend their ways. However, should there eventually be real movement, and should the attempt to find a solution succeed, it would be the most satisfactory recompense and vindication that I could hope for.

Index